PLAY
MONEY

PLAY MONEY

My Brief But Brilliant
Career On Wall Street

**Laura Pedersen
with F. Peter Model**

CROWN PUBLISHERS, INC.
NEW YORK

Published by Crown Publishers, Inc., 201 East 50th Street, New York, New York 10022. Member of the Crown Publishing Group.

CROWN is a trademark of Crown Publishers, Inc.

Manufactured in the United States of America

Library of Congress Cataloging-in-Publication Data

Pedersen, Laura.
   Play money : my brief but brilliant career on Wall Street / Laura Pedersen with F. Peter Model.
      p.   cm.
   1. Floor traders—United States—Biography.   2. American Stock Exchange.   I. Model, F. Peter.   II. Title.
HG4621.P44   1991
332.63'228—dc20   90-20312
[B]   CIP

ISBN 0-517-58227-9

Book design by Chris Welch

10 9 8 7 6 5 4 3 2 1

First Edition

For Peder Hjalmar Pedersen (1902–1990)
and
Peter J. Heffley and Peter J. LaBadia

It isn't given to us to know those rare moments when
people are wide open and the lighest touch can
whither or heal.

F. Scott Fitzgerald

We can't turn back the days that have gone. We can't run life back to the hours when our lungs were sound, our blood hot, our bodies young. We are a flash of fire—a brain, a heart, a spirit. And we are three cents' worth of lime and iron, which we cannot get back.

Thomas Wolfe

Opening Bid

LTHOUGH THIS BOOK deals extensively with my experiences on the trading floor of the American Stock Exchange (AMEX), it will not necessarily make you rich(er), or smart(er)—at least, not intentionally.

As an options trader on the AMEX, the country's second-largest marketplace for stock options, I participated in the greatest bull run in Wall Street history. Now that I am a lecturer on the college circuit, I have found the mechanics of options trading to be of little or no interest to the twentysomething generation. They couldn't care less about puts, calls, spreads, straddles, and strike prices.

Instead, what most of them want to know is: How did I do it? How could someone as young as I make it to the top of my chosen profession so fast? Wouldn't I now like to share with them the secret of my success? Sure, if only it were that simple.

From January 1984 through October 1989, I'd kept a pretty good running diary of my experiences on the floor. I never thought that one day my entries would prove useful in the writing of my "memoirs," such as they are.

As the tone of the subtitle makes clear, *Play Money: My Brief But Brilliant Career on Wall Street* is neither a how-to manual nor a historical treatise on the Gilded Age II. It is simply a personal narrative of things that happened to me in and out of the trading pit at the AMEX over a period of nearly six years, which closed with both a bang and a whimper the day I decided enough was enough—and quit, without so much as a twinge of regret.

I have never liked grapes, least of all the kind that leave a sour aftertaste. So don't read *Play Money* expecting to find another bill of indictment. It contains not even the whiff of smoking guns, none of the tantalizing "insider" tidbits that might get some zealous first-year SEC staff attorney to gleefully shout "Eureka!" and call his chum over at Justice. There will be no cutting of government travel orders, destination "Club Fed," on account of these recollections.

Nor will *Play Money* appeal to the reader's prurient interests. As movie material, this book carries a "G" rating. That's because, within my experience, the games adults play down at the AMEX are more of the kindergarten variety—childish, harmless pranks that help to break the daily tension and thus lower the stress level. Author Tom Wolfe was wise to do most of his research for *The Bonfire of the Vanities* at the New York Stock Exchange. At the American, he'd have found they seldom got past the flash point.

I suspect that when it came down to choosing between sex and money, most of the men I worked with went for the money, too tired after the closing bell for fleshier temptations. "Go very light on the vices, such as carryin' on in society," warned the late, great Cleveland Indians pitcher Leroy (Satchel) Paige, upon being inducted into the Baseball Hall of Fame. "The social ramble ain't restful." He might as well have had us in mind.

My reason for writing *Play Money* is that I wanted to record what I perceived to be the final gasps of a tradecraft that has been rendered almost superfluous by high technology.

Historically, stock exchanges grew and thrived because of their dependency on the interaction of *people*. In the 1990s, the people are fewer and so are the occasions for interaction. Look at London or Hong Kong, where the chaos has been done in by cybernetics. The price of this "progress" is already being paid in the loss of quirkiness. Trading is no longer as much fun as it used to be. That's too bad, because it's this very excitement that drew me down to 86 Trinity Place in the first place.

These days, the AMEX trading floor is about as stimulating as the programmers will tolerate; that is to say, it's not very stimulating at all. Revisiting the floor a year after leaving it, I found it a much quieter, sadder place. Against the efficiency of the mainframe computer, traders don't stand much of a chance to strut their stuff. So, if the shouting isn't yet quite over, I suspect it soon will be. By the year 2000, round-the-clock, globe-girdling trading will be in place at the AMEX, NYSE, and Chicago Board of Options Exchange (CBOE). Consequently, many of my fellow traders won't be. In September 1990, the New York Stock Exchange approved a five-phase program that, according to the *New York Times*, "would for the first time bypass the exchange's specialists, who keep orderly markets in assigned stocks, often by using their own capital. Rather, buyers and sellers would be matched by brokers or the exchange electronically."

Nor will their backups be there—the clerks, runners, and reporters—the people without whom we couldn't have functioned for longer than five minutes. I have spared the reader pages of recitation about how hundreds of these faceless men and women loyally put in thousands of backbreaking hours to let people like me shine—and make the Exchange a more effective trading institution. If the Exchange's governors feel I have shortchanged the troops, let me assure all concerned that I have not done so intentionally. I too was once a clerk.

| | | |

It is said of nightclub comedians that they are often crude, cynical, vulgar, and insensitive for zeroing in on human foibles. I'm not so sure of that. As a semiprofessional stand-up improv comic, now semiretired, I have had to sit through hundreds of other comics' routines until it was my turn to jump on stage. I too used to groan audibly, hearing them tell us life's but a cabaret. Audiences pay to hear how the world is skewed; they find no humor in hearing of perfect vacations, happy marriages, straight-A students, good deeds rewarded, handsome men and beautiful women, balanced budgets, trade surpluses, deals that work out— and *professionals doing their jobs precisely and correctly.*

"Why can't the media report the good news, the happy news?" wailed that political philosopher Spiro T. Agnew, ten years before Ronald Reagan declared it to be morning again in America. Agnew's was a silly, rhetorical question, a pathetic (cynical?) attempt to muzzle the "nattering nabobs of negativism." He knew as well as anyone that you don't sell many papers that report that the sun has risen on schedule at 5:41 A.M., that all the trains are running on time, and that street crime has fallen off precipitously.

I happen to think it's not the products or the systems but the *people* that make the Exchange such a terrific career-launching pad. Many of these people became my friends, some of them my personal heroes, whom I would like to celebrate, here and now, for their creativity and ingenuity, but above all for their innate decency and humanity. They know who they are. In my book, they're nontradable. As to the villains, they too know who they are, and I don't want to dignify their existence any more than I have.

Finally, I want to thank those who made this book possible, starting with my parents, John A. Pedersen and Ellen E. Pedersen, who more or less endured my growing up; also, the family and friends off whom I have been freeloading for the past twenty-five years: the Abbates, Beth and Cathy Barish, Suzy Benzinger, the Borenzos, Burveniches, Castles, Joanne Condon, Bob and Renee Condon, Figuras, Fisks, Elisa Fromm, the Greenans, Greenblats, Heffleys, Herrmanns, Hohags, Beth Kleiman, the Kohnstamms, LaBadias, Tom Larsen, the LeFauves, Lieses, Christine and Rob Murphy, the Osgoods, Betty Ann Pedersen, the Pynes, Russell Ram, the Rankes, Ricketts, Schrecks, Sciandras, Howard Smith, Lt. Jim Stewart, Mary and Jerry Suszynski, Jim Watson, Sue Watson, the Wallens, and the Wessels.

Above all, I have a special sense of gratitude for my literary agent, the tweedy Robert I. Ducas, who looked at my diaries and saw the makings of a book; my wordsmith, the unghostly F. Peter Model, who turned that vision into a working manuscript; and my editor, James O'Shea Wade, who deftly shaped it into the book you now hold in your hands.

1

The Pit

I MADE MY FIRST million dollars as an options trader on the floor of the American Stock Exchange before I was legally old enough to buy, sell, or own a single share of stock.

The Securities and Exchange Commission requires that a person be twenty-one to participate directly in the stock market; the attorney general of the State of New York forbids anyone younger from acting in a fiduciary manner. In other words, at the age of twenty I was not allowed to handle other people's investment funds—nor, for that matter, my own.

Yet for nearly six years, from 1984 through 1989, I not only traded many millions of dollars' worth of stock index options, but at twenty I got my own seat on the Exchange— that is to say, my employer rented it for me—becoming the youngest person in Wall Street history up to that time to have done so.* Had I wanted to celebrate by buying my colleagues a full round at the bar downstairs, I couldn't have; I was underage.

| | |

I started at the Exchange in January of 1984 as a $120-a-week clerk on the main trading floor of the country's second-largest stock exchange, mindlessly feeding transactional punch cards into a data-processing machine. Two weeks later, after I had demonstrated my uncanny coffee-getting skills, I was recruited by the firm of Dritz, Goldring & Company—now defunct—to work as an assistant in the Market Value Index (XAM), one of several new products the Exchange introduced in 1983 to help the new breed of portfolio managers hedge or protect their stock positions during particularly turbulent trading sessions. I was raised to a munificent $150 a week. Eight months after that, when the XAM fizzled out for lack of customers, I switched to the outfit next door, Spear Leeds Kellogg/Investors Company, to work on the Major Market Index (XMI). This new index is an average of twenty blue-chip stocks, also known as a "market basket." Seventeen of these stocks help make up the Dow Jones Industrial Average (DJIA): American Express, AT&T, Chevron, Coca-Cola, Dow Chemical, DuPont, Eastman Kodak, Exxon, GE, GM, IBM, International Paper, Johnson & Johnson, Merck, Mobil Oil, Philip Morris, Proctor & Gamble, Sears,

---

*Seat prices, determined by the law of supply and demand, have been known to lease for as much as $6,200 a month after and sell for $420,000 (the week before the 1987 crash, a record high). That same $420,000 seat went for just $100,000 in September 1990, the month after Iraqi strongman Saddam Hussein forfeited Big Oil's post–Cold War "peace dividend." When I arrived at the AMEX (January 1984) the going price was $255,000. The greater the trading volume, the costlier the seat. Thus, during World War II, when the average daily volume was down to a mere 89,000 shares—a fraction of today's average of 12.4 million—seats could be bought for as little as $650.

3M, and USX. By taking a position in the XMI—betting whether the prices of these stocks would rise or fall—one didn't have to buy individual shares in each of the stocks (which one could only trade on the New York Stock Exchange, in any case).

Spear Leeds Kellogg/Investors Company, then two years old, was a joint venture of a well-known Wall Street firm, Spear Leeds & Kellogg, and a group of small trading firms, including that of Ronald Shear, the man who hired me.

Unlike Dritz's Market Value Index, the Spear Leeds XMI was a winner almost from the start. Because it generated more volume than any other product being traded, it was the only one to be accorded its own trading pit. Actually, "pit" is a misnomer: It more resembled a low-slung amphitheater for standees only—studded with and surrounded by video monitors and overhanging electronic tote boards. All the other new products were assigned to existing firms operating at trading posts.

Whenever a new product—stock or option—is ready to come to the trading floor, the Exchange conducts a lottery among all its members for the right to manage or "run" the product. Acting as a franchisor, the AMEX's allocations committee will accept applications from all paid-up members and make its decision on the basis of the applicants' past performances, their cash positions and willingness to expend capital, and similar hard-nosed criteria. It, too, has an investment to protect: its reputation, not to overlook the fact that in exchange for setting up these new operations, the AMEX gets a small cut of every single transaction, money that helps defray overhead costs.

As one of the XMI partners once explained it to me, "It's sort of like all the players in a Monopoly game getting together to vote on someone playing banker. You still trade as before, and just because you're sitting on the treasury doesn't mean you get to play under different rules."

Both XAM and XMI were market-basket products representing underlying stocks, thus enabling risk-minded investors to "trade" in these common stocks without actually having to buy or sell them individually. Where XAM's basket was just too big and cluttered with marginal issues to be of any value to the institutional investors, XMI was just what these heavy hitters were looking for to hedge their portfolios. It soon became the hottest new product to have been introduced in the history of the American Stock Exchange—in precrash 1987 trading as many as seventy-five thousand contracts a *day*—and Spear Leeds kept adding new traders, each of whom needed at least two clerks. Several weeks after going to work in the XMI pit, I found myself trading while the partners went out for a smoke or were otherwise preoccupied.

For the four years, three months, and thirteen days I traded— initially as a pinch hitter, then as a credentialed specialist—I did everything my parents told me never to do. Bad enough that I would antagonize, curse, spit, slug, kick, and terrorize, and fight with my colleagues—many of them older and probably wiser than I—but that I would do these things gladly and for a price struck me as ironic, given my abhorrence of confrontation of any kind.

Although I stand five-foot-ten, and as a teenager developed a pretty impressive set of biceps shoveling snow—de rigueur where I come from in upstate New York—I was the sort who would seldom pick a fight. Yelling, screaming, stomping, as my mother constantly reminded me, would never get me any- where. Yet, after I'd gotten my seat on the Exchange, one of the guys I'd just finessed came up out of the pit and congrat- ulated me. It's that sort of crazy business. "You've got a great future in options," he predicted. "You know why?" I shook my head. "You can scream loud, jump high, think fast, and count without using your fingers." And I can also read without moving my lips.

He turned out to be right. I *did* have a great future in options, as did the people I worked for. During those four years, three months, and thirteen days of trading, I generated more than $5.3 million in profits for Spear Leeds Kellogg/Investors Company. In turn, they rewarded me handsomely with an ever-expanding compensation package that, by the time I was twenty-three, came to more than $ 800,000 before taxes and that enabled me to *really* make money. For, as they say, what counts is not the money you make but the money you get to keep—to reinvest. Early on, I would take what little money I had left after living expenses—in New York City, not very much on a gross salary of sixteen thousand dollars—and buy some penny stock, silver futures, tax-free bonds, and options. In the Reagan bull market, my personal trading account grew exponentially. By early 1987, it carried a market value of one hundred thousand dollars. Added to a quarter of a million or so I made in year-end bonuses, these funds allowed me to get into real estate, which seemed to me a lot safer in the long run and, as it turned out, far more profitable.

Right after the October 1987 crash, which left my personal trading account gasping for a transfusion, I'd made up my mind. As did millions of other amateur players, I'd concluded that the sport had gone out of the game. The rules had changed; in the hands of the big boys, it had gone professional. More to the point, I also believed I could no longer march to the sound of two different drummers while on the job. So, for the good of my firm, which had by now made me a partner, I decided I had best protect the positions I held for the partnership by focusing all my energies on doing what I did best—trading index options—and to hell with everything else. I stopped reading the *New York Times* and *Wall Street Journal* stock-market tables and closed out my personal trading account.

It's no secret I "got out of the market" well before I left Wall Street for good. To those not in the securities business, this may smack of either heresy or a lack of faith. I submit it is nothing of the kind. Despite the famous biblical admonition, I know of few physicians who heal themselves, or lawyers who plead their own cases.

It was in my second year at the AMEX that I began investing ever so cautiously in real estate. I was hedging, putting some of my stock-trading profits into some residential properties in suburban New York and New Jersey. I got a real-estate license, enabling me to buy and sell. Along with some floor brokers, I bought multifamily units at foreclosure, fixed them up, then either sold or rented them for more than the mortgages. I then began adding undervalued commercial properties in upstate New York in anticipation of the boom that is bound to transform Erie and Niagara counties once the free-trade laws take full effect.

Thomas Wolfe was wrong: You *can* go home again.

| | |

Home was Amherst, New York (population 117,000), eleven miles east of Niagara Falls and the infamous Love Canal. For reasons I still haven't been able to get my parents to understand to this day, I'd dropped out of the University of Michigan after just one semester. If I'd wanted to be a movie star, I suppose I'd have headed west, to Hollywood; as I only sought to make a fortune, I flew east, to Wall Street. By the time I finally left the AMEX in October 1989, I was making close to half a million dollars a year as one of the AMEX's 217 specialists (or "broker's brokers"). As one of four partners of Spear Leeds, by then a forty-person operation, I'd received a modest salary topped by a gratifying year-end bonus. Once I became a partner—starting at one percent, then two—the better the firm did, the greater my rewards. The reverse also applied: If the firm posted a loss, which it did only once during my association with it, I shared in that, too. It wasn't easy giving back $50,000 that year. And don't let them kid you when they say it becomes easier the higher you go: On the Friday of the October 1987 crash, I made $100,000 for my firm, but on the following Monday lost $1.3 million and, the next day, another $350,000. True, I'd make it back within six months, but try going to sleep feeling guilty because you've just blown over $1.6 million of your company's money due to a wrong guess or bad timing.

Along the way, I'd enrolled at the New York University School of Business and, in my junior year at NYU, was invited by the New York Institute of Finance to run an investment-analysis course.

| | |

Seen now in the harsh glare of posteighties guilt, denial, and reprobation, the last decade seems light-years off in the galaxy. I am sure that one hundred years from now, when the hapless American taxpayer has finally paid for the unregulated sins of the junk bond–financed yuppie years, scholars will treat this period about as kindly as today's historians view the Great Dutch Tulip Mania of 1636–1637. But for us traders down on the floor of the Exchange, it was anything but a delusion. It was all so very real. If something was amiss, if capitalism was running amok, we didn't want to hear it. We were having too much fun. We intentionally shut our eyes to the shenanigans going on Out

There, beyond the heavy-metal mesh curtains covering the dirt-caked windows of the great hall.

If our superiors had any inkling about the amoral antics of those whose breaches of public trust would inevitably unleash the Furies of U.S. Attorney Rudolph Giuliani, they didn't share their misgivings with us.

Some of the better-known market manipulators like Michael Milken and Ivan Boesky ended the "Me Decade" awaiting sentences or serving time in such white-collar prisons as Lompoc or Allenwood. Others paid for their sins with tax-deductible fines or dictating self-serving memoirs, which speciously argued that whatever crimes had been committed were done in the name of market efficiency.

They were the more egregious examples of what went wrong in the Roaring Eighties: greed gone rampant. The junk bonds that Milken had "invented" ostensibly helped raise money for companies to expand or to be acquired through leveraged buyouts (LBO). The LBO can best be described as using borrowed money to buy a company you want at whatever the price because you want the company's assets. Once it is yours, you use the company mercilessly, often selling off its individual parts, in order to pay back the money you borrowed to buy it in the first place. Most of these target companies could not get bank loans: They were either credit rated B or lower or their plant and equipment were so antiquated that they could not be used as collateral. Although some companies did benefit, in most instances they failed, so that the stockholders were left holding the bag—if that—once it became clear that these takeover artists had in fact destroyed America's industrial infrastructure for their personal enrichment.

The coming decade will be harder for the young admirers

of the LBO set, those fuzzy-cheeked kids who, just a few years out of business school, succeeded-in-business-without-really-trying. Many are now out of work, lucky not to be in jail like that overpaid Drexel Burnham Lambert underling who thought it heroic to bite the bullet. Should she and the others still want to make a career on Wall Street in the stripped-down nineties, their reentry is bound to be a great deal tougher, because you can only start at the top *once*. They had a hell of a run.

Actually, so did we all. The only differences were that down on the floor, there could be no insider trading as we operated as middle men taking daily positions in order to fill and match buy/sell orders placed by the Exchange's customers. As it was all spur-of-the-moment, ours was a reactive business that simply made such hanky-panky impossible. What's more, down in the XMI pit, we worked unbelievably hard, making the primary markets, which the red-suspender brigades in their fancy uptown-skyscraper trading rooms played so adroitly during the debt-propelled Reagan years. All they had to do was to show up for work each day, whereas we floor traders—independent contractors—had to account for our losses. Daily. And make good on them.

We also subjected ourselves to the kind of physical abuse that no sane person this side of Teheran would long tolerate. We may have drawn the line at self-flagellation with whips and thorny rose bushes, but otherwise we did a pretty thorough job of wrecking our health. Burnout became the rule, not the exception. The stress alone should have disqualified most of us from getting health and disability insurance.

One day, fifteen of us from the floor went up to Mount Sinai Hospital to give blood to another trader who'd had heart surgery.

We were all rejected for colds, liver problems, high cholesterol levels. Two of my fellow traders were even asked to check in to undergo further testing.

| | | |

Completed in 1930, the fourteen-story American Stock Exchange is seldom mentioned in books extolling New York's architecture, probably because its nondescript art deco facade is overshadowed by the stately presence of Trinity Church, a true landmark, and its cemetery—the resting place of Alexander Hamilton. Were it not for the huge blue and white AMEX banner jutting out over Trinity Place, the industrial images of a ship, train, factory, bridge, windmill, and tractor sandblasted into the limestone, and the historical marker identifying it as the site of the old Curb Exchange, this could easily pass as just another downtown Manhattan office building. Appearances are deceptive: Step through its center doors and climb up a flight of stairs, and it's an altogether different story. You step into something as huge and as noisy as the flight deck of the carrier *John F. Kennedy*. They call it, with touching simplicity, the trading floor.

From the opening bell at 9:30 A.M. to closing at 4:15 P.M., I could be observed jumping up and down, appearing to be, to any rational outsider, either psychotic or demoniacally possessed. Flapping my arms like a seal, making frantic, funny, often obscene hand signals and gestures, I would routinely address my fellow traders as "shitbrain," "asshole," or "fuckhead." On some days, I'd work myself up into such a frenzy that I'd end some sessions literally foaming at the mouth.

What made it worse were the floor acoustics—sound bouncing around this huge, 33,000-square-foot, cavernous space, high enough to envelop a five-story apartment house. Built for a generation of traders far more sedate than today's, the hall was devoid of sound-dampening materials; as a result, it had all the charm and ambience of an immense aircraft hangar. After a while, we didn't even hear ourselves yell and scream.

We were traders: We were addicted either to the action or to the money that comes from being good at it. The *Dow Jones–Irwin Business & Investment Almanac* defines traders as "individuals who buy and sell for their own accounts for short-term profit." That's too simplistic a definition for what we did on the floor.

In the beginning, whenever people asked what I did for a living, I would tell them, "Buy and sell options at risk," which of course meant nothing to people who hadn't the foggiest idea of what happens on the floor of the stock exchange. After the blank stares, they'd say, "That's interesting, but just what is it you *do* all day long?" and without waiting for the answer, they'd get to the nub of the question: "What's it *like?*"

I often resisted the temptation of saying something glib like, "Oh, you know, sort of like crossing a six-lane freeway on foot at rush hour." Actually, the freeway simile is not all that outlandish. In the pit, as an options trader juggling millions of dollars in nanoseconds, I would often also double as ringmaster over an unruly mob of bawling, often brawling human animals —sweating, gum-cracking, foul-mouthed men (and three women) in their twenties and thirties—capable of leaping over the barrier dividing us, ready to kill. I was expected to think and act and anticipate all at once, employing all my wiles, all my senses, including or especially my sixth. If I so much as hesitated, showed an iota of indecision, I'd risk being financially obliterated.

On the floor, where I began, we traders would determine the price at which AMEX-listed stocks, bonds, options, and treasury bills should trade the instant we were handed buy-sell orders pouring in from brokerage houses, banks, and institutional and even private investors from all over the world. We would determine *price*, not value. There's a big difference between determining what something *should* sell for and what it *might* be worth.

One reason the Exchange floor turns into bedlam is that when it comes to value, no two people will ever agree. The determining factor is that enigma called "prevailing market conditions." The plural is used because the conditions change from minute to minute, depending on interest rates, trade deficits, inflation, wars, revolutions, and the results of the president's annual physical at Bethesda.

Who determines the current price? Few people bother to ask. The answer is whoever placed the last order. It's nothing more or less than the highest amount somebody was willing to pay (or receive) for a share of stock at the precise moment the order ticket was handed up to the man or woman trading that particular issue.

Think of the trading floor as some sort of gigantic auto showroom in which three hundred or so competing dealers are trying to clear out their models from last year, along with last year's trade-ins (kept discreetly out of sight), while still keeping enough inventory on hand in case some cash-carrying customers walk through the door ready to make a fast, on-the-spot deal. When not watching the door, the dealers are pondering *their* prevailing market conditions—steel prices, latest Labor Department employment figures, consumer lending rates, travel trends, and so forth—while keeping a wary eye on their own costs of doing business, overhead, commissions payable, carrying inventory, and outstanding customer loans.

Where stock traders and auto dealers differ is that our customers "walk in" every few seconds and turn over the entire inventory in less than an hour of trading. We might make as many as five hundred decisions in that time and pray that half of them will be sound, so that we can still trade the next day.

Also, a stock trader may often buy a "dog" of a stock, even though there may be no demand at the present time for this particular equity or he may already have more on hand than he could possibly unload at that particular moment. Unlike the market for new and used cars, the stock market—being cyclical—is more predictable. With rare exceptions, what goes down eventually goes back up, and so it's always better to have something to trade than to be caught empty-handed. With few exceptions, anything bought at the right price in a business predicated on the principle of "buy low, sell high" is a good investment, because eventually someone will come along and want it. And as long as there are hungry bankers willing to lend "on margin," most firms believe it pays to keep a larger inventory than they can possibly use up.

Like our proverbial car dealer, most of the time traders will calculate how much they can get a customer to pay before the customer walks away. Knowing the breakpoint comes with years of practice of analyzing customers and knowing their markets. Of course, at some point everyone miscalculates. Given such unpredictable calamities as the two October crashes of 1987 and 1989, even the best trader can end up with a huge inventory that is going to be hard to unload. When that happens, the trader goes belly-up. In a flash.

| | | |

The place where I ultimately ended up working, the so-called pit, is a space set apart from the rest of the trading floor. Its sixty-five square feet of space are filled with more people than you could cram into a subway car. The XMI pit, however, was no auto showroom. And the only cup of coffee you got while waiting for the next trade came flying through the air. I was pummeled, stepped and spat on, jostled, hassled, and grabbed. At the end of some of the wilder trading sessions, after we'd moved a couple of million dollars in a single hour, I'd drag myself home wearing clothes encrusted with dried ketchup, my panty hose shredded. Some days the damage would have been done after the first mad hour of trading. My sweat-stained blouses would either be torn to ribbons, punctured by unguided ballpoint pens thrown like spears, or soaked by spilled cans of soda thoughtlessly parked in the way of my flapping arms. My working outfits would often have to be discarded after only one wearing. (Early on, after going through ten sets of panty hose a week and several Ann Taylor suits, I switched to battle fatigues—cotton slacks and seven-dollar shirts from a nearby discount-clothing outlet.) We all suffered from the Count Dracula syndrome. Because the giant windows of the Exchange are covered with gray mesh screens, after a while it became impossible to tell night from day. With so little natural light, many of us started wearing sunglasses whenever we had to go outside ("ARGGHH, that *sun!*"). Some of us would keep them on even after we were inside, because they served to protect our eyes from flying paper clips and staples.

We faced more hazards than just those Identified Flying Objects. We'd be routinely jabbed and poked with pencils, pretzel sticks, and calculators. The staples were the worst; they'd often lacerate my skin. The configuration of the XMI trading pit didn't help. Body heat accumulated rapidly, inverted, and became trapped like smog in the Los Angeles basin, forcing the governors to unofficially exempt us traders from having to wear those light-blue pinstriped jackets. This made our shirts targets for anyone wielding a rubber stamp ("Just what is it you do for a living?" my exasperated dry cleaner asked me one day. "Train circus lions?"). We'd get paper cuts from handling price-reporting cards and order decks, requiring a quick trip over to Beekman Hospital for some stitches. We'd get slammed by fists and elbows of clerks and brokers trying to maneuver in and around the masses of screaming traders and specialists. As half-empty cans of soda that were jammed between monitors tipped over, their syrupy contents would pour down my legs and run into the sneakers I wore to give my aching feet some relief from standing on them for hours on end. When I walked, I would hear the squish-squash, reminiscent of sloshing through the marshes, hunting for frogs in day camp.

There was never time either to worry about it or to wipe it up. No time to do a quick body check for blood or bruises; there were plenty of both. As long as we could still make out the blue plastic badges and hear trades being made, we'd keep going. You learned to walk in extremely tight circles: Swerve too fast and you'd collide with another hurrying trader or, worse, a heavy metal time clock or large computer screen that you'd swear wasn't there yesterday.

I'd get hurt but would be in such a backbreaking rush that it would be hours before the shock would wear off and I'd feel the full impact of the concussion. One night I looked in the mirror and saw a bruise on my forehead three inches in diameter. I tried to remember how and when, that day, it had happened.

Then there were the plain old occupational hazards; for example, fire. On one particularly hectic afternoon, the electrical wiring overloaded and set a pile of paper trash smoldering. With so much money at stake, none of the traders dared leave the pit, making it impossible for the clerks and others to evacuate. Then the pile of paper ignited. As the billowing smoke filled the pit, my boss, Ron Shear, and I tied handkerchiefs over our faces—he

breathing and moaning, and told us that it's impossible to breathe properly and scream from the diaphragm "ven you are angry or excited." I wonder how well Frederika von Stade would sound if, each time she sang an aria, she lost one hundred thousand dollars?

Actually, the lessons weren't a total bust. I can now hail a taxicab from ten blocks away.

2

The Bimbo Contest

ESPITE ALL THE residual discomfort that will dog me for the rest of my life, I wouldn't have wanted to be anywhere else. It was great while it lasted. Years from now, we'll be regaling our children, and theirs, with war stories of what it was like when people rather than machines still handled trades. Chances are they won't care. They'll probably be more interested in hearing about Black Monday, Terrible Tuesday, and where we were, what we did, the day the bubble burst.

Some bubble. For longer than anyone dared to hope, it kept growing bigger, shinier, and probably more transparent—as if nobody could foresee that every upward curve has its downside.

It was a time for sheer decadence, debauchery, and occasional depravity. All of us were living it up in grand style. Name any of the seven deadly sins—pride, covetousness, lust, anger, gluttony, envy, and sloth—we practiced them all. Joyfully.

Even the overworked price-quote reporters and underpaid clerks had caught the spirit and were living well beyond their means. Why worry about tomorrow? *Borrow!*

As a result, in the roaring Reagan 1980s, *everything* was up: the Standard & Poor's 500, the Dow Jones industrial average, bar tabs downstairs at Harry's, year-end bonuses, stress levels, cholesterol counts, bomb scares, psychiatric referrals, and the demand for limousines—waiting out front, engines purring, at the close of trading to rush anyone willing to pay the cost of going uptown or out of town.

Commuter-rail and mass-transit ridership was off, as was attendance at Wednesday PTA meetings, Friday-night temple, and Sunday-morning church services. God wasn't so much dead as conferring after-hours with his portfolio managers. Proof of that came the day John Cardinal O'Connor of New York came on the floor, walking around and blessing wedding rings, hastily extracted baby pictures, boxes of Dr. Scholl bunion pads—anything and everything that could possibly be blessed.

But the minute the bell rang and the action got under way, the cardinal's faithful abandoned him. He became the Maytag repairman, the loneliest guy around. On that day his entourage came down from Saint Patrick's, I last saw him out of the corner of my eye, shuffling rather forlornly toward trading post 11, reaching out to people who hadn't the time for His Eminence. The word must have come down, because on the next payday, a number of his flock wrote checks made out to the Society for the Propagation of the Faith.

The day after the October 1987 meltdown, when the Dow plunged 508 points and $1.7 trillion in paper assets simply evaporated in a span of seventy-two hours, Peter LaBadia, a "two-dollar" floor broker from New Jersey with whom I'd become friendly during my clerical training, remembered the cardinal's curtailed mission. Though Catholic, he could not resist calling out, to no one in particular, "Hey, Your Eminence, where are you now that we need you?"

| | | |

Of all the characters I met during my years at the Exchange, the hyperkinetic, bantam-sized LaBadia is surely the most unforgettable. And generous. To an eighteen-year-old, footloose and friendless, in Manhattan for the first time and having to make her way in a large, hostile city—LaBadia, his wife, Beverly, and their two children became my surrogate suburban family. I spent so much time over at their house that I soon became known as their third—"rental"—kid. If one could pick one's father, older brother, and best friend in one and the same person, there'd be no contest: Pete would win hands down. In fact, looking back now, I don't know how I could have survived the first year without his irreverence, his sense of the ridiculous. Maybe that was what drew us together: the shared feeling that one had to be crazy to do what we were doing for a living.

He'd been at it a lot longer than me, having come to the AMEX in 1960, at age twenty, after starting out as a professional jazz drummer. He never gave that up. Every time there was a recession, LaBadia would pick up different "revenue-enhancing" sidelines—managing a band (1969–1970), playing solo in a piano bar and lounge singing (1974–1975), selling residential real estate (1980–1982). Finally, in May of 1990, a victim of automation, Pete packed it in and, with another broker, Al Abbate, went into the printing business in New Jersey.

Pete takes his share of kidding because of his slightly apelike posture, which was not the result of foraging for food but of spending thirty years walking fifteen miles a day around the trading floor, eyes darting to and from the sheafs of buy-sell orders clutched in his hands, always going, going, going.

A Staten Islander, Pete speaks a Kojak-style English, clearly residual from his band-playing years. "Hey, baby," he'd say to a sixty-two-year-old Groton- and Harvard-schooled broker, "you're a cool cat! Love ya but I gotta run!" He once dismissed Arthur Levitt, chairman of the Exchange: "I'm beepin', man, gotta split. Catch ya 'round." His dress mode is strictly the antithesis of U.S. Army Quartermaster issue—a riot of conflicting patterns and screaming colors, sort of like the Grand Canyon at sunset.

ı   ı   ı

No question about it. Downtown Manhattan was awash with money. Wall Street was raking it in about as fast as Washington could print it. The old joke about wearing out your credit cards from overuse ceased being funny when one of the city's three tabloids discovered ladies of the night working the South Street Seaport, carrying charge-plate imprinters in their handbags.

We paid others to do everything for us except eat, sleep, and of course trade. Take that away and we were nothing. Rather than complain, we bragged about how much we had to pay in taxes. One year, my federal, state, and city taxes came to one hundred thousand dollars—more than twice what both my working parents took home in salaries during their best year.

Before the days of reckoning, employment on Wall Street more than doubled, as did business-school enrollments. The lure of being able to pull down six-figure incomes with just two years' (or less) experience proved irresistible to graduates who, in any other era, might have gone into environmental law, biomedicine, inner-city education, or Third World nutrition.

It was no coincidence that during this time the *Wall Street Journal* added a third section and nearly doubled its circulation and newsstand price. There were nearly forty thousand corporate takeovers, mergers, and buy-outs. Pensioners, as yet blissfully unaware that their plans were being bled dry by the junk-bond mania, realized the best possible returns on their investments and plunged back into the market.

Those with long memories of the Great Depression, too skittish to entrust their life savings to the booming stock market, played it safe—they thought—by putting their money into unregulated savings-and-loan institutions that promised them, at the very least, the moon.

On Wall Street, the simple Friday-afternoon ritual of asking people what they intended to do that weekend would elicit such conversation stoppers as, "Oh, not much. I might take the Concorde to a party one of the Bear Stearns guys is having in Soho"— the one in London, of course. Guys who just a few years earlier bought their shirts by the gross from Sears or K-Mart now thought nothing of being fitted by Ascot Chang uptown, who would then have the shirts cut, monogrammed, and couriered in from Hong Kong.

Those who had once made a production out of taking the subway to the blue-collar beach at Far Rockaway now were routinely jetting down to Martinique or Cozumel for a weekend of snorkeling.

When I started clerking, *Options As a Strategic Investment* by Larry McMillan was the bible for traders. A year later, McMillan had been supplanted by *Chapman's Piloting, Seamanship & Small Boat Handling* by Elbert S. Maloney. (It begins with the question "What is a boat?")

Everyone was either buying a boat, trading up to a boat, making their old boat the dinghy on their new boat, or getting a Bell helicopter (and pad) for the top of their boat, just like *The Highlander*, the late Malcolm Forbes's boat. Or else they were flying down to South Carolina and Florida for some comparative boat shopping. Discount, of course.

Outside the Exchange, it was clearly a seller's market. The guys on the floor made the most of their newfound spending power, only they balked at paying retail. One of them came in one morning flashing a flawless three-carat white emerald-cut diamond ring he'd bought his girl the day before, uptown at Van Cleef & Arpels, and when he showed it off, the guys hooted at him for having acted like a dumb tourist. Smart traders didn't go to Van Cleef, they went instead to drive hard bargains on West Forty-seventh Street, Manhattan's famous diamond district where deals are made with a handshake.

But that wasn't the end of his troubles. Soon after New Year's, when he got home, his *wife* flashed something else. American Express had just introduced its "detailed charge report" for the previous year. These annual summaries probably were responsible for driving up the divorce rate that year.

Who got the diamond ring? the wife demanded to know. *When* were you in Aruba? And just *what* is this charge for room service at the Plaza? All over the tri-state area men went packing off to Manhattan hotels. A bunch of them marched down to American Express headquarters in the new World Financial Center and tore up their cards. AMEX must have gotten the message: Soon thereafter, those who requested it were sent their annual summaries at work.

As the markets became busier and more volatile, it became impossible even for the company big shots to escape for lunch. But instead of running out to the nearby Burger King or sending one of the runners for a Sabrett hot dog from the pushcarts on Trinity Place, they'd order in—deli containers of beef Wellington, lobster bisque, chocolate mousse. One guy even arranged to have his lunchtime martinis sent in a coffee cup, with olives on the side.

Clearly, money was no object. There was so much of it floating around that it was becoming a commodity, *play* money. Many could not even wait for the opening bell to move it or lose it. During the Super Bowl games, for instance, just before trading began, high-stakes gambling took place right in the open. There'd be several betting pools, as high as $100,000, that one could get into for a minimum of $125. Some of the fiercest bettors turned out to be the clerks, the guys who could least afford to blow half a week's wages for admittance into the pool. They would do so because winning could mean instant retirement. One could always tell when a clerk won the pool; he wouldn't hang around until closing but be off the floor in ten seconds flat.

Then there were other indoor sports, such as the "bimbo contest," held one week during the summer when trading slowed down to a crawl. You could tell that something was under way just by looking at those trading posts that seemed to be teeming with tall, skinny blondes wearing enough pancake makeup to drive up the stock of the company that currently owns Max Factor and enough hair spray to shellac the deck of one of Elbert S. Maloney's small boats. Normally, they could be seen down in Harry's Bar & Restaurant in the Exchange building on Friday afternoons, hoping to connect with traders who were looking particularly flush and prepared to paint the town with green— greenbacks, that is. Now, here they were, touring the floor like a bunch of visiting dignitaries.

Two traders had bet each other that they could get the most "bimbos" to come for a tour of the floor in the span of one week. The bimbos were assigned a value of a thousand dollars each, which meant that if each trader brought in twenty, the contest was declared a tie and nobody won; but for every bimbo over the tie figure, someone would gain, or lose, a thousand dollars. And of course there was side action similar to a basketball game with point spreads that constantly shifted as the week wore on.

The trader corralling the greatest number of candidates would take his winnings and treat them all to cocktails at Harry's downstairs and perhaps dinner—accompanied by those bettors who didn't have to go home to their families.

On this particular occasion, faced with a shortage of candidates and the certainty of losing to his rival, one of the traders marched by our post, trailed by a bevy of seventeen leotarded women who didn't quite fit the occupational MO. As others gaped in disbelief, he leered, saying, "I got it locked up. This makes it forty-six to his thirty-three" (a cool thirteen thousand dollars of weekend spending money).

"Nice," said the broker next to me approvingly. "Where'd you get them?"

"Hah! Down the street at that fitness center—entire aerobics class. Promised them all a vegetarian dinner in Chinatown." As there was no time to take the dispute to arbitration, the judges gave it to him for sheer bravado and creativity.

"Think of the bimbo contest as a preemptive strike," one of the traders confided to me the first time I saw one getting under way. "Instead of them picking us off, one by one, we go out after them, wine 'em and dine 'em and take first dibs. It's more efficient that way. Sorta like program trading."

| | |

Harry's, which was shut down for good in the summer of 1990, supposedly to create more trading space, had long served as the AMEX's unofficial nerve center. With its wood-paneled walls, its dark nooks and crannies, and subdued lighting just made for conspiratorial tête-à-têtes, Harry's was where all of us used to hatch our practical jokes, our trading strategies, and complain about our love lives.

For years Harry's served admirably as a combination co-ed locker room, dating bureau, recovery ward, and officers' club that had been grudgingly opened also to the enlisted men and women. The food would never win any culinary prizes—dinner was okay, but the hors d'oeuvres were abysmal, the Swedish meatballs (AKA sodium balls) particularly loathsome and probably lethal. But people didn't go there to eat, they went there to talk. Wildly exaggerated talk, usually. Baron von Münchausen, the eighteenth-century soldier of fortune known for his braggadocio, would have been quite at home here as, with every drink, the big trading exploits seemed to gain in magnitude what they lacked in veracity. In all the times I spent down there, I can't recall running into any losers.

Most of the action at Harry's would take place after the closing bell and would generally be confined to either the bar or the dining room across the way, also known as the Inventor Room. This moniker came about because this was someone's idea of what an intimate bastion of capitalism should look like—Leatherette banquettes, bookcases jammed with faux leatherbound books extolling business and industry, hunting-green walls festooned with the names of inventors (Guglielmo Marconi, Robert Fulton, Eli Whitney, Thomas A. Edison, Alexander Graham Bell, Cyrus McCormick, among them). By eight o'clock, a different crowd would settle in, the regulars having moved on to other nearby watering holes, such as the Pink Pussycat Lounge at Greenwich and Rector or the South Street Seaport.

There were two ways into Harry's—down a flight of stairs from the main AMEX trading floor or through the front door on Greenwich Street. Which door you used determined true status:

The "civilians" would, of course, have to come in from the street, past the checkroom, where Orestes, the eagle-eyed captain, kept a supply of ill-fitting jackets and garish neckties for those found failing the dress code.

The richest guys there weren't necessarily the customers but the veteran waiters and busboys. Some of them must have been descendants of Jay Gould, the legendary Wall Street robber baron. They often pocketed tips bigger than the tabs. A few of them had been passed down, like family retainers, from father to son, and one could tell their length of service by the degree of intimacy bestowed on their clients. Some of them didn't wait for the customer to leave to take up the collection. For example, the Asian busboy in charge of bringing out the "free" pizza squares after 5:00 P.M. pretended to be deaf and dumb, but we knew better. I don't know about his English, but certainly his hearing came back dramatically whenever some hungry trader would wave him over, a five-dollar bill jammed between his fingers. No fin, no pizza, it was as simple as that.

Often customers would leave without settling their bills, but these were the regulars and nobody worried about being stiffed. Orestes, the captain, knew most of the six hundred or so steady patrons by name; most of them had open accounts, so the waiters would tote up the bill, add a *very* generous tip for themselves (and something for Orestes, as well), and that would be that.

Not that they didn't earn their money. The regular waiters welcomed insults, just as long as they got paid for it. In that respect, they were no different from the clerks upstairs, who quickly learned that forty percent of their take-home pay went for the actual physical labor, sixty percent for taking unmerited abuse.

Orestes, especially, earned what he made. He may have had

the most thankless job of all. Not only was he the overall circus master but also chief telephone operator, taking calls from traders and clerks still stuck upstairs and relaying them to the right person (who sometimes didn't want to be found, meaning Orestes would have to come back to the phone and say the individual wasn't there). Knowing most of the maître d's in Manhattan also helped when it came time to make reservations for VIPs who didn't want to be caught dead eating Harry's food. Orestes also took care of ordering limos, pouring the habitual drunks into summoned taxis, and knowing who not to seat next to so-and-so.

As long as everyone was getting theirs, and then some, the camaraderie knew no bounds and led to a bull market in practical and not-so-practical jokery—especially during occasional trading lulls, when there was nothing to do but wait for the action to rebound. One favorite pastime was pie throwing. Mind you, we were all grown-up professionals, but were a visitor from one of Europe's staid bourses to walk in unannounced, he might be forgiven for thinking he was witnessing a college fraternity hazing or the Keystone Cops.

Pies would be thrown for any occasion, no matter how trivial. Actually, the white stuff was Cool-Whip, the brilliant inspiration of a local baker who figured out he'd make a lot more profit filling his pies with canned glop than with fresh fruit and marking it up to an exorbitant twenty dollars a pop. Or more accurately, *plop*. Should the scene be interrupted by circulating floor officials, the perpetrators could expect to be hit by a series of fines, which began at fifty dollars when pie throwing was still a novelty and rose incrementally to one hundred as more money poured into the market. By the time of the 1987 crash, a complex penalty system had been enacted, calling for graduated penalties—so much for first offense, second, third, and so on. But what's a hundred or two hundred bucks in fines to fellows taking home two or three million dollars a year?

(It was a lot different back in the 1870s, but then so was the take-home pay. While the rough-and-tumble brokers of the Curb Exchange were whooping and hollering in the street, the top-hatted and swallow-tailed swells over at the New York Stock Exchange were expected to comport themselves like gentlemen. If not, they'd pay. The fine for smoking a cigar was five dollars; standing on a chair, ten bucks, as it was for throwing a paper dart. That's why most brokers settled for knocking off the other fellow's stove top. Fine: fifty cents.)

One trader, the dean of the AMEX specialists, liked clowning around and had more tricks up his sleeve than a magician. But like so many on the floor, he was a sucker for good-luck charms. Otherwise-sophisticated traders are under such relentless pressure and have so few hard facts on which to base their buy-sell decisions that they have to grab at *something* for stability.

This guy's was a toy rubber mouse named Mitchell (after Mitchell Energy Development Corporation, which apparently had been very, very good to him). Daily, he would rub Mitchell's nose for good luck, before heading into the fray.

One day, Mitchell disappeared. The poor man thought he'd lost his charm. In fact, the mouse had been kidnapped by one of his cronies, who must have sat up all night to painstakingly assemble one of those anonymous ransom notes. The bereaved parent was told to leave one hundred dollars with one of the security guards. He refused. "It's the principle of the thing," he said, "not the principal." Whereupon the kidnapper—no doubt inspired by the Getty kidnapping in Rome back in the 1970s—cut off Mitchell's ear and sent it up to the post where this man traded. He still refused to pay. By the time the gag was over he needed epoxy glue to put his mouse back together.

Sometimes even the most elaborate jokes get out of hand. There were two rival trading partners near the Merrill Lynch post up on the mezzanine. Let's just call them Bill and Joey. For weeks, Joey had been trying to get even with Bill, who had somehow lifted Joey's thirty-foot cabin cruiser out of Long Island Sound and relaunched it in his friend's brand-new Olympic-size swimming pool the day before Joey's birthday party.

Now, Bill was accustomed to sending his clerk out each morning to the nearest cigar store on West Broadway for fifty New York State one-dollar lottery tickets. After observing this ritual for several days, Joey learned that New York State lets you choose your own six numbers. So, one day, Joey got this fiendish idea. He picked up the *New York Post* and jotted down the winning numbers. Bill as yet had not come in. When he did, Joey knew, Bill would plunge right into trading, break for lunch, and just before the 2:00 P.M. lull would reach for either the *New York Post* or tune in radio station WINS and then check the numbers on his tickets. So Joey took Bill's clerk into his confidence and had him run out to get a ticket with *that day's* winning number on it, which wouldn't be good until the *next* day. He then slipped it into Bill's stack of tickets, sat back, and waited.

Sure enough, at 2:00 P.M. Bill leaned back against the side of the post and began flipping through the stack of tickets. The odds were 1 in 25.8 million.

"Holy shit!" he bellowed, turning his ticket this way and that to make sure of the numbers. Still shaking his head in disbelief, he had his clerk call the neighborhood liquor store to confirm the winning numbers.

The clerk dutifully dialed and wordlessly handed Bill the receiver. Bill listened, then dropped it. "Sixteen million dollars! Sixteen million fuckin' dollars! Call my wife. *No,* I'll call my wife!"

He announced his resignation on the spot. Joey and the other guys took him downstairs to Harry's for a round of farewell drinks. Naturally, Bill had a few too many. His pals prevailed upon him to resign formally from his firm. They followed him upstairs, where he confronted his boss. He began by telling him how rich he now was and, almost as an afterthought, said, "You little p———. I've really hated you and all your scumbag executives . . . and this stinking firm." The boss's wife, he said, had "the depth of a pie pan." He rambled on and on, ignoring the brays of laughter behind his back. Enough, already. Joey took him aside and confessed. Bill promptly passed out.

When he came to, he pleaded with management. His boss wasn't ready to forgive or forget. This was the same Bill who, the year before, had placed a piranha in his boss's fishtank, expensively stocked with rare tropical fish. Bill had made good with eight thousand dollars' worth of fish replacements. But in the end, the boss relented and tore up Bill's resignation. He had no choice: Bill was making too much money for them.

No MBAs Need
Apply

EVEN TODAY, AFTER nearly two years of decompression, of going over my daily journals and vicariously reliving the life that I led as a post-teenage trader, I'm still not exactly sure where all the money came from. Not that it makes much difference now. I took my money and ran. It was there for the taking. You had to work for it, but you were assured it was there. Some of the young traders, late to the game, made the mistake of believing it would *always* be there.

I was once told by a gambler friend of mine that, in order to feel comfortable about having money, you first have to get over the fear of losing it. Gambling is what the floor of any options exchange is all about. Its business is to make primary markets in stocks, options, and bonds. This means determining the price at which a company should be trading, based on all the information available.

Trading index options was quite different. We *avoided* digesting all of the news. "Too much information clogs the brain cells," my mentor Ron Shear of Spear Leeds Kellogg/Investors Company observed on numerous occasions, "just enough to understand the Big Issues of the day." Like, that when interest rates go up, the Dow Jones industrial averages go down.

Then it becomes a race as to who can figure out the price the fastest. Some people use computers, some use their brains, and some go by instinct. As I've never known how to use the computer for anything but word processing, I must fall into the last two categories.

It's purely a game of speed, and the ones who can do the valuation in their heads without having to punch numbers into a hand-held calculator usually win.

Some of it is innate, and the rest is acquired through experience and repetition—in short, trial and error. Trading can't be learned in school or from books. Trust me. I tried.

| | | |

You can visit the casinos in Las Vegas or Atlantic City and the very worst that can happen is that the house takes back every cent you bring to the table or feed the slots. But on Wall Street, you not only forfeit your investment but everything you use as collateral—your house, your car, the kids' college educations, sometimes even your spouse of many years' standing. Your loved one may have gotten so used to the good life that, when it ends abruptly, so does the marriage. It happens more often than you might think.

And, as if that weren't bad enough, if you're like some heavy traders I knew, you're likely to spend the next ten years paying off the loans. That's because, when you bet on options, only a small percentage of the pot is yours; the rest is either borrowed or someone else's money. Typical was a big trader I'll call Dennis, a three-time loser with whom I struck up a conversation one afternoon down at Harry's. He was nursing a whole pitcherful of martinis, looking disconsolate as hell, when he poured out his tale of woe. He'd just lost a cool million upstairs, "only fifty thousand of which was mine; the rest I'll have to scrape up somewhere." He told me he loved "living on the edge." What he didn't tell me was that this was his third go-round; he still owed on the first and second.

For the salaried trader, which I was before being made a partner in December 1987, there was additional stress. At the end of each trading day, the senior partners would phone or visit to ask, "How'd you do today?"—translated, "Did you make us money or lose it?"

Lose too many deals, too often, and you'd also lose your job. I have seen traders drop three-quarters of a million on a Tuesday and by Wednesday be gone, never to be seen again. You don't even notice they're gone until you happen to pass the bulletin board in the members' lounge and see the posting of the latest seat transfers. A new player's shoes quickly fill the empty cubbyhole in the coat room.

Given the median age of an option/futures trader—32.7 years—the stress-induced burnout rate would seem to be one of the highest on Wall Street. It's said to be the highest of any occupation, save that of air-traffic controller. One often encounters floor brokers (who execute orders for another firm or individual and work on commission) in their late sixties, but seldom an options trader who has hit fifty.

Few of my friends understood what all the excitement was about last year when Nolan Ryan became the oldest no-hit pitcher in baseball history. "At forty-two," one of them told me, "he's in better shape than some of the thirty-year-olds I trade with."

During my five-plus years in the XMI pit, I recall few, if any, fortieth-birthday parties—forty being to options trading what sixty-five is to just about any other profession.

Whenever a trader pushing thirty-five would ask to be excused in order to take his mandatory annual physical, some younger wise guy would recite that old joke about the doctor telling his patient, after the annual physical examination, that he was in remarkable shape for a guy his age, "but if I were you, from now on, buy only one suit and shirt at a time."

Should a trader make it to the ripe old age of fifty without having to undergo a quadruple bypass, it's usually cause for a big celebratory dinner downstairs at Harry's. Most traders I know don't like doctors, because each time they go for a physical they're told to quit what they're doing and seek other employment. Which is why, I suppose, so many of them depend on patent medicines and seek their own home remedies for everything that ails them, from stress fractures and bleeding ulcers to nearsightedness and tonsillitis.

My friend Frankie Borenzo, a specialist in the XMI pit, says he once "made the mistake" of seeking professional medical advice about his loss of hearing. *Mistake*, because "the crazy doctor accused me of deliberately jabbing a knife in my ear."

| | | |

At twenty-two, I often dragged myself home feeling fifty. Oddly, at the same time I could not wait to return to combat the next day. Part of it was the same feeling one gets from coming back a winner from Las Vegas or Atlantic City—the elation of having more money in one's pocket at the end of a day of trading than one had that morning.

Even more energizing, I suspect, was the feeling of instant gratification, the exhilaration of creating options strategies and knowing instantly, or by the latest the next day, whether I'd been right or wrong. Corporate executives make big decisions that don't pay off for five, perhaps even ten years, and sometimes never. I've often heard it said that a floor trader makes more decisions in a single day than the average CEO makes in a year.

The people I traded with on the floor bore little if any resemblance to the caricature Wall Street yuppies of the movies. Sad to say, I never ran into anyone as sympathetic as Kris Kristofferson in *Rollover*, as smooth and lovable as the Harrison Ford hero of *Working Girl*, or as reptilian and messianic as Michael Douglas as Gordon ("greed is good") Gekko in *Wall Street*.

Most of the big operators I ran into would tend to sputter, grunt, curse, or mumble—in that order. Articulation, poise, and charm were hardly their strong suits. Most of my bosses and, later, partners were strictly blue-collar working guys. These guys didn't mind brown-bagging their lunch or chewing while barking orders, and they liked talking cars and sports, laughed a great deal and loud, and openly expressed their contempt for the yuppie investment-banker types uptown; they went to church or synagogue and spoke the Queens (New York) English—with a couple of "dems" and "doses" thrown in. And they had all traded baseball cards and played stickball as kids. They didn't kiss anybody's ass for anything or look up to the millionaires on the floor (and there were a lot), and they didn't look down at the janitor sweeping away their mess. Sure, they would talk down to their clerks and anyone who was on the payroll, but that was all part of being an underling. Yet, compared to others I've dealt with since leaving Wall Street, I'd be inclined to say they were among the most brilliant, gutsy, generous, straight-shooting, and witty people who had to elbow for a living. In the heat and passion of multimillion-dollar trading, we might fight and vow never to have anything to do with each other again, as-long-as-we-both-shall-live. But, afterward, we'd be pounding each other on the back on our way out.

| | | |

Unlike me, most of them did not set out to make a career on Wall Street. They only came to the AMEX because the market was a place where they could make big money without fancy degrees or climbing up the slippery slope of corporate life. A number of them had been cops, truck drivers, plumbers; many were high-school dropouts. Others, better educated, had given up promising but boring jobs in law, dentistry, landscaping, accounting, education, and industry. A few had interesting previous or present positions, such as bounty hunting for banks tracing deadbeat debtors or collecting human skins for hospital burn centers.

The skin collector would be trading hot and heavy when his beeper went off, indicating that a potential donor had died, at which point he'd dash off to collect the donor's skin and rush it over to the designated medical-center burn unit. I can only assume he did not personally participate in the peeling process, or watch it.

Because of such diverse backgrounds and the incredible resourcefulness of people who worked on the floor, we didn't have to go far to have our taxes done, close on a house, put in a swimming pool, pave the driveway, or, for all I know, have our bodies vulcanized.

Everybody was a trader, wheeler, dealer, schemer, or dreamer. This became evident whenever the trading slowed to a trickle, leaving everybody with little to do but dream up new mischief. As a breed, traders suffer from an incredibly low boredom threshold. Whenever there was nothing to do, someone would break out a couple of backgammon boards. We usually played for money. Once, when I hadn't yet gone to the bank and had even run out of subway tokens, I played a vegetarian trader for twelve pounds of seedless grapes and a bag of alfalfa sprouts. I lost.

My friend Michael Gann was a normally crazed broker who virtually lived in the pit. He was so good at pushing his way through the bodies and getting good executions for his customers that he had enough business to keep him constantly frenzied. It's such a high-tension job that, in the thirty seconds between receiving orders, Michael would reach for his trusty crossword puzzle just to keep his brain from slowing down for a second and possibly starting to sputter and smoke.

Others went in for less cerebral distractions, like scalping concert tickets, booking travel, or structuring real-estate partnerships. I was never convinced they did it for the money— they had to give themselves something to do. It's that kind of business.

If nothing else, the floor is about the interdependence of money and momentum. Even the clerks would get into the entrepreneurial mode by selling hats, sneakers, wallets, coats, anything that could be transported into the Exchange. I once bought a men's 36-short camel's-hair overcoat simply by hand signaling to a clerk way up in the balcony. He held it up, modeled it, and tossed it down. Free delivery but no receipt.

All these guys had come to the AMEX because they were fed up with punching in and out of time clocks. Most wanted to be independent contractors, to be their own boss. More to the point, all had an instinct and a proficiency for down-and-dirty gambling. They knew all the theory of risk and reward—risk one to make three. That alone set them apart from the floor brokers, who made their money by executing orders. So when these adventurous men got wind of the big bucks to be made downtown, without any entrance qualifications such as a college degree or an aristocratic background, they reinvented themselves as screaming, jostling paranoids.

Most people don't think in terms of risk and reward. It's not the safest or surest way of making money. In fact, it's probably the chanciest. They're either afraid or too lazy to think through the odds, so they look for the sure thing—the bigger, the better. That also holds for Wall Street.

Have you ever noticed how few men who make it through the Merrill Lynch or Prudential-Bache or PaineWebber broker-recruitment programs are slight of stature, and how many of them are built like football players, even if they've never so much as held a pigskin in their lives? For some reason, Wall Street recruiters think that large, beefy, well-built men will bring in the customers; that being big, they're apt to sell stock by the carload—none of this sissy stuff for them. They always seem to be pushing the big blue-chips over the more offbeat, interesting stocks that have a great deal more volatility. I suppose that's one way of minimizing risk. In the pit, as on the floor, you accept risk as an essential fact of life. You're no good if you can't live with high risk—so many traders try not to think about it too much. As far as I was concerned, the only advantage I saw to hiring big guys was that they were better able to muscle their way through the crowds in the pit when the trading got really hot and heavy.

| | | |

Most of the guys who purchased options seats between 1983 and 1988 were games players. It's what made them such superb options traders. Options are, essentially, a pure bet. An option gives you the right—but not the obligation—to buy or sell one hundred shares of stock. In return for time to decide to go through with the deal, buyers pay a nonrefundable amount of money, whereas sellers are subject to unlimited downside risk.

In many respects, the options traders are cut from the same cloth as professional gamblers and card counters. It is Wall Street lore that Jack Dreyfus, progenitor of the Dreyfus Fund—one of the oldest and most successful mutual funds—learned to pick stocks by using the same stratagems and sensibilities that made him such a first-rate bridge player.

The linkage first hit me on a day's excursion down to Atlantic City. The only difference between that casino and ours was that their dealers got to go to the bathroom at regular intervals, enjoyed routine coffee breaks before resuming their shifts, and wore clean aprons.

I suspect that if you're any good at winning at blackjack (also known as twenty-one), you may be ready for a Big Time career as a stock-options trader! At least in theory. You may need a little practice, nerves of steel, and a poker face.

Like the options market, blackjack is one of the few games of chance that still allow players to have an "edge" or advantage over the house, as long as there are only a few decks in play. Having a good memory is what counts. At least it makes a good card counter, top of the list of undesirables at any casino.

Any game of chance is based on the principle of statistically determined probabilities. Whether you win or lose depends on which cards (1) are face up, (2) the player cannot see, and (3) are likely to come out of the undealt deck.

Card counting operates on a system that must be committed to memory and played by rote. There is a predetermined move for each different set of circumstances. Naturally, when there are only one or two decks in play, it's easier to remember all the cards that have been dealt. The card counter compares all hands that are showing with the unplayed cards that he remembers are still in the deck. This quick analysis determines whether he will stand pat or take a hit. It is a mathematical decision, as opposed to feeling "lucky" or having a "hunch" that he'll get the correct card.

The next part of the blackjack problem is the bet. It is easy to spot the professional card counter because he will sit at a table with a five-dollar minimum and a five-hundred-dollar maximum, repeatedly placing the five-dollar bets. After thirty minutes, the probability of getting the necessary card with which to beat the dealer increases dramatically.

At this point, the pro will plunk down the five-hundred-dollar table limit. After winning a tremendous amount of money with that hand, he will go back to five-dollar betting until the cards in the deck or decks line up for him again.

Sounds easy, right? Well, if you practice at home and are pretty good with numbers to start with, it's not too difficult. The tough part is to avoid overtly concentrating on the cards being played. Maybe, instead, lean over and start up a conversation with the player next to you, order another cocktail, or flirt with the waitress. But whatever you do, *don't* ask the dealer to "Go a little slower please" or "What was that last card?"

The minute you "flag out"—show that you're a professional counter—Donald J. Trump himself may sidle over, bend down, and politely ask you to leave the table. Or the management may just offer you dinner for two, a show, comp you with a room and, if you're alone, maybe even some female companionship. But, "Please, sir, no more blackjack."

Some options traders on the floor actually have their picture on file at different Atlantic City and Las Vegas casinos and can't even sit down at a table without being spotted and shown the door. Being tossed out of the gambling casino is perhaps the greatest compliment an options trader can receive.

Ironically, the very human characteristics that make options traders such effective alchemists would, in any other field of high finance, prove their undoing. Take the hallowed teamwork principle that drives your typical, successful *Fortune* 500 company. The concept is utterly foreign to the options trader, even subversive. Classic loners, the inner-directed, steely nerved options traders live up to their image as gunslingers. When you have to make split-second, life-or-death trading decisions, you don't have the luxury of sending out for research or calling on the guy down the hall for a second opinion. Most options traders I've worked against wouldn't even give me the correct time if they thought it would help me trade.

Some I've caught resourcefully spreading *dis*information, just to confuse their opponents. Early on, I was warned never to invite an options trader to play tennis doubles, or Trivial Pursuit. I quickly learned why.

Next to the euphoria of scoring clean and big, options traders enjoy nothing so much as seeing the other guys annihilated, *wiped out*. It follows that if your opponent has just lost his bundle, chances are good that most of it has ended up in your trading account. Options trading may be the last form of *mano-a-mano* combat left on today's computerized trading floor.

At the same time, if given a choice with whom to be marooned on a desert island, bankers or options traders, I'd take the latter. The options traders would build a raft, rustle up coconuts, and set up a short-wave radio in order to get back for trading the next day, before the bankers could even send out memos to organize a meeting, break into subcommittees, and allocate parking spots.

4

The Last Frontier

IF THERE IS SUCH a thing as a dog-eat-dog workplace, the options trading pit comes pretty close. When the trading is in full swing, one of my friends used to say, "The only rule of thumb is to stick it in the other guy's eye before he can stick it in yours."

But the days of the trading floor may be numbered: The entire concept is bound to become an anachronism once the markets become fully automated early in the twenty-first century. Electronic trading has already revolutionized the Cincinnati Stock Exchange, embracing approximately five hundred stocks listed in the U.S., and overseas, with electronic trading, the antiseptic London and Hong Kong stock exchanges now exude as much excitement as a grocery store, even during the busiest trading days.

Over the next five years, both the New York Stock Exchange and a consortium led by the American Stock Exchange and Chicago Board of Options Exchange expect to swing into twenty-four-hour-a-day worldwide electronic trading. Already the New York Stock Exchange has launched a program that would effectively bypass its members with an electronic system matching buyers and sellers, a function that has been performed by the specialists for most of the past two hundred years. The mere confirmation, in September of 1990, of these plans for around-the-clock trading sent shivers of fear down the backs of thousands of floor brokers and traders who could clearly see the handwriting on the wall. Many already feel obsolete as they see their paychecks—reduced by the industry-wide imposition of negotiated commissions—further eaten into by the automated execution systems. Today, a clerk in the Little Rock, Arkansas, office of Merrill Lynch need only push a button to buy ten thousand shares of stock or twenty options direct from the specialist halfway across the country, completely bypassing the floor broker. Will the trader be far behind?

For the time being, the traders are still safe and the floor remains one of the few places on earth—a last frontier—where it is still possible for a high-school dropout to start as a runner, quickly rise to clerk, make as much as a hundred thousand dollars a year and learn to trade, and by the time he's twenty-five end up owning a multimillion-dollar specialist firm.

Not everyone can become a specialist, though many try. For one, it takes a great deal of hands-on trading experience. For another, it takes a lot out of a person, physically and mentally as well. According to Exchange statisticians, the average forty-one-year-old specialist brings to the job twelve and a half years of floor-trading experience and another four and a half spent elsewhere in the securities industry.

The introduction of index options trading, however, has tended to accelerate the learning process. I was told I would learn as much in six intensive months of hot-and-heavy clerking in the pit as I would in twelve years as a broker on the trading floor. They were right.

Index options trading caught on and multiplied in volume more quickly than anyone at the Exchange had anticipated. Stock indexes were designed to protect investors trading large portfolios. Thus, mutual-fund managers controlling large blocks of stock use index contract "sell" positions as insurance against declining stock prices, much as farmers use cotton futures to protect themselves against falling cotton prices. Conversely, investors planning to buy stock in the future can lock in a price by taking an index contract "buy" position. One reason for the unexpected success of the indexes was the emergence of a new breed of speculators who were willing to be either buyers or sellers, depending on whether they thought the stocks in an index would rise or fall in value.

Just like other stocks and options, the index options were given to the specialist firms to run. All it takes to start up one of these firms are two or more traders, operators of specific stocks or options with proven track records, and a lot of capital. Compared to the big full-service firms that provide their clients with all sorts of amenities, such as research, mailing of monthly statements, and investment seminars, the specialist firms are bare-bones, minimal operations. All they do is trade, and selectively at that.

Under the rules, regulations, and bylaws of the Exchange, the specialist firms are mandated "to conduct fair and orderly markets" and to "be the buyer and seller of last resort" in their allocated product(s). Ours was XMI, the Major Market Index. Even if we had wanted to, we couldn't have taken on any other products, so big did XMI become during the time I was at the AMEX. As it was, the Exchange had to rebuild the XMI pit several times to accommodate the soaring volume; by the time I left, XMI occupied most of the northwest quadrant of the main trading floor.

Because their *entire* business takes place on the floor or in the pits, and their staffs have no dealings with investors other than the order-bearing brokers, the specialist firms have no need to maintain offices away from the Exchange. That's why the investing public seldom hears of them. (The only reason we kept offices at 115 Broadway, as well as at the Exchange, was that Spear Leeds & Kellogg, which owned almost fifty percent of our firm, had its headquarters there.)

Most specialist firms tend to be very small, fiercely independent, turf-protective, and quite profitable. They do virtually nothing to build a public identity off the trading floor, but are well known inside the securities industry, as are the equities or options assigned to them by the Exchange.

The specialist's role originated long ago, with the explosion of stock trading during the post–Civil War speculative frenzy. Prior to 1869, the vice-president of the Curb Exchange would read aloud to the throng of brokers gathered around him the entire list of New York Stock Exchange stocks being traded that day, reeling off current bids (the highest price anyone was willing to pay at that moment) and asked price (the lowest at which anyone was willing to sell). This he did three times during trading hours. Lacking today's electronic tote boards and fast-moving "tapes," a broker with orders to fill might have had to wait for hours for a particular stock's name to be called. It was one thing if the broker had been ordered to buy at the going price (market order), but during a period of volatility, many investors unwilling to risk sharp price changes in the time between placement and execution of an order imposed upper and lower limits on their buy-sell orders. With more and more new issues to trade, no broker had the time to hang around, instead handing such "limit orders" to a new breed of sub-broker—soon to be referred to as "the specialist." To make it worth both their while, the floor broker would split his commissions with the specialist. Naturally, as new stocks were introduced, the role of specialist grew in importance—and power—and soon assumed the role of a market maker. Once the Exchange moved indoors in 1921, instead of mingling at curbside the specialists began congregating at set locations, or "trading posts," forcing the trading partners to come to them.

Today's specialists actually have to wear four different hats in order to accomplish their market-making functions—often at the same time, so frenzied have things become: *broker*, *dealer*, *auctioneer*, and *referee*.

As a *broker* the specialist holds orders that can't be executed at the price stipulated by the customer until an opportunity arises.

The specialist must, according to Exchange rules, act as a *dealer* in his allocated stocks and options. In doing this he must risk the firm's capital by buying and selling for his own account whenever there is a temporary imbalance between buy and sell orders. To close the gap between bids and offers, the specialist, trading for his own account, may have to offer to buy at a higher price than anyone else is accepting, and sell at a price lower than anyone else is offering.

As an *auctioneer*, when the bell rings the specialist establishes an opening price for the stocks or options. If a reopening is necessary because of a trading halt, the specialist presides and manages order imbalances while setting the new prices.

Specialists are involved in every trade, even if they do not participate financially. That's how they operate as *referees* or, on busy days, as traffic cops. Somebody has to separate the brokers, representing public and institutional orders, from the traders, who establish positions for their personal accounts. Priorities are usually set on a first come–first serve basis—actually, first *yell*– first *heard*. It's up to the specialist to monitor the cacophony and determine who was first and who *claimed* to have been first. Though specialists are not required, under Exchange rules, to risk life and limb by breaking up brawls, they are empowered to levy fines ranging from five hundred to one thousand dollars— assuming a floor official approves.

Operating a specialist firm on the trading floor can be very profitable because you're ideally situated to react to fast-breaking news, often at the moment it happens. The tradeoff is that by your pledge to "make markets" and risk the firm's capital, you can be wiped out in a single afternoon, as indeed a number of specialist firms were during the October 1987 crash. They were done in by the market's unexpected free-fall, unable in time to clear out their tremendous inventory of stocks and options or meet their margin calls.

So stressful is the environment in which these traders operate that, on the busiest days, it is not uncommon to see traders tear up their position cards or pick up the keyboard to their Quotron (computers displaying real-time market data) and smash it into the terminal screen. I saw one guy pick up the entire unit and hurl it to the floor.

Telephones seem to be the most vulnerable to fits of pique: Not a day went by when at least five of them weren't ripped off the walls or hurled across a trading post. Things got so bad that it was rumored that New York Telephone, fed up with having to constantly replace phones, finally demanded that the Exchange buy them by the gross and do its own installation work. The Exchange now has its own army of installers out on the floor, doing triage in much the same way Army medics roam the battlefield after the fighting.

| | | |

Imagine turning over the set design for the war room of the starship USS *Enterprise* to an undisciplined fourteen-year-old owner of the world's largest Erector set, whose father has cornered the market in video monitors, and you can begin to picture our working environment. An octagonal pen, off to the side of the main trading floor, the pit is actually an enclosed series of raised, rubber-matted tiers and platforms bisected by several passageways leading to the main floor of the Exchange and hopelessly cluttered with computer keyboards, monitors, time clocks, order racks, banks of telephones, half-filled Styrofoam coffee containers, hundreds of unopened foil packs of ketchup and plastic envelopes of soy sauce, empty soda cans, coils of insulated wire, Plexiglas boxes resembling hamster cages, stacks of note pads—and, standing largely unused near the exit, huge garbage cans and a couple of push brooms.

Wherever you went, you'd run into big metal pipes and girders bristling with odd-size video-display screens and terminals—our "data banks." The screens ranged in size from a six-inch personal-size monitor to the kind of tote boards found in most high-school or college gymnasiums. The first impression of a visiting friend of mine was, "Gee, just like the TV display wall at Sears!" There were so many video monitors stacked seemingly willy-nilly that, unless you were looking down from the balcony that runs along the side of the main AMEX trading room, it was impossible to see what was going on inside the pit. I suppose it could be argued that the Exchange's governors wanted it that way, but that presupposes they'd actually hired a space designer.

Actually, the pit *evolved* from a glamorized trading post and, like kudzu vine, ran amuck, consuming more and more real estate as XMI volume shot up. Changes came about through necessity. In the beginning the pit was littered with twenty or so fruit crates and cardboard boxes, courtesy of Greenwich Gourmet Deli, on which short traders and clerks used to stand in order to read broker badge numbers when it came time to record the trades. Built to transport fruit across the country, these boxes could not sustain the weight of people jumping up and down and so usually didn't last the day. It could be embarrassing for the clerks to stand atop a box, signal frantically, and find themselves suddenly sinking from sight as, one after another, the boxes collapsed. That sight must also have offended the governors' sense of decorum, as one morning a space-design consultant showed up with a clipboard to ask us all sorts of questions on our work habits. Not long afterward, the cardboard boxes disappeared. In their place, the house carpenters built and installed a number of wooden boxes covered with industrial "no-slip" black-rubber matting. We all fought over the new boxes like tigers foraging for their cubs—our clerks. They needed to be kept happy. Turns out this was the least of our problems.

Like a Broadway theater, there was the "stage"—in our case, a high platform on which the specialists stood, looking across a chasm at the hordes of traders who were stationed atop a series of graduated tiers. In between, in the orchestra section, was a long passageway, ostensibly reserved for the waves of brokers who, during trading hours, moved in and out of the pit like spawning salmon. At least that was the way it was supposed to work, on paper. It never did. Chaos is not the sort of thing that lends itself to space allocation.

One thing that went wrong almost from the start was that the carpenters were designing this thing from blueprints instead of from observation. Had they bothered to see us in action, understood human greed, they'd have seen instantly that what mattered more than unobstructed vision—sight lines between traders and specialists—was (a) the proximity between the two groups, and (b) the need to be in voice contact with the specialists, to catch the hand signals, eye movements, and so forth. The problem was that the higher the traders and specialists were placed, the greater the distance. The communications gap became a chasm in which a lot of hand-to-hand combat took place. To keep the brokers from being overrun by the surge of frenzied traders, it became necessary to install a long metal railing, similar to the one found in every zoo around the polar bear cages. Actually, the analogy isn't that farfetched. Before the railing was built, the poor brokers found themselves quite literally bulldozed up the other side of the pit by a swarm of angry traders, pinning us specialists against the makeshift wall behind us, and leaving us no choice but to use our feet to violently shove these bodies back down. There were days it looked like that famous castle-siege scene in any one of half-a-dozen Hollywood epics. Thanks to all those discarded ketchup packets, we even had the "bloodstains," to show our battle worthiness.

Efforts at noise abatement proved equally futile. The "walls" of the enclosure were wrapped in thick industrial carpeting to muffle the ungodly combination of noises that emerged from there. On top of the roaring of three hundred or so maniacal traders, there was the noise of the beeping monitors, the overhead public-address system, and thirty phones incessantly ringing off the hook. All at once.

Even before the opening bell, well in advance of trading, the players would jockey for position in the pit so as to be the first to be recognized by the specialists, standing slightly above them on the podium overlooking the floor of the pit.

The best way for X to get a front-row position was to finagle Y out of the pit. This was often accomplished by the simple expedient of arranging for Y to be paged out front—usually by X's clerk standing two feet away, using a wall phone. The minute Y left, X would slip into the vacated spot and stay there, not budging an inch. By the time an infuriated Y returned to the pit, he would find it impossible to worm his way back in.

Given that sort of competitive environment, mistakes were bound to occur that could test the best of friendships.

One particularly active day, my clerk jotted down that I had bought "*fifteen* options contracts at the price of thirteen and a half," while the opposing trader yelled back that he'd sold me "*fifty* contracts at thirteen and a half."

The difference between saying fifteen and hearing fifty led to a $47,250 misunderstanding that had to come out of one of our pockets the following day. What made it particularly awkward was that the aggrieved trader was a rather good-looking guy I'd had a date with the evening before, one of those rare occasions when my restricted life-style allowed me a night out. Because the transaction reporter standing next to me during the trade also swore to having heard me say "fifteen," my opponent had a tough time proving the error to be mine.

Either of us could have sought a ruling by a floor referee or gone to formal arbitration, which would have put a crimp in our budding romance. Moreover, arbitration is not a viable alternative for settling such trading arguments, because it can take hours and cost both traders precious floor time, often a sacrifice of more money than the amount being disputed.

So, instead, we grudgingly agreed to split the loss. The pit had been too loud for anyone to hear correctly. My adversary left with his copy of the rejected trade notice, but not before calling me a "first-class bitch." At least he still thought of me as first class. But not enough to resume dating me. In fact, he told me afterward that whenever he looked at me, all he could think of was losing $23,625.

❘　❘　❘

Considering the overwhelming number of young men compared to the handful of women on the floor, it's surprising how very little of the old hanky-panky went on during my time on the trading floor. I suspect the guys were either too busy making big bucks or too tired to do anything but flirt.

I admit to having my share of admirers, most of whom proved eminently forgettable. A nice exception was my friend Roger Fenn from Merrill Lynch, a real gentle giant who took a protective interest in me and kept my podium stocked with candy bars. On the way back from an AMEX marketing presentation one day, on impulse, he bought all fifty balloons from a street vendor for twenty-five dollars and handed them to me. Then he left to do some errands. As I walked down the street, people approached me and asked if they were for sale. Naturally, I said "Of course," and sold them all, at two bucks apiece. One of the women in the marketing department had seen Roger buy them for me and was shocked at my callousness. "How can you do that to Roger?" she said, voicing her disapproval. "Okay, okay," I said, "I'll tell him." I did more than that. I handed him fifty dollars—half the profits. He beamed. "Atta girl!" After all, a trader is a trader.

For those of the boys who went in for the bachelor life, there seemed to be no shortage of women down at Harry's on a Friday night. These women probably didn't get the *Wall Street Journal*, but they knew that in a bull market the after-trading action stayed downtown.

From nine to five they were secretaries, demurely working in uptown corporate headquarters and law offices. But once the Friday-night five o'clock whistle blew, something happened. They became Diana the Huntress, rushing out the door lickety-split, heading by bus or subway to Harry's at the American Exchange.

Sitting with some of the guys in the bar, I'd see them arrive, like stragglers off a tourist bus, entering through the 113 Greenwich Street door, clutching their plastic shopping bags with the spiked-heeled, open-toe shoes, makeup, and curling irons, and heading straight for the ladies' room, where they'd put on their makeup and jazz up their outfits. Some would even restyle their hair and replace the small pearl earrings with big gold hoops.

Maybe I should have hung around more often to see what happened when an irresistible force meets many movable objects, but, frankly, come Friday night I was just too shot to indulge in voyeurism. Besides, there was better stuff to be seen in Woody Allen video rentals. I also didn't feel like competing, nor did most of the other young women I worked with. As it was, to be a woman on the floor of the Exchange was a daily nine-hour grind, having to look good and feel comfortable and still be strong enough to engage in gymnastics whenever the market got busy.

The idea of women doing something besides clerking was still relatively new when I first arrived on the scene. Most of us were still hung up on the notion of looking the way we thought men expected us to look—all put together, something straight out of the pages of a magazine. We learned fast that in that kind of combative environment most of the men didn't look at us as anything but what we in fact were—working bodies. And so we quickly adapted to reality, making not so much a compromise as an adjustment. I started out wearing black leather pumps, switched to loafers, then to sneakers. My Farrah Fawcett tresses were replaced by a shag cut, then a ponytail. In the beginning I would spend a lot of time shopping for the right perfume; I soon became an expert on which deodorant lasted longest and which brand of lip balm tasted least offensive. I got rid of the rings and bracelets after being caught once too often by the voracious time-stamping machine. Finally, I kissed off long polished nails, stockings, and most accessories. So much for glamor on the job. It took too much out of me.

Naturally, not everyone felt the way I did. A number of the women obviously subscribed to comedian Billy Crystal's "Dahling, it is better to look good than to feel good." You could tell who they were by what they brought to work with them—clear nail polish for mending stocking runs, emery boards, spray cans of hair lacquer and Static-Guard, earring reinforcements, purse-size vials of drop-dead cologne, breath deodorants, vanity mirrors, you-name-it/they-had-it. And they would generously offer to share their beauty supplies. Let *them* compete with the girls downstairs, I kept telling myself, without much conviction, as I secretly admired their determination to stay utterly, beguilingly feminine. I was still too much of a tomboy and unwilling to make the effort to be a knockout. For one thing, I would have had to get up much earlier and spend a lot of time at the ironing board.

I I I

As I accumulated wealth, I knew it would be hard to resist living lavishly, but I was determined to do it. I was neither emotionally nor psychologically equipped to adopt a life-style that ran counter to all the upstate–New York small-town conservative values— frugality, moderation, and so forth—that had been instilled in me by my working-class family. I thus found it very difficult to do the things that Helen Gurley Brown of *Cosmopolitan* said I was supposed to be doing.

At work I wore off-the-rack clothes from Loehmann's, Labels for Less, and The Gap. I stuck to my Reeboks. I lived in a succession of dingy flats in decidedly déclassé sections of Greenwich Village. My home furnishings were strictly Salvation Army Modern in a "recent-cyclone" arrangement. When I could at last afford to buy that obligatory condo—in this instance, a $300,000 pad overlooking the South Street Seaport, a few blocks from Wall Street—I chickened out at the last minute, believing I'd just been wiped out by the crash of 1987.

I flaunted my trusty Mickey Mouse Timex; not for me one of those ubiquitous fourteen-karat-gold Rolex Oysters. I even resisted the $59.95 knockoffs those sidewalk equal-opportunity Senegalese hawked to wannabe yuppies in front of Tiffany's.

I got around town by subway, bus, and a souped-up fiberglass skateboard (which got me a write-up in *Thrasher* magazine and spared me from having to garage my nonexistent BMW 725i). Whenever I needed a car, I'd take the train out to Long Island and borrow my eighty-seven-year-old grandfather's bronze 1980 Camaro.

My only luxury was going to the theater, courtesy TKTS, the discount-ticket operation, which had just opened a downtown branch at the nearby World Trade Center. I didn't mind sitting in the cheap seats.

Later on, whenever my extracurricular role as the AMEX's marketing representative for index options trading required me to put in cross-country personal appearances, I usually chose to fly coach on the Red Eye, which would almost guarantee me a "sleeper"—three seats across.

My American Express card was green, not gold, certainly not platinum, and got little wear because my favorite neighborhood bistros—McDonald's, Burger King, and Wendy's—did not take plastic. And during those "power breakfasts" the Spear Leeds partners used to spring for, so we could all fiendishly plot that day's underhanded trading strategies, I would embarrass my colleagues by passing up the croissants and shirred eggs, as I had already finished a bowl of Cap'n Crunch and a sliced banana. Not everybody objected, especially on those days when the cereal box produced such useful premiums as tiny plastic binoculars, which came in handy for magnifying the news monitor.

"Laura," my boss Ron Shear once said, sighing in total exasperation, "we can't take you *anywhere*."

It didn't matter, really. By the time I finally did come of legal age and sidled up to the bar down at Harry's for my first drink, the damage was done. What I didn't know about sybaritic behavior couldn't hurt me.

I had basked in the warm glow as a sort of mascot, everybody's baby sister. Men would take a brotherly interest in me and would fret about my safety and well-being. Then, suddenly exposed as being even younger than they'd dreamed, I would find myself becoming the butt of jokes all over the trading floor, not just in the XMI pit.

How often I would hear, "Did you know that at her first birthday party, Laura traded her stuffed elephant for two teddy bears?" or "Laura arbitraged her first case of Gerber's at the age of two and a half, threw in her tricycle, and on top of that made a cool twenty-five dollars."

As it turned out, my bosses didn't really give a damn whether I was twenty or seventy-four, just as long as I got to work on time and made them lots of money. When Ron Shear learned how young I was, he joked, "Good—if you do anything wrong I'll send you off to reform school."

5

Mine and Other People's Money

WITH THE EXCEPTION of John Kenneth Galbraith, I know of no funny economists. No wonder their calling is referred to as "the dismal science." Yet Dr. Herbert Stein came close to displaying genuine wit when he observed that Michael R. Milken, late of the equally late Drexel Burnham Lambert, "had not increased the net flow of capital into investment so much as he altered the direction of the flow." A fitting epitaph, it seems to me, for the volatile Reagan years.

I'm somewhat ambivalent about Milkenomics. On the one hand, there's no question that the boom that made me a millionaire at twenty-two was largely sparked by the junk-bond mania of the 1980s. On the other hand, so were the two October meltdowns that wiped out a lot of my friends and ultimately got me to take early retirement from my brilliant career as an index trader, at what was then the top of the market.

The disenchantment began during my last summer on Wall Street, when I caught an off-Broadway morality play, Jerry Sterner's *Other People's Money*, on the very subject of corporate restructuring and asset stripping. Sterner ridiculed and satirized not just the raiders but the public's curious indifference to such predatory practices. There was nothing subtle about his message. Even the playwright himself expected nothing more than a short, seasonal run at the Minetta Lane Theater, near where I lived in Greenwich Village. But just around that time, the government came down on Drexel and the show's press agents were surprised and delighted to spot among the audience some of the very people Sterner savaged. The gossip columnists were quick to pick up on word that among those who laughed the loudest were folks like Carl Icahn, T. Boone Pickens, Henry Kravis, and Asher Edelman. Donald J. Trump, then still riding high, was reported to have "discovered" this gem of a play and talked it up to all his friends. Word of mouth turned it into a hot ticket, led to a movie sale, yet—interesting enough—it bombed on the road. But that was before the enormity of the looming savings-and-loan crisis was brought home to grass-roots America.

| | | |

It was around the same time that the beleaguered Drexel ran its shamefully manipulative TV commercials in defense of junk-bonding. I'm sure I wasn't the only one to find this last-ditch attempt to put a positive spin on Milken's dubious accomplishments cynically transparent. It generated a lot of talk in the pit. One of the guys raised an interesting point: Why hadn't the same TV moguls, usually quick to offer politicians equal time, shown viewers the *other* side of the junk-bond certificate—the shuttered factories and "restructured" company towns?

Now that some of those Very Important Predators are being released for good behavior—I wasn't aware they'd been indicted for lack of manners—Wall Street's revisionist historians are suggesting that what they did wasn't all that bad when you consider the alternative. Like Richard Nixon insisting he wasn't the first to bug the Oval Office, they would like us to remember that what went on during the heyday of the robber barons did far greater lasting damage to the national economy. Perhaps so. But at least the Goulds, Vanderbilts, Fricks, and Rockefellers, to name but some of the legendary miscreants, built something other than those mountains of debt that will never be scaled in our lifetimes or those of our kids. What's more, unlike this crowd, they left behind great universities, libraries, art museums, and philanthropic foundations. Now the guys on the floor joke, "You go to the store to buy a toaster and they'll throw in an S & L to thank you for your business."

So, I wonder, who'll be the first professor to occupy the Milken Foundation–endowed chair of high-risk economics? Which graduate school of business administration will set up such a teaching post?

| | | |

Although the figures show the crash of 1987 to have had no long-lasting effect (except, perhaps, to the fourteen percent of the Wall Street work force let go in the aftermath), for us in the XMI pit much of the excitement vanished soon afterward. Any enthusiasm we could work up during the market's recovery did not make it past the second crash, in October of 1989, when the market plunged 190 points during the last hour of trading. For me, that was checkout time.

Interestingly, none of us were ever able to put a precise finger on the cause of the ennui that clung to the pit like the acrid smell that lingers after a forest fire. Perhaps it was the realization that there really was a computer named HAL (see Stanley Kubrick's *2001*) which was taking over Wall Street; that the people in charge of the machines were either incapable or unwilling to pull the plug on program trading—the computer-based buying-and-selling programs that have come in for heavy criticism. These computer programs are triggered automatically when prices reach a predetermined level and are responsible for accentuating wild and sudden swings in the price of stock, reverberating throughout the market. It took no great prescience to see that in time we traders would become irrelevant. We who had long fancied ourselves as master market-makers would eventually have to answer to a higher authority—not God but a tiny but all-powerful silicon microchip.

ǀ   ǀ   ǀ

The two crashes were tantamount to that old saying "Death is nature's way of telling you to slow down." The party was definitely over. It only remained for someone to tell all the guests to leave.

Even before the second meltdown, the hunt for scapegoats began. It didn't take long for all those self-righteous Cassandras who had long railed against the futures markets to say, "See, we told you so." No doubt about it, they had. But in targeting the program traders instead of the people who had worked long and hard to develop the technique—and I don't mean the computer programmers—the self-appointed reformers did what so many reformers have always done: shoot the messengers.

According to former General Motors chairman Roger Smith, appointed by the New York Stock Exchange to head a blue-ribbon panel of Wall Street insiders to produce the definitive study on market volatility and how to contain it, there's nothing inherently wrong with the system other than the fact that the press (as usual) has bollixed things up. How? By not properly explaining program trading to the public.

During 1986, when the New York Stock Exchange's new computers were reprogrammed to rapidly trade entire market baskets of stock, recorded volume soared to 35 billion shares, double the 1982 volume. More to the point, during that year, a record 26.5 million stock-index futures contracts were traded, a fourfold gain, while index option trading, my specialty, increased one thousand percent.

We didn't have to read the end-of-day printouts to see what was happening. The evidence was all around us. As we filed out one Friday evening, a phalanx of carpenters arrived to build us a bigger, jazzier XMI trading pit. But no sooner had we settled into the new ampitheater than it was time to move to newer, larger, state-of-the-art space.

But larger wasn't large enough. There were days when we felt like we'd gotten out of one subway car only to get into another. Into a space built for one hundred people, as many as three hundred were packed so tightly, shoulder to shoulder, that no one could shrug, much less raise their arms.

So the traders raised their voices instead and clawed for breathing space. It is no exaggeration to say clerks had to stand *sideways* just to remain next to the specialists to whom they'd been assigned. Or that "lefties" were kept next to "lefties" in order to maximize space. I know, because by then I was doing all the hiring for XMI, which had signed me up as a clerk in September 1984 but by 1986 was giving me a variety of different managerial responsibilities.

It was at one of our breakfast meetings that someone suggested, half in jest, that I go out and recruit only thin people. "What," I said, "and risk being called before the Equal Employment Opportunity Commission on charges of weight discrimination?" Someone else chimed in, "Why not? It's about time Randy Newman came up with a new twist on 'Short People.'"

Actually, I was sufficiently worried about where to put all these new people to ask them, early in the interviews, "Don't apologize for not having gone to Harvard, what I need to know is, how much do you weigh? Do you plan to put on any weight?" At one point, there was even talk of enticing new people with health-club memberships at the Vista Hotel in the World Trade Center or making the job contingent on going there three times a week.

Soon, territorial imperatives were set. "That's *my* spot," bellowed Chris DiFabio, one of the clerks. He could prove it, too, having staked out his spot, "right where the gum is stuck to the second step from the top!" Passions ran so high that actual bare-knuckled fights would erupt on the flimsiest of provocations. One man even threatened another by muttering audibly about ordering a contract hit. I didn't doubt for a moment that he had the connections to arrange a real killing on the market.

| | | |

As I dealt almost exclusively with options, at this point I suppose I should point out that not all options are alike—there are *equity* options, *currency* options, and *index* options—and I should explain why they're often traded by specialists. (When they made me a specialist in January 1986, I remember calling home, all excited. My mother, a nurse, reacted typically: "But Laura, honey, how can you be a specialist? You didn't go to medical school.")

Options are simply contracts that entitle the purchaser to buy ("call") or sell ("put") shares of a stock or a group of stocks, like those included in the Dow Jones industrial average, at a stated price on or before a fixed expiration date.

An option *contract*—equal to one hundred shares of stock—can be for several months ahead and expires at 11:59 P.M. on the Saturday immediately following the third Friday of the stated month. Listed stock options appeared on the exchanges during the early 1970s. They allow investors to hedge against sudden and sharp market fluctuations. They can be thought of as low-cost but risky "term insurance" to cushion precipitous plunges. The risk comes from the volatility of the options markets.

An *index* options contract gives the holder the right to buy or sell a stock index at a fixed price within a specific period of time. If the stock index either rises or falls in the direction you predicted it would, you make money. If the stock index doesn't do what you expected, you lose the bet and you lose your money.

The advantage is that index options are much more cost-efficient than trading individual stocks. A small amount of capital can give the player the ability to buy or sell a large number of shares of stocks. And commissions on one transaction are obviously less costly.

| | | |

The American Stock Exchange first began trading "calls" (buy options) in 1975, adding "puts" (sell options) two years later. The reason calls were introduced first was because, for some reason, three times as many calls are traded. In 1987 alone, fifty-one million calls were bought as against seventeen million puts. I guess that again proves we're a nation of shoppers.

The idea was to let investors, large and small—mainly large—"play" a market average of blue chips as if they were one stock.

Instead of putting buy orders down on all the different exchange floors for hundreds of stocks, it only took one phone call and a few seconds while a broker ran into the pit and made one quick transaction. The investor now "owned" all the stocks in the basket and fully participated in the fluctuations, just as if all the stocks were in his portfolio. Of course, he did not receive dividends, get certificates, or have voting power in the individual companies, as he would have if he'd bought the underlying stock. The market-basket approach also let the technical analysts— people who chart stocks and market trends—study market performance in order to detect market trends in the making, which none of us civilians could spot on a sunny, cloudless day in May.

The advantages of options—low cost, high elasticity—help pension-fund operators and investment-fund managers capitalize on the indexes. They can sell options against their already existing stock positions or just insure their inventory against market fluctuations. In this manner the options markets offer them a great opportunity for enhancing their fund's performance.

To make things even easier, it is not necessary for the individual investor to understand the specifics of the underlying companies. The game is to gauge the short-term movement of the Dow Jones industrial average. Before index options came along, one had to make three decisions: (1) What direction will the market be taking? (2) In what industry group should I invest? (3) In what stock in that industry group should I invest my capital?

Indexes took away all those financial decisions and made it a game that anyone could understand and play. All you had to decide was whether the market was going up or down, place your bet, and see if you'd been right or wrong.

There are traders who buy or sell options based on how they feel about the underlying stocks or the general direction of the market. But given the high and wide market fluctuations of the past few years, this has become a dangerous game. Unless they happen to be seasoned technical analysts, these traders are usually flying by the seat of their pants and, according to the law of averages, eventually losing not just their shirts but their pants as well.

Nowadays a trader can only score a big hit in the indexes by catching the beginning of a huge swing. This means determining when a program trade is about to hit the floor and set off a deluge of buying or selling.

The biggest difference between the card counter in Atlantic City or Las Vegas and the probability theorist who trades options for a living is the *risk-reward* of the bet or the stake.

As already noted, all the casino player can lose is whatever he puts on the table in any particular game. By contrast, the options trader—the most undercapitalized businessman in the capitalist system—can lose *everything*. With a fifty-thousand-dollar bet he can easily lose more than a million dollars—and be responsible for having to pay this back to the clearinghouse in real money by liquidating all his assets.

The clearinghouse acts as the accountant for all transactions made on the floor. It receives and distributes all monies from purchases and sales of stocks, options, and bonds. This system makes bookkeeping easier and prevents traders and brokers from having to bill each other on an individual basis.

My friend Tom found himself in just that unfortunate losing position the day after the 1987 crash had run its course. Sitting at Harry's Bar, nursing his fifth Mai Tai of the afternoon, Tom was furiously scribbling on a cocktail napkin when he turned to me and blurted out the number "five hundred and seventeen."

I asked, "What's that, your weight?" He said, "No, that's the number of years I'll have to work at my old job, making forty thousand a year." "Why is that?" I asked. "To pay back the three million I just lost on Teledyne," he replied.

But for every spectacular loser like Tom there must have been five winners like Kevin, guys who were able to retire on the strength of just a couple of afternoons of being fast on their feet. When last heard from, Kevin was out of the game, living in a lakeside chalet in Switzerland. He fascinated me because, up until I'd met him, I'd never before encountered a twenty-eight-year-old who became a double-digit millionaire after just one year on the job—a six-and-a-half-hour, five-day work week at that.

| | | |

Back in the innocent times of 1980, the new CBOE/S&P product proved such a runaway success among portfolio managers and institutional traders that acceptance marked the start of what we now describe as "program trading" or "risk arbitrage."

Not to be outdone by the Second City boys, the New York, American, Philadelphia, and other major exchanges launched their variations of stock index options. A few did well, while most of them bombed out rather quickly. They were either too "vertical"—there were indexes for airline stocks, oil companies, computer tech, and other narrow-gauge categories—or insufficiently promoted to draw any kind of volume. Upshot: skewed index figures that made little sense.

The XMI was the AMEX's first entry and from the outset outdrew a second index (XAM) on which I cut my eyeteeth as a clerk for Dritz, Goldring & Company. XAM was an index of *all* the stocks traded on the AMEX and proved too unwieldy to be attractive. But the main reason XMI scored while XAM didn't may be that the former more accurately mirrored the DJIA, because seventeen of the twenty stocks within it were also in the Dow Jones industrials.

Since its launch seven years ago, XMI has shown a ninety-seven percent correlation with the DJIA and eighty-five percent with the S&P 500. For every five points the Dow advances, XMI moves one point.

The difference between stock and index options is in the way they're settled. An ordinary stock-options contract is exercised by delivering one hundred shares of the underlying stock, while the more arcane index-option contract is settled with the payment of cash—the dollar difference between the contracted price and the closing index value on settlement day. For example, if the holder of a July 370 XMI call option exercises it the day XMI hits 380, he's ahead (and due) $1,000. [($380 − $370) × 100] = $1,000.

Despite what your broker may tell you to the contrary, there exists about the same degree of risk in regular stock as in index options. You can lose your shirt or make a fortune equally fast in either. The risk for the XMI index-option seller lies in the price fluctuations of all the twenty underlying stocks rather than just one of those twenty.

You may well ask why stock index options proved so immensely attractive to so many investors, particularly institutions, portfolio managers, and pension planners.

Let's start with pension planning, another oft-misunderstood term. Back in the 1960s and early 1970s, MBAs all wanted to become pension planners. Only, back then, pension planning was seen to be about as glamorous a profession as public accounting. So the early practitioners called themselves "money managers." As a money manager one could charge heavy fees without having to do any heavy work.

Then, along came ERISA—the 1974 Employment Retirement Income Security Act. Under this legislation, the new self-styled money manager was prohibited from putting all of his clients' money into one pot. It required corporate and private pension plans to minimize risks by diversifying both their investment management and investment strategy. From that time on, pension-fund managers could manage only *a portion* of each pension fund's portfolio.

This led to the strategy of portfolio diversification and brought to the game newer, also leaner and meaner, investment firms, not necessarily steeped in the WASP culture that dominated Wall Street for so many years.

Historically, the money manager's mandate was to select those stocks that were expected to outperform the Dow and S&P averages. Easier said than done, because now, in the wake of ERISA's passage, who should show up to crowd the field of experts but a new breed of theorists, chartists, call-them-whatever-you-want. They were mainly academicians, the kind who wear Harris-tweed jackets with leather elbow patches.

These scientific bookworms retreated to their ivory towers to brood over reams of yellow foolscap. Every once in a while, they'd emerge to run down to the mainframe computers the university kept under lock and key. Steven Jobs and Steve Wozniak had not yet built their first Apple desktop, so any number-crunching would have to be done at night, after the physics department had gone home.

In studying and charting the efficiency of the marketplace, they concluded that it was a dreadful waste of time to hand-pick stocks for investment by sitting and poring over annual and quarterly reports, in which discouraging words are seldom seen. Nor would clients be served by having the money managers visit the home office or plants, sample products, or talk to customers.

The well-paid money managers, they concluded, could do as well or better selecting winners by throwing darts at the *Wall Street Journal*'s daily stock tables.

The brain trust, in other words, had not merely questioned the validity of the money-management profession; they had declared war on it.

| | |

As it happened, the gauntlet was being thrown down at the precise moment the Organization of Petroleum Exporting Countries launched its first strike. The resulting recession led many corporate chieftains into ordering some belt tightening, and guess which consultants were among the first to go? All over America, CPA-trained chief financial officers began asking themselves, "Hey, why are we paying such high fees to these guys when the best they can do is barely keep up? Let's index the money ourselves."

Which is precisely what they did.

Now *Business Week* and market watchers were going around pronouncing "the death of equities." The stock market was in the doldrums, causing institutional buyers to sit tight, which of course sent stock prices drifting downward—often worth less than the break-up value of the underlying company.

Instead, the deal makers started buying bonds. Enter young Michael Milken, then a hotshot researcher with the sleepy firm of Drexel Harriman Ripley, which was about to be taken over by Burnham & Company. He was the one who figured out a way of converting equity into debt, and you know what happened next.

So, faced with the threat of overnight extinction, the money managers regrouped, cut (or hid) their fees, and gave their clients exactly what they wanted: *at par* market performance. They started placing most of their entrusted funds with the thirty Dow and five hundred Standard & Poor bellwether issues, leaving the dregs to be invested in whatever their research departments happened to be pushing that day.

By 1985, the year after I got to Wall Street, ninety to ninety-five percent of these discretionary funds were being indexed. In some of the classier investment houses, the remaining five percent was allocated to investments inelegantly referred to as POSSUM, a phonetic acronym meaning "piece of shit of the month."

The money managers also sought additional safety by creating and investing heavily in mutual funds. As long as the Dow was rising at an annual twenty-nine percent, anyone in a natural-fiber suit could randomly pick stocks for his entrusted portfolios and do it about as scientifically as the racetrack tout who bets on a horse because he likes the owner's colors.

In a raging bull market, they simply couldn't lose. They didn't. In fact, it left them feeling so good that they next came up with indexed mutual funds. They gave these funds such trust-inspiring names as "Grosvenor," "Buckingham," and "Picadilly," bracketed with such confidence-building descriptors as "Developing," "Growth," "Increased Income," "High-Yield," or just plain "Value-Added."

These funds were, and continue to be, up-and-up. They did especially well when everything went up. Moreover, they let investors get in the game for much less than regular stock-purchase commissions, and their margin requirements were a lot more flexible—as much as seventy-five percent of the purchase price could be paid for with borrowed funds.

In the era of junk-bonding, these money managers were given a new problem to deal with. The brokerage-house institutional clients were suffering an embarrassment of riches—newly pumped-in cash—and a new investment vehicle would have to be found. Market researchers and product developers found that vehicle parked in the S&P 500 index, which is widely used as an indicator of stock-market trends. They would now create a tradeable index product using options.

| | | |

It was around this time that the desktop computer found a place on virtually every desk on Wall Street, creating a vast new army of number-crunchers and instant analysts. They, in turn, devised the dreaded monster, Program Trading.

Here's how that evolved.

Take any stock index—there are now about eight of them— and plug into your computer the price of every stock in that index. Now add in the stock index future and instruct the computer to react every time the future drops below the index price.

In the beginning, things were a bit primitive. When the gong sounded, a recently hired MIT graduate got on the phone to his broker in the Chicago pits to buy futures and to his broker in New York to sell stocks in an equivalent ratio so as to offset each other, retaining the difference. The same procedure was often also profitably reversed by selling futures and buying stocks.

In time, the technology gained sophistication. Each day, it seemed, the computer whiz kids came up with a new wrinkle so that, by the time the MIT grad had finally mastered the sequence, he was replaced by a Rensselaer Polytechnic grad who no longer had to reach for the phone. All he did was push a button. He, in turn, was supplanted by Mr. Cal Tech, who programmed the mainframe and desktops in sync, so no one even had to push a button. The computer did it all by itself, freeing the portfolio managers to do what they do best: leave the office to shop for condos and Porsches.

Computers spawned a brand-new type of wheeler-dealer, the techno-trader. Those I dealt with in the XMI pit, the tyrant-traders, were truly a breed apart. We dealt by instinct tempered with a bit of probability theory, while they went strictly by rigid mathematical formulas.

The more complex the computer programs got, the happier the techno-traders became, and the less I liked them. In the beginning I was a lot more tolerant, because they were so damned good at math that I was willing to overlook their acrylic dress code, plastic pocket-protectors, and Hewlett Packard hand-held computers.

| | | |

News travels fast on the Street, and "free money" isn't just news but great news. Junk bonds. Cheap going in, high returns—if you don't mind the risk.

A lot of investors didn't mind, and they came in droves, pitting Wall Street against the banking establishment, whose product—including government-backed securities—was suddenly found rather unexciting and uncompetitive compared to what Drexel and Goldman, Sachs and PaineWebber were serving for lunch.

Invariably, Wall Street goes with the flow. But here we had these billions of dollars flipping back and forth between the stock and futures markets, with traders buying whichever was cheaper at any given moment and simultaneously selling its opposite in the other market.

The public began reading about these new hotshot deal makers, who shed their frumpy wives for younger, more decorative versions—as *Fortune* would dub them, "trophy wives"—cavorted in high society, and were the darlings of the charitable fundraisers and gossip columnists. Some of these tycoons left their Quotrons long enough to put in a guest appearance on Johnny Carson's "Tonight Show," to unburden themselves on the trials of Sudden Riches. Right after the live performance of the tree-climbing dog.

Greed was not only good; it had become fashionable.

6

The Making of
an Entrepreneur

I WAS FIVE, GOING on six, when I first became a commodity trader, the first of my many brief entrepreneurial ventures. This one lasted two weeks and three days.

My partner and best friend was Mary Pyne. Mary was my age and lived in the house right behind ours, in Amherst, just across the street from SUNY, the State University of New York at Buffalo.

We'd get up at the crack of dawn, "borrow" my mother's homegrown tomatoes, and sell them from a roadside stand set up in front of my house.

It took Mom a couple of weeks to figure out that the question of why her garden wasn't producing tomatoes was answered by where we were getting our supplies. That's how I went belly-up in commodities. It must have been the only start-up company that year whose CEO was grounded for two weeks by parental action.

Then I set out to become a card shark. Mom taught me how to play poker, seven-card stud and five-card draw. I played with my family and friends for change, mostly quarters, and candy bars. I would try to determine when the others were bluffing and call them on it with a big raise. But Mom ruined it all by refusing to lie. She considered bluffing dishonest, so she would fold every time. She'd have made a lousy Wall Street trader.

While I liked the action, I liked the racy language even more. My Uncle Jim was a newspaperman at the Buffalo *Courier-Express* and talked like a Damon Runyon character ("Ante up," "One-eyed jacks are wild," "Cut 'em thin and win, cut 'em deep and weep"). Whenever I dealt I'd call for two wild cards. It must have been an incongruous scene: To be high enough to be able to place the cards on the table, I had to prop myself up on the chair by hook, crook, and telephone book. I began to think there must be better ways of making money.

So, at age eight, I entered the business world as a wholesaler of greeting cards. By ordering in bulk, I was able to farm the sales out to four of my friends. The aggravation of keeping track of inventory, maintaining a sales force, and handling customer relations was seriously denting my social life. I figured I'd rather go to the movies or skateboarding so, unable to make any mergers, I sold the business to a competitor for a modest gain.

| | | |

Eventually, I got revenge on Mom for shutting down my earliest ventures. When I was thirteen, I read my first how-to book, *How to Prosper During the Coming Bad Years* by Howard J. Ruff (who also published a newsletter called *Ruff Times*). It so affected me that after only three chapters, I was buying canned food and stockpiling it in the basement as a hedge against inflation. My mother told my Aunt Sue and Uncle Jim and they all laughed at "Crazy Laura."

But I had the last laugh when during one particularly vicious Buffalo blizzard, Mom asked me if I still had those cans. I did and sold them to her—a 50-cent can of Green Giant corn for $3.00 and a $1.50 can of Hormel corned beef hash for $5.00.

By the time I entered junior high school, I had settled comfortably into *arbitrage*—buying at one exchange and selling at another with consistent profits, small transactional costs, and at no risk to the broker. I'd buy candy bars by the case at the Food Warehouse, a local wholesaler, and mark them up anywhere from fifty to one hundred percent. Admittedly, the bookkeeping was a bit sloppy but the profits came steadily and the stock turnover was so brisk that I was told I might have to get a New York State tax resale number.

But before that could happen, the old gambling urge was rekindled. I sort of gravitated toward illegal card games, becoming particularly interested in blackjack. Unknown to my classmates, I'd been studying probability theory—the percentage chance of a particular card appearing at a specific point in the deck—and so had a definite advantage over them. I suppose that had I not gone to Wall Street—the biggest casino with the fattest purses—I might have ended up being a dealer in Atlantic City or Las Vegas.

Ironically, those who watched me trade down on the Exchange floor and thought of me as a whiz at numbers never knew that I was not particularly good in math. I couldn't even tell time until the end of the third grade. My parents and my teachers despaired. Fortunately, digital watches weren't invented till the 1970s, or I never would have learned how to read analog numbers. I even flunked algebra. Most of us kids in Buffalo learned basic math in church-sponsored bingo games and at the local bowling alley. It was only when there was a dollar sign in front of the numbers that I could perform calculus in my head.

Whenever a bookstore had a big clearance or a public library burned down and the city held a fire sale, Dad would bring home five or ten bags stuffed with books he'd purchased, ten for a dollar. Of course, they were never on any subjects that his only child happened to be studying. There'd be books on astronomy, deep-bore zinc mining, plastics extrusion, soap making, dendrochronology, Esperanto, and similarly exciting reading fare. The science books were usually colossal bores, but I was intrigued enough by the others at least to want to skim them.

One day I came across *Standard & Poor's Guide to Your Investments*. I don't know why, but I read the book from cover to cover, even though I only understood the verbs. I certainly didn't comprehend municipal bonds, corporate buy-backs, and T-bills, so I looked up what I didn't understand. What I *did* grasp, almost off the bat, was that they all paid more than the five-and-a-half percent interest offered by the local savings banks.

Shortly afterward, I started reading *Barron's* and *Forbes*. A friend of my mother's was a stockbroker at Kidder, Peabody & Company, and he'd give me all his old copies of business magazines. I learned something about how the economy works, how business operates, and how different people achieve success. It was the best education money couldn't buy, full of real people and the deals they were pulling off. I sensed that somehow I wanted to be a part of it all.

| | | |

Easy money. The phrase had a nice ring to it, and I first heard it the day my Uncle Jim took me to the racetrack at Fort Erie, across the border in Ontario, Canada. It was my twelfth birthday, and I was entranced.

Uncle Jim had started me on what became a five-year betting habit. Surprisingly, Mom and Dad were open-minded about my skipping school to ride across the Peace Bridge and make the one o'clock post-time at the track. As long as I produced a decent report card at the end of each semester, my parents couldn't argue with my extracurricular activities. In fact, at dinnertime my dad would sing, "What did you learn in school today, in school today?" (it was part of an old folk song, I think) and I would reply, "I didn't make it to school today, but I won thirty-two bucks at the racetrack." He would then just smile and say, "Be sure to put it in the college fund."

Wide eyed, I took it all in—the track, the grandstand, the concession booth, the stables, the sweating horses, and the little jockeys. But I kept coming back to the big electronic tote board and its flipping numbers. I quickly figured that every time someone placed a two-dollar bet, the track had to be keeping twenty-five or fifty cents of that. No matter which horse came in first, which lost, the track owners would win. So that night, back home, when I scanned the stock tables and saw a 35¼ bid, offered at 35⅜, I realized that *somebody*—probably at the stock exchange—had to be keeping the money, and that if I were serious about becoming a millionaire, forget the track. Play the stock market by *being* there.

| | | |

Of course, when I finally got to Wall Street, I soon learned it wasn't all what I had cracked it up to be, or that easy to hold on to the difference. One day when I was passing through the Exchange's coat and shoe room, I happened to pick up a discarded

Wall Street Journal that had been folded and marked up the way only a real horse player would do it—with certain items scratched, others edited with numerical changes, and a few company names circled as that day's potential winners.

"Hey!" I shouted. "Who's the horse player here?" At which point, seventy-ish Michael Pascuma, one of the oldest of the floor brokers, emerged from the racks, excitedly waving a picture of a horse. "How'dya know?" he asked. I told him that I could tell from the way he read the paper and also that, when he walked, his eyes never left the floor. I kidded him: "Still looking for dropped tickets?"

Around that same time I had a sudden hankering to see the ponies, and I arranged to have a date take me out to The Meadowlands track in New Jersey. What a letdown! I found myself incapable of placing a bet; it was too similar to what I was doing from 9:30 to 4:15, five days a week. I walked morosely around the grandstand. I enjoyed the race but was depressed by the realization that gambling, my life's one enduring passion, had now been reduced to a respectable way to make a living working on Wall Street.

| | | |

In my teens, I discovered the school library's microfiche room. I don't know who was more surprised: me, to stumble across the *New York Times* stock tables of the 1950s, or the librarian, who'd seen me as a regular guest only in the school's detention room.

The stocks definitely had cycles. When I found representative stocks from several different industries I made charts to keep track of them. Being only fourteen, I had no idea that there were a lot of grown-ups making charts just like the ones I was improvising and to which one could easily subscribe. So, with my trusty geometry compass, I naively went about inventing the wheel, a regular teenage chartist.

Penny stocks—companies with virtually no value other than their speculative potential—soon acquired for me the same aura the horses had previously held. I had Mom open a custodial trading account for me at Kidder, Peabody. Later as a twenty-year-old AMEX trading-seat holder, I *still* wouldn't have been able to trade shares for myself without first getting Mom to call my broker and say it would be okay.

I began by trading small, upstart mining companies and Alaskan oil stocks on the NASDAQ Stock Exchange. They would go from one dollar to two dollars in a matter of months. Risky stuff for the unwary, but I had the U.S. Bureau of Mines on my side. They publish a lot of useful information about new geologic strikes and technological developments, which I used to good advantage as I tiptoed into the over-the-counter market. Though anyone can send away for the reports, I don't think many bothered to do so that year because they responded immediately, so happy were they to hear from *somebody*.

| | | |

Enter Peter Jay Heffley, my eighth-grade social-studies teacher. He wore bow ties and would sometimes wrap a sweater around his head, turban style, while he taught Arabian history. Sometimes he would teach while balancing himself atop the room divider or do somersaults and handstands to dramatize a historical detail. The only thing he absolutely couldn't do was operate the school's movie and slide projectors. He was all thumbs.

Heffley began paying attention to me the day he asked me what I wanted to do when I grew up, and I replied, "Live in a hotel." Not just any hotel but the Plaza in New York. I wanted to be Eloise, Kay Thompson's impish, troublemaking princess. "If not her, what do you want to *be?*" he next asked. The other kids wanted to grow up and be president, while I said I only wanted to be as rich as Rockefeller—*any* Rockefeller. I didn't have the heart to tell my classmates that I'd already checked out Jimmy Carter's salary and didn't think two hundred thousand dollars was very enticing, even with all those presidential perks.

Careerwise, though, the second most influential man in my life was a much older man, a retired stockbroker. Every summer my family used to go to Hampton Bays, Long Island, where this man was a regular. He would sit in a webbed chair on the dock, a fishing rod in one hand and a cocktail in the other. Almost every day at about noon he would fall into the bay—followed by chair, pole, and martini. I was nine years old when he taught me how to dive into the Edgewater's kidney-shaped pool that first summer. I thought he was a retired swim coach, but I soon figured out that what he really wanted was to have someone reliable around who would dive off the dock after lunch every day and retrieve his eyeglasses, which had sunk to the bottom.

One afternoon I was on the veranda trying to coerce my mother into buying me a single share of Pepsi Cola for my tenth birthday. It was trading at 13½ that summer. The gift she had in mind for me—a cat clock with moving eyes, whiskers, and tail—cost twenty-four dollars. My broker friend was sitting a couple of chairs down and was startled to hear his deep-sea diver talking about stocks. Soon he started telling me about what it was like working on the floor of the American Stock Exchange. We then got to discussing the market together, combing the *Wall Street Journal* for undervalued companies.

Four summers later, in 1980, I told him that I was going to the visitors' gallery of the New York Stock Exchange. He told me to go to the AMEX instead and gave me a list of six of his cronies and an introductory letter scrawled out on the back of a fishing-bait price list. I showed up at 86 Trinity Place in shorts—nobody had tipped me off to a dress code—went to the front door, and proceeded to have everyone on the list paged. Four guys on the list were dead (that should have warned me about life and death at the AMEX) and another had retired. But when I paged the last one, Joe Petta, his son came down instead. I showed Joe, Jr., my friend's "letter of introduction," and he agreed to give me a tour. The guards handed me the largest broker's jacket they could find, which came down to my knees and made it appear that I had a dress on underneath.

It turned out to be the best day of my young life. Joe was very busy doing his brokerage, and I ran alongside him, carrying a stack of his orders and watching him do his executions. For all I could tell that day, we must have traversed ten miles. It certainly *felt* like ten miles. Not so to Joe, Jr. Built like a football linebacker and in something of a perpetual crouch (as if waiting for the ball to be snapped), he was in his element, lumbering across the floor in huge strides—one for every three steps that I took.

The place itself overwhelmed me. It was huge, as busy as a small city at morning rush hour, and very, very loud. Down on the floor, I gaped at the huge bright-green electronic ticker tape, indecipherable letters and numbers marching smartly across the wall, just as I had seen on TV. I looked up to the ceiling, seemingly a mile high, and was taken by the white sculpted three-dimensional bulls and bears.

The natives were all screaming at the top of their lungs. I couldn't make out a word of what they were yelling. It seemed to be some sort of foreign language. They were also flapping their arms and shooting out their fingers. They seemed so angry at one another. I had no idea what they were doing but, whatever it was, I wanted to do it also. It seemed like great fun.

Then Joe took me to post 11, the exact spot where they traded Chibogama Mines, the first mining stock I had purchased when I was ten. He showed me where it traded and introduced me to the specialist. I was totally, utterly entranced. I instinctively knew that, come what may, I would have to end up here, at the American Stock Exchange. I was ready to go to work right then and there. Unfortunately, I was only fourteen; there were no other kids my age working the floor, not even as runners.

| | |

During the halcyon summer of 1979, Pete Heffley introduced me to Milo Mindbender, the entrepreneurial mess officer in Joseph Heller's *Catch 22*. To this impressionable teenager, young Milo was everything that I wanted to be: the quintessential trader, cleverly profiting from chaos, creatively exploiting the insanity of organized death and destruction.

Milo made good sense to me; he was absorbed by mathematical relationships and driven by the profit motive, just as I was. Politics took a back seat to business while he provided goods and services for everybody, regardless of whose flag they happened to be fighting under. I was particularly enraptured by his arcanely triangular commodities trades and K-ration arbitrage. I thought he had a very glamorous life and figured that unless another world war broke out by the time I was ready to graduate, I'd settle for something more mundane. Like Wall Street.

| | |

Looking back those ten years, I can't remember overall what I actually learned in high school. Something about Phoenicians building ships. I think that's all anyone remembers. You don't exactly know when or where they lived, or how they got there, but as soon as someone mentions Phoenicians, most people know they built ships. Most of us don't have ships. If I had one, and it needed repair, I'd definitely call in a Phoenician.

Heffley would teach me things I obviously wasn't picking up at the Fort Erie racetrack. He would drag me to antique shows, art galleries, and estate auctions. He made me recite the significant works by prominent artists and the merits of each painting in particular. He quizzed me on different park designers and whatever passed for good architecture in Buffalo, a city more famous for its chicken wings than for its skyline.

He sent me to the library to read about furniture styles, so I could differentiate between a Sheraton and a Hepplewhite. Heffley also required me to know rugs, so I could distinguish between a Kirman and a Bokhara. He made me learn how cloisonné was crafted and what made antique clocks tick.

After Heffley forced me to understand some essentials about the fine arts, he packed me off to the library again, this time to read plays and classical literature. Going to the theater, opera, or symphony wasn't so much a treat as a trial: He demanded I know *everything* ahead of time about the work and its creator, so that afterward we could discuss theme and socio-historical significance. He just wouldn't give me the time to get into trouble.

It paid off. Within three years he had taken this member of the Buffalo *lumpenproletariat*, an incorrigible truant with so-so passing grades, and turned her into a straight-A Pygmalion, member of the National Honor Society, and winner of a New York State Regents scholarship.

I suppose I should have gone to SUNY Buffalo, but I was tired of shoveling snow. So in September of 1983, I left for the University of Michigan at Ann Arbor. I had applied, knowing that several friends were also going and I would probably be able to get a ride with one of them, thereby saving money I didn't have. Mine was the logic of a seventeen-year-old. I'd actually wanted to go to Wharton School of Finance at the University of Pennsylvania, but Penn didn't want me. Maybe I shouldn't have put down "Unitarian" on the application where they asked for religious affiliation. Had I written "Sunni Muslim," I'd probably have gotten in as part of their minority quota.

I arrived in Michigan feeling poor. I was. I had no pocket money to speak of. As there was no racetrack nearby, I turned to scalping football tickets to earn some spending money.

I also signed up as a human guinea pig at the science school, which paid fifty to one hundred dollars per experiment, depending on how rigorous it would be. I participated in a test linking lack of sleep with the common cold. At the end of the week I lacked sleep and had a cold. My fifty dollars went toward Comtrex and chicken soup for the cold and earplugs and a sound cassette of waves crashing on the beach to lull me to sleep. None of these nostrums worked.

After just a few weeks, I felt like one of thousands of students reading the same books, taking the same classes, and writing the same papers. How could I be successful, I wondered, when the four years of mind-bending knowledge would be cloned thousands of times at this school and across the country?

I picked up the yellow pages and started dialing stockbrokers, asking them what I had to do to become one of them, what sort of training was required, and how old I had to be. They all told me, "Twenty-one." I was seventeen and couldn't wait. Then, on a lark, I called the personnel department at the American Stock Exchange and asked if they had any entry-level positions, and how old would one have to be? They said they always had such openings, but I'd have to be at least sixteen.

I next phoned US Air and booked a flight from Detroit to New York to fill out the application. Flying east, I figured out how to handle my parents. I'd transfer to either Columbia, Fordham, or New York University. My mother, having gone to night school for her degree while working as an RN, surely couldn't object if I were to do the same.

Upon landing at Newark I was greeted by a screaming *New York Post* headline announcing a dorm shooting at Fordham, so that quickly narrowed the short list to two. After filling out the application at the AMEX, I took the Broadway IRT line up to Morningside Heights to check out Columbia. On Broadway near 116th Street, six burly greaseballs in cut-off T-shirts were removing the wheels from a parked Lincoln Continental, looking rather menacingly at passersby who wondered about this quaint local custom. This was early in the afternoon, while just up the block I saw a lone New York cop ticketing a double-parked car. I never bothered to ask for the admissions office. Instead I headed back down into the IRT and took the next train down to Greenwich Village, where I picked up the NYU forms.

I finished the semester at Michigan and packed up all my gear in the trunk of my Rent-a-Wreck. No matter what happened, I wasn't going back. *Ever.* I picked up the four other kids I was driving to Buffalo. I'd rented the car for sixty-five dollars and was charging them each twenty-five—meaning that after gas I'd be pocketing a fifteen-dollar profit.

7

Kindergarten Revisited

I WAS SUMMONED six days before Christmas of 1983. I'd been home from Ann Arbor for four days but hadn't the heart to tell Mom that I really had no intention of going back to the University of Michigan. When the phone rang and the woman on the other end identified herself as someone from personnel at the American Stock Exchange, I feared the worst: more rejection, Wharton School all over again.

Quite the opposite. The AMEX was actually offering me a job! I didn't even ask what sort of job it was or what it would pay. I was told to present myself at the Exchange at 9:00 A.M., three Mondays hence. That would make it January 16. Of course, I had no way of knowing that I had just agreed to plunge into AMEX's pool of high-school dropouts who carried no expectations of advancement.

On Friday, January 6, the week before I'd planned to fly down to the Big Apple, I got another call. The woman from the NYU registrar's office didn't miss a beat and plunged right in, as New Yorkers always do, telling me lickety-split that Miss Pedersen had been accepted for the spring semester as a sophomore because of college-credit courses I'd taken upstate in my senior year.

She then apologized. "We're running a bit behind. I should tell you that registration is today and tomorrow." I never had sent in my preregistration deposit, so I was immediately impressed by a school that didn't require a deposit and wasn't anxious to earn interest on my money. They must have some whopping endowments! I said I couldn't move that fast and would take potluck when I got there.

Early on Monday morning, the sixteenth, I flew into Newark on "People's Distress" Airlines. I took a Jersey Transit bus into Manhattan's Port Authority terminal, checked my bags in a locker, and hopped a cab down to the Exchange. The taxi cost fifteen dollars. I now think there should have been an option to buy the cab at the end of the ride.

Someone in the AMEX personnel department had decided that my "qualifications"—none—were just right for the vacancy of data clerk at trading post 13 on the floor. My identification badge picture was taken, as were my fingerprints, and then I was issued a regulation dark-green cotton jacket.

I went uptown to Greenwich Village to register at NYU. The process took only fifteen minutes, which was a pleasant change from the three-day ordeal at Ann Arbor, where I literally had to camp out in a pup tent and cook on Sterno cans while waiting to sign up for the classes I wanted. NYU even served free coffee and donuts—a nice touch that didn't escape the attention of a local bag lady, who snuck in and shoved about a dozen into her "I Love New York" plastic shopping bag while the security guard looked the other way. I would run into her repeatedly at other campus functions. I was told she had "unofficial tenure."

I encountered only one problem: NYU wouldn't give me housing because—would you believe?—I was a resident of New York State and therefore didn't qualify. I slapped my hand to my forehead. How stupid of me! Why hadn't I thought of that and put down Copenhagen as my hometown? What infuriated me was that kids from Hoboken, New Jersey, on the other side of the Holland Tunnel, were getting dorm rooms, while I—an eight-hour train ride from home—was told to go find myself a warm bench in Washington Square. So I gathered up my courage and telephoned Hjalmar Pedersen, my paternal grandfather, out in Huntington, Long Island. I had seen him only sporadically over the years, usually during the summer.

Retired after thirty years as a restaurant waiter, Grandpa generously insisted that I come out that very night. He didn't tell me the Long Island Railroad stopped at every other apple tree on the way out to Port Jefferson and that the train trip to Huntington Station would take over an hour.

I reported for work the next day. Personnel had asked me, "When do you want to start?" and they were taken aback when I replied, *"Now."* I was told to ask for John Shoy, the man in charge of the AMEX floor staff. The security guard pointed him out to me, standing on the steps leading up to the main trading floor—chewing someone out, I gathered from the heat of the conversation. I tapped him lightly on the sleeve and said, "Excuse me, Mr. Shoy..." He turned around, scowling, then brightened. His first words to me were, "Call me Johnny." The man was old enough to be my grandfather. I said I couldn't call him by his first name, no less the familiar diminutive, that it would not be respectful and, besides, we'd just met. I told him that I almost got thrown out of the Girl Scouts back home when I once addressed the leader by her first name.

"Lesson number one," he told me, "this ain't the scouts. You're not here to do good deeds. Lesson two is that everyone—*everyone*, regardless of position, income level, social status—is Billy, Joey, Sammy, Johnny, Bobby, Tommy, Georgie, Ralphie, Jimmy, and so on. And it's not a sign of endearment," he added. "You don't have to like them."

Johnny then took me over to meet Gene, my supervisor, whose last name now escapes me. I remember him as an easygoing guy in his late thirties, who seemed alternately amused and bemused by my mishaps and sort of took me under his wing, this naive kid from upstate who was obviously in way over her head. Can't say I blame him.

Gene could have fired me right off the bat the day—my fifth— I showed up late for work.

"What kept you?" he demanded. "What's your excuse?"

"I got lost," I whispered, looking down and shuffling my sneakers.

"You got wha-a-at?" It's as if he'd never heard that line before.

I took a deep breath and began just as if I were late for homeroom. "Well, I always look for the big American Stock Exchange flag to find the building. It's raining out. There was no flag."

He seemed taken aback. It was clearly one of the more original if lame-brained excuses to have been run by him.

"Well," he said in the tone of a kindergarten teacher dealing with a not-too-bright child, "we'll keep this between the two of us. Maybe you should buy yourself a Hagstrom map of Lower Manhattan, what do you say? We can't just have you here on sunny days."

I remembered from my teenage visit that the Exchange floor was big, but just *how* big didn't hit me until I was standing in the middle of the main hall trying to figure out how to tell one trading post from another. Joe Petta, Jr., was nowhere to be seen. But then I lucked out by striking up a conversation with an attractive, energetic man in a powder-blue jacket. I think it was about the third day.

"Hi, I'm Pete LaBadia," he said, "who are you? You look lost." I told him my name wasn't Lost but Intimidated. He laughed. "What you need, baby," said he, grabbing my hand, "is Dr. Pete's ten-cent tour. So, tell me, what's your *real* name?"

He didn't walk, he *strode*. Though long-legged, I was forced to break into a trot just to keep up. What I most remember of that first whirlwind tour—there'd be several more before Dr. Pete allowed me to fly solo—is the number of people who knew LaBadia by name, and he them. He introduced me to everybody as if I belonged. I began to feel I did. Pete seemed to have a good word for everybody and, as we left them behind, an anecdotal story about most of them. I asked him what he did. "I'm the last of the two-dollar brokers," he replied, lapsing into this nonstop description of what life was like back in the good old days before negotiated commissions cut his income by seventy-five percent. Then, for each buy-sell trade LaBadia would bring to the specialists, he'd collect a two-dollar commission. Now he was lucky to make fifty cents. I said that, to me, that didn't sound like a lot of money. "To my generation, it *was*," he shot back. Given the volume, "it did add up," he added somewhat wistfully.

By now we were on one of the two escalators leading up from the main trading floor to the mezzanine, which a few years earlier had housed the visitors' gallery and now held four new trading posts. The escalators go about three times as fast as those in a department store, but LaBadia was leaping steps three at a time. "Time's money," he insisted. "You'll learn."

I began to follow him on his rounds. There was too much activity to be able to understand everything that was going on. LaBadia must have seen my expression, as he suddenly grabbed me by the shoulders, propelled me to the right, and said, "Here, you'll get a better perspective of what this crazy business is all about." We were standing at the edge of the mezzanine, with four trading stations behind us. I stood at the railing, looking down on the vast expanse of the main trading floor. I counted about fifteen trading posts, each a beehive of activity, though some appeared busier than others. Nobody was standing still. Everybody seemed to be looking up at the monitors that ringed each post, except for the brokers who darted from one post to the next.

After going back down the escalator, we visited about three of the long trading posts and around twenty small booths. At the posts—actually long, rectangular work stations measuring about ten by twenty feet, with counters facing out and manned, on both sides—there were about twenty specialists, clerks, and transaction reporters. At the end of each counter stood a number of bored-looking exchange employees, feeding data punch cards almost by rote into a device that processed them and converted the material into quotes and last sales on the monitors above.

Nobody talked in normal speaking tones. Everyone shouted, made notations, and looked up at the numbers blinking overhead on the monitors.

Behind them, suspended from a network of steel girders and stacked atop horizontal shelving, sat all sorts of hardware: computer terminals, time clocks, phones, and—blinking and beeping—a panoply of different-size video terminals and market monitors, many with split screens, in both color and monochrome green and amber.

LaBadia stopped at a couple of them, barking out figures—I couldn't tell a buy from a sell order—furiously scribbling something on the palm-size note pad that never seemed to leave his hand, either handing it to one of the people behind the counter or crumpling it up and discarding it.

Flanking the edges of the floor, and up the steeply rising balconies on the north and south sides of the great hall, were a number of newsstandlike booths, measuring about four feet square. In each, I counted two or three people, mostly guys but a few women, crammed into the small space along with stacks of order pads, six or seven phones—each with ten different lines—a time-stamping clock, and a big calendar. Lining the wooden sides were small cubbyholes holding orders scrawled on playing-card–sized pieces of paper marked BUY or SELL.

I asked, "Why do you keep going back to the same places?" It seemed as if we were making a continuous circuit, going from booth to booth around the perimeter of the floor, sometimes bisecting it and stopping to make a trade, then back up the escalator to stop and trade at one of the upstairs posts. Pete explained that the action takes place at all the big trading posts out in the middle and that the booths serve as way stations for the brokers. Each brokerage firm has its own operations booth at the Exchange. Most firms have several: The big houses, like Pershing, Charles Schwab, Oppenheimer, Merrill, and Bear Stearns, have as many as five or six scattered all over the place. It's where the clerks sort out incoming orders from the ones already executed. Pete would drop off reports on what he had accomplished and pick up any new instructions that had arrived in his short absence. It's through these stations that company headquarters communicates with its floor staff; it's also how the back office gets information for billing clients and preparing account statements. The floor brokers also use them as R and R stops, taking their coffee breaks there and stashing their brief-cases.

One day, years later, Pete came bouncing up to me, sporting one of those K + R pedometers for measuring mileage. "My average today was thirteen and four tenths miles," he proudly reported, adding, "for all the good that does me." I asked what made him say that, since the American Heart Association recommends walking over most other forms of exercise. "Yeah, but I figure the stress of the business will kill me."

It didn't. A few months after the October 1989 crash, after toting up his daily expenses and his take, LaBadia realized all this vaunted automation was costing him more to come to work each day than it returned in commissions. He'd given the AMEX thirty years of his life, all of them on the floor—eleven as a broker, nineteen as a clerk. Overnight he made up his mind to quit.

| | | |

Whenever the TV networks do a routine story on a calm day in Wall Street trading and need "background color," they use stock footage of the New York Stock Exchange. When things go crazy, they send over crews to the American Stock Exchange options pit. That should tell you something, but the footage doesn't begin to convey the bigness, loudness, and sheer madness of the place during trading hours.

I'm often asked to describe what it *felt* like, being here, and have always had trouble conjuring up a word picture. When you look down on the floor from the mezzanine, it's one vast blur of multicolored movement. And when you're standing in the middle of the floor, with hundreds of people rushing by from booth to post, bells ringing, the PA system blaring, you feel like you're bouncing around in a pinball machine.

The noise is equally hard to describe. I suppose it's what one would get individually taping and simultaneously playing back the sounds of Grand Central Station at rush hour, a big-city municipal swimming pool on summer weekends, and Niagara Falls after it rains. I finally appreciated the meaning of the descriptions "mind-numbing" and "stone-deaf," especially during those occasions when a new issue started trading.

Worse were the acoustics, which made sound bounce around the huge space, the lack of baffling materials, and the reflective rubber-tiled flooring, raised so that several thousand miles of computer cables and conduit could run beneath. It didn't take me long to grasp why everyone seemed to be gesticulating. They were unable to hear each other over the constant waterfall of noise, let alone understand what the other guy was yelling. As I would later painfully discover, when you're juggling millions of someone else's dollars in a series of swiftly executed trades, you'd better be damned sure of what the other guy wants, or it's *your* execution. To further complicate life, nobody spoke in complete sentences. Everything was framed in a sort of verbal shorthand, delivered in staccato, machine-gun-like bursts.

Not long after I got there, another clerk working for Dritz, Goldring, named Anthony, who would not answer to his Christian name unless it was properly pronounced—"Ant'ny," with the accent on the broad A, as in aunt—took pity on me and gave me a crash course in sign language, AMEX style. The brokers use it to "speak" with their clerks, positioned off the floor, sitting in the sharply rising balconies.

"You can learn all the expressions you'll need the first day. Then go home and practice in the mirror. It's a snap." He was right. We began with the core program, swear words. I soon mastered three different ways of signaling "Fuck you!"—all of them variations of the signals for the number 4 and letter Q, and all of them indispensable.

The Exchange's system of hand signals dates back to the days before 1921, when the curbstone brokers, who had been conducting business outside since the 1830s, finally moved indoors. The New York Curb Exchange (renamed the American Stock Exchange in 1953), and its predecessors, had always been perceived as the raffish cousin of the powerful and elitist New York Stock Exchange (a perception that made the place more appealing to me in the first place). Historically, just as the AMEX would later give life to a lot of start-up companies in computer electronics, nuclear chemistry, genetic engineering, and other esoteric industries, it was the curb market that was always the more daring of the two when it came to backing enterprises with uncertain futures—like a canal system for barges or digging for gold in the California Sierras. These days, the AMEX has to be on the cutting edge in order to compete with all the blue-chip stocks listed on the NYSE, which will always be its bread and butter.

Back in olden times, before the Exchange had moved indoors, on windy days the traders at curbside couldn't hear one another, so the clerks inside, perched precariously on windowsills several stories up, would lean out over the street below and, by hand signs, relay the information. They had first tried shouting, but that worked about as well then as it does now.

The signals are a modified version of American Sign Language with a few additions to incorporate fractions. Over the years, traders and brokers have also added their own proprietary signals for "Where's lunch?" "Going to the bathroom," "Phone for you," "Get me two tickets for tonight's ball game!"

I noticed that the signals were even carried over to the cafeteria. A quick wave of the hand tells your buddy, "Large Coke, chicken salad, no mayo."

If not for the different-colored jackets, it would be difficult to tell who is who and who does what. Even then, it's not always clear whether the blue-jacketed person you've just grabbed by the sleeve is a data clerk or a broker, because the shades are so similar—a difference of, say, $220,000 a year. And if you're color blind, forget it. Supervisors have lime-green jackets, transaction reporters wear dark-blue jackets, spread brokers, orange; and some of the firms have their own colors, like Merrill Lynch's canary yellow, PaineWebber's beige, and Wagner Stott's cranberry.

(The jackets themselves are remnants of the old curbstone trading days when, during the dark, rainy days, clerks had trouble recognizing their brokers outside until someone came up with the idea of giving them different hats to wear. The AMEX photo archives show people sporting opera hats and those squarish baseball caps that are now making a comeback in some major-league clubs like Oakland and Pittsburgh. Of course, once trading went indoors, the wearing of hats was deemed socially unacceptable.)

During my time at the Exchange, the place seemed to be in a state of perpetual reconstruction, sort of like Boston's Route 128, which began as a WPA project during the Depression and is still being rebuilt half a century later. The first year I worked at the Exchange, trading volume hit 1.5 billion shares; during my last year, it surpassed 3 billion shares, or 12 million a day. During these boom years, the AMEX corps of engineers struggled mightily to keep up with the demand for more work space. Ultimately, they had to carve out nooks and crannies way off the trading floor to accommodate the crowds of traders. Because by this time everything was state-of-the-art electronic, the old line-of-sight requirements had long gone by the boards.

When New Jersey Governor Brendan Byrne tried to seduce us to quit Manhattan for beautiful downtown Hoboken, New York's governor, Hugh L. Carey, reportedly made a counteroffer to have the state finance a new home for the Exchange. The AMEX governors didn't think Carey could deliver (they were right) and thought long and hard about moving to New Jersey. Then it was pointed out that they couldn't very well leave the NYSE behind. If the NYSE had been ambivalent about pulling up stakes and moving to New Jersey, the 1987 crash stopped them cold by forcing a reevaluation of the existing financial system. I would not have been surprised, once the market recovered, to have come to work one morning only to find someone had opened up yet another trading post in the ladies' room.

My initial job required that I take large index cards, which had been filled in by the price reporters assigned to the various posts to record the latest trades, and feed them into a machine that looked like a photocopier but wasn't. The data would be simultaneously logged in and flashed on a large overhead screen for all to see. Real drudge work. Looking back, I can't recall a more tedious, dreary job than having to stuff the machine's maw, one card at a time. We clerks were the *braceros* of Wall Street. At least it wasn't stoop labor and we weren't paid at piece-work rates.

The high spot of the day for me was when the pesky machine would start spewing out rejects. That happened at least five or six times a day, and it meant a blessed break in the routine. Oh boy, what fun it was to reinsert the same card over and over again until the machine accepted it. Sort of like stuffing empty cans into the compactor at the A&P: You never knew when they would come shooting back out.

Whenever trading got particularly heavy, I imagined I was Lucille Ball doing the assembly-line number in "I Love Lucy"— trying to keep ahead of the candies that came spewing out of some mysterious black hole. Only, in our situation, we wouldn't be able to stuff the incomplete orders into our cheeks.

In that skit, Lucy Ricardo had her supervisor to worry about. We had Sheila. British to the core and demanding, Sheila was our den mother and drill sergeant. She took a personal interest in "training" me, although I was sure a baby orangutan with a hearing problem could have learned the complexities of the job in just under three minutes. And been happy with a banana.

"Regulations, luv," she explained.

Sheila's regular job was to rant and rave at the clerks in order to keep them feeding those cards into the machine. She was a forceful motivator for anyone who qualified as a slow self-starter. Once, when I told her this harassment was insanity, she looked at me: "I'm insane, but what's your excuse?"

Sheila also took an interest in seeing that I was familiar with all the gadgetry that was supposed to simplify life—hers, mainly.

Back in the 1950s, while the rest of the financial world was first becoming aware of computers replacing men with quills and abacuses, the Curb Exchange installed one of those department-store pneumatic-tube systems that snaked underneath the cavernous trading floor and connected various outposts. In just a few seconds, rubber-bumpered brass-and-plastic cylinders would whisk buy-sell orders and any other document from here to there and back again.

Never having seen such a system, much less played with one, I was naturally elated as I loaded my first cylinder to shoot it up to my new friend, Pete LaBadia, way out there in left field. Gee, this was going to be a lot of fun. I could see delivering candy bars and other snacks by plastic tube.

That vision lasted about as long as it took Sheila to set me straight. She informed me, with what seemed to be utter seriousness, that the tubes are plague carriers and they act like pistons, pushing polluted air out into the trading room. Because there are no windows that can be opened to admit fresh air, the air in the tubes hadn't been changed since the system was installed. "Think of it, luv," she said, "you could be breathing the same air that some tubercular trader infected back before you were born." Pause. "By Friday, you'll probably be coughing up black mucus."

On hot summer days, when the air conditioning was sputtering on reduced power because of "brownouts," a shortage of power citywide, I used to sidle up to one of the tube stations, surreptitiously look around, then pry open the spring lid with my fingers extended, and let the cool air whoosh up my sleeve, an armpit at a time. Definitely not what the engineers had in mind when they ordered up the system.

When the AMEX personnel lady had called me at home during Christmas, she'd said nothing about the opportunity for advancement. It turned out that there wasn't much; at least not on my rung of the ladder. The Exchange does not operate like an ad agency or network, where it's an article of faith that the mailroom is only a temporary but necessary entry-level assignment and that anyone staying there longer than six months obviously has nothing up there and nothing to offer the employer, and so is therefore eventually eased out to make room for someone who does have potential.

Not the AMEX. Instead of offering hope, AMEX management recruits clerks by dangling before them a generous benefits program unequaled elsewhere on Wall Street. Company loyalties have been built on far less. It's not in the Exchange's best interest to have a lot of turnover among staff electricians, carpenters, data clerks, price reporters, and other support troops. They keep the machinery in place and running.

So, looking for an opportunity, I talked to different people on the floor to find out what they did all day. In this way, I could set my sights on what I really wanted to do down there. Jobs ranged from janitor, tube-room operator, mailroom supervisor, floor broker, independent trader, to owner and operator of a multimillion-dollar specialist firm.

| | | |

I just *had* to get out of kindergarten, so I began sounding out people on the floor to learn how one would go about working for one of the specialist companies.

I got to talking with Arthur Langel, a specialist in about thirty-five stocks with Dritz, Goldring & Company. Artie is an avid sailing enthusiast. He reads a lot of sailing magazines in between trading millions of shares. To be honest about it, Artie is so good that he can trade millions of shares in the intervals when he is not reading sailing magazines.

One day, a frenzied two-dollar broker named Sammy came running up to Arthur's post, sweating profusely, seeking to buy thirty thousand shares of Texas Air at the market price. Arthur looked up from *Sail* magazine, feigning annoyance at having been disturbed by so mundane a matter, and asked, "Did I break a mirror? What are you doing here?" Perfectly aware that Artie only buys at better men's clothing stores, Sammy ignored the insult and fired off his riposte: "My, you're looking very Sears, Roebuck today." Backed up with orders and anxious to get moving, Sammy was clearly not in the mood to dawdle. Which is precisely why Artie turned to another page in *Sail* and asked, "Nice tie, couldn't the guy at the carnival guess your weight? Sammy, what do you think of this thirty-footer?" Knowing that nothing annoys Arthur so much as a discussion of *motor* boats, Sammy shrugged. "Nice, but it seems like a hell of a lot of money to spend on something that doesn't go on its own power." Without another word, Artie executed Sammy's trades and looked up. "What are you hanging around here for, anyway, waiting for hairstyles to change? Get outta here!" And, as Sammy ran off, Artie threw in, "And don't ever trade with me again!" Artie laughed as he resumed turning the pages of his magazine.

I asked Arthur, "Who was that?" He replied, "Oh, one of my best friends. Sammy's been around here since the Flood. If it weren't for me, he'd still be driving a Cadillac."

Arthur is best known as the originator of the Broker Olympics. Working from his corner post, a few feet away from the Prudential Bache booth, Artie one day noticed that when the Bache telex disgorged its orders, clerks would rip and read and simply toss the carbon papers on the floor. The waxy buildup struck Artie as being a nifty skating rink, and during lunch one day he handed each of his clerks cardboard signs numbered one to ten in such categories as "grace," "artistic development," "form," and, of course, "number of orders tossed in the air," as the brokers came barrel-assing around the corner and slipped and slid to the floor. Whenever that happened, Artie, as master of ceremonies, would give the high sign to his jacketed judges, who then would display the score they felt the hapless victim had earned. It would be very embarrassing for the brokers caught with their dignity down. Once Artie bagged a guest—a woman in high heels and black leather skirt. She was not amused, but the boys were quite impressed. Recalled one of them, "She had on the kind of heels you'd want to drink Dom Perignon out of."

After I had correctly brought Artie and his clerks their coffee order three days in a row, he took notice of me. One thing led to another when he suddenly asked, "What's your IQ?" I replied,

"One fifty-eight." Wordlessly, he picked up the phone and dialed an extension number.

"Mike? Artie. Got someone you gotta see." He listened, cupped the mouthpiece, and asked me, "Monday morning okay with you for an interview?" I nodded vigorously. He hung up. "Go for it!"

8

Basic Training

IKE TURNED OUT to be Michael Dritz, name partner
in one of the floor-based specialist firms handling
stocks, stock options (Storer Communications,
Coastal Corporation, Hercules and Union Carbide), and the
Market Value Index (XAM)—the second of the AMEX-
sponsored option indexes and one which the Exchange mis-
takenly thought would do well.

Fiftyish Mike Dritz was a trader-turned-owner/manager and
not given to small talk. Standing roughly five-foot-six, lean,
balding but with a rim of curly gray hair, he was also the nattiest
dresser I would ever encounter during my years on Wall Street.
God knows how he did it—maybe he kept identical suits stashed
away upstairs—but he'd make it through the day looking as
immaculate as he did starting work. His suits were never wrin-

kled, his shirts seemed to repel sweat. No hair seemed out of place. He looked like a walking GQ fashion spread.

One day after I'd gone to work for him, Dritz demonstrated his occult powers when he spilled a cup of coffee. *Spilled* doesn't tell the story. *Saturated* does. The coffee splattered everything within sight—piles of reports, computer terminals, time clocks, people standing nearby. But not a drop landed on Dritz. I asked his partner Artie Langel how that was possible. "Easy, that coffee wouldn't *dare!*"

In making the switch I felt a little apprehensive. Fewer than four weeks had passed since I started as a data clerk and already I was getting ready to jump ship—or at least cross the aisle to look for more meaningful work. If Sheila the drill sergeant guessed what I was up to the morning I showed up for my sub-rosa interview with Mike Dritz, all spiffed up in my Sunday best, she did not let on.

I'd allowed my entire lunch period for the interview, but I needn't have. The interview, behind post 13, took all of three minutes and went sort of like this:

DRITZ: Artie here says you're smart. That's good. The pay is $150 a week plus bonus. You have to be in by 7:30 A.M. to work on rejected trades. Do you want to start Friday or Monday?

ME: (*Thinking*) I haven't yet told this guy my name and here he's offering me a job at thirty bucks more a week. (*Speaking*) Monday is George Washington's Birthday. I guess I'll start Tuesday.

DRITZ: Mmmm, I forgot about that. You should have said Friday and you'd have gotten paid for the holiday.

ME: Okay, okay, I'll start Friday.

DRITZ: (*Walking away*) Too late, kiddo, see you Tuesday. You just made your first trade.

Already I could see that this business was going to be a lot like playing chess with my Uncle Jim up in Buffalo: Once you took your hand off the piece, it was all over.

Apparently I'd gotten a firm offer and just as apparently I'd accepted. I hurried off to inform Gene, my floor supervisor, wondering how I was going to handle this two-weeks'-notice matter when I was expected at Dritz, Goldring five working days hence.

Dritz, Goldring had been given the XAM allocation the year before. As the franchisee, Dritz was to get from the Exchange the space and support services needed to make the index go. The franchisee would pay for the specialists and clerks and, for every contract or hundred shares traded, would pay the Exchange a percentage of every transaction.

XAM was a broad market-product based on a weighted average of *all* the common stocks listed on the AMEX—then about 940, give or take a few either way. There was no way of my knowing it at the time I joined Dritz, but XAM was destined to be the Edsel of options indexes. The problem with XAM was that, unlike XMI's lean and mean twenty-blue-chip-stock underpinning, it reflected too many stocks in too big a basket to interest the fast-action crowd—the portfolio hedgers and program traders, then gaining strength in numbers. This was made abundantly clear once the XMI revved up to become the Exchange's single most successful product.

XMI had been allocated to Spear Leeds Kellogg/Investors Company, another specialist firm, as its only product. Its trading post, not yet quite a pit at that point, was close enough for me to observe in action.

In addition to XAM and XMI, the Exchange would in time also offer two more broad-market indexes—the Institutional Index (XII), embodying seventy-five of the leading institutional portfolio stocks), and the International Market Index (ADR) of fifty leading foreign stocks that trade in the United States, primarily in the form of American Depositary Receipts. It also added several narrow-based indexes, among them the Oil Index (XOI) and the Computer Technology Index (XCI).

To give you an idea of what Dritz, Goldring was up against, consider that in 1984, the year I joined them, the Market Value Index (XAM) traded only 142,179 contracts, while across the floor, at Spear Leeds, XMI traded 5.8 million contracts. In 1985, by then having been fobbed off by Dritz to another specialist firm, XAM traded only 22,000 contracts. That same year, XMI zoomed to 12.2 million, in 1986 peaked at 17.6 million contracts, while poor XAM mustered fewer than 200 contracts.

That year, AMEX quixotically moved the Dritz, Goldring post next to that of Spear Leeds, perhaps in the forlorn hope that XMI's frenetic activity would rub off. It struck most of us as being as pathetic a gesture as parking a Ford Pinto next to a Rolls-Royce so that it would transmogrify into a Bentley.

Early the following Tuesday I reported for work at Dritz, Goldring. Mike turned me over to John Torres, a small, wiry, twenty-six-year-old street-smart Italian from Brooklyn who talked in what I later came to recognize as an East New York accent. He could be as deadpan as Buster Keaton, which I suppose made him excellent at what he did—as well as at occasionally bluffing his fellow options traders.

Torres—or J.T., as he was called—was one of the Exchange's 661 regular-member seat holders and one of a handful of traders specializing in both stocks and options.

In addition to these 661, there are also 203 seats for options principal members who trade only in options, and 36 limited-trading permit holders who traffic only in the XMI and XII index options. Trading is, as American Express would put it, "a member privilege." To trade you've got to be a member of the Exchange; that is to say, hold a seat. But you don't necessarily have to buy your seat; you can lease it, or your employer can lease it for you. (A fourth category, associate membership, provides wire and telex access to the trading floor, to regular members who then execute orders.)

There are a little over twice as many seats on the New York Stock Exchange, where prices have come down considerably since the Reagan high of 1987, when a single seat sold for $1.15 million. In fact, according to the *Wall Street Journal*, it's now cheaper to buy a Big Board seat than a McDonald's franchise.

As one of the firm's specialists, J.T. clearly preferred the fast action of options over stock trading, which convinced me I'd better stick closely to him and observe, if I wanted to learn the more arcane points of options trading.

My job, he explained during our first chat, would be to record all of the XAM trades taking place. Sounds do-able, said I, brimming with confidence, figuring as any rational human being would that the traders would inform the clerks when a trade had or was taking place, who was trading, how many options contracts, and at what price.

Did I have a lot to learn! I'd soon discover that traders traded, period. That they either didn't have the time for the post-op paperwork or didn't give a damn. I quickly suspected it was the latter. At the sound of the closing bell, they rushed down the stairs to Harry's, leaving to us hapless clerks the unenviable task of putting the entire day's pieces back together. Given the number of transactions the average trader handled during the day, reconstruction was often impossible. So the clerks had to be there while the trading was going on, intently following the play-by-play as if they were refereeing the National Open Tennis matches. This meant catching the hand signals, listening to the shouts, and afterward grabbing brokers by their lapels on the way out for eyewitness testimony.

The way it actually worked can be illustrated hypothetically. J.T. might bellow at another trader, "Leon, I'll buy twenty at seven and a quarter!" whereupon it would behoove me, as his clerk, not only to see whom he was yelling at ("Twenty from whom?") but also to figure out, "Twenty of what?" J.T. wasn't about to stop and tell me.

"Twenty at seven and a quarter" was trader shorthand for "Buy twenty April 325 calls at seven and a quarter"—$725 per contract, each contract being the equivalent of one hundred shares of common stock. All of the options had a different "strike price" (the price level that the underlying stock or group of stocks had to reach in order for the options to be worth anything at expiration). In this particular case, expiration would be the third Friday in April.

For J.T., this exercise was a "trade." It was what he did all day, every day, all year. It was what everybody around him—traders, specialists, and brokers—did either for themselves, their clients, or for institutions. Trading is the *only* way of making money on the floor. If you don't trade you starve, since overhead just slowly eats away at your capital.

The way traders make money on some transactions is by what they decide to do *after* selling or buying the contracts.

"Option trading," J.T. would explain to me, "is no different, actually, than buying a Van Gogh at Sotheby's, except it's cheaper. Question: Do I hold on to it and hope the value goes up or try to sell it right away to some other guy?"

Conversely, were he to sell the painting, should he buy another right away? Should he take the money and bank it or invest it in something else? So, having just spent $14,500, J.T. had to make some quick decisions while cranking up the next trade: Should he keep the options in inventory and hope they'll appreciate? Should he insure himself against losing a lot of money by selling stock, another option, or futures, in order to hedge the bet? Should he try to get out of the position right away by making a quick profit or taking a loss? All this within a span of seconds.

In our hypothetical example, it was a tough call. There didn't seem to be any traders jumping up and down wanting to participate, so J.T. threw the twenty calls into his account as part of inventory. He'd wait thirty minutes, and if it didn't look like it would be profitable, he'd sell some futures against it for insurance.

"If you find yourself running your hands through the telephone cord like it's a rosary and praying for the market to go your way," he would often say, "then it's time to bite the bullet and hedge your bet. Professionals let their profits run and cut their losses short. Only dopes cut their profits short and let their losses keep going"—or words to that effect.

In a busy market with a lot of volume it becomes more like the game we used to play as kids called Hot Potato. It's frustrating to keep a position in inventory, because it's expensive and you have to monitor it. So all the traders try to keep flipping trades out as fast as they make them, trying to "scalp" for eights and quarters and taking their losses when they're wrong.

| | | |

Over time, I got to figure out what to listen for and recorded the time, amount, price, broker's badge number, and company in a special book.

As the options market was slow that first day, J.T. and I began talking about what it took to become a specialist clerk. He told me that he too had started as a clerk, for "a really big trader. He was selling stock on the New York [Stock Exchange] and the reports came in over that phone. Well, half the time I'd pick up that phone before it even rang and got the reports. I could feel when it was about to ring. Sheer mental telepathy, I swear. He couldn't get over it, and I saved him a lot of dough, so he made me a trader."

So that was it. I'd have to be *discovered*, the sooner the better. I'd have to figure out an effective attention-grabbing device. It gave me something to think about.

I asked J.T. if there were any hard-and-fast rules for a beginner like me. When he said there were, I pulled out a spiral-bound notebook. This he didn't expect, a serious student. He cleared his throat. "Rule number one is never get involved in a land war in Asia . . ." As I dutifully wrote this MacArthurism down, J.T. guffawed: "No, no, fercrisesakes, I'm only kidding. That's for my other course, on strategic *military* options at West Point."

Adopting a more serious tone, he told me, "Actually, for clerks there are really only three things to remember. One, record all trades as they occur, not afterward; two, don't make any mistakes; and, three, take the blame for everyone else's mistakes and any other things that are apt to go wrong. Murphy's Law by way of Torres."

I was scribbling away when he abruptly said, "That's all for today, kid. Now go out and buy the McMillan book so you'll know what I'm talking about when we get to lesson number two."

As soon as I could, I went up to the NYU bookstore and picked up Larry McMillan's *Options As a Strategic Investment*. It set me back thirty bucks, but I figured it was my first strategic investment. Besides, I told myself, all those lunatics in the pit seem to swear by it, and, when in the heat of trading, most of them only grunted in one- and two-syllable words anyway, so how difficult could it be?

They happened to be right. I'd read much harder books for college credit. Once you understood the basic underlying principals of options trading, the rest sort of slid into place.

The way I understood it, options are options, whether in real estate, in Hollywood, or on Wall Street. They all essentially work the same. Let's say you want a house costing sixty thousand dollars. The broker may give you one month to decide and charge you one hundred dollars. You don't get that hundred dollars back if you decide not to buy; nor does it go toward payment if you do. It just means the realtor can't sell it to anyone else until your month is up.

At this point, the best thing that can happen to you is that the state announces it is going to put in a highway one mile away from your property, because that highway will certainly spur growth in that part of the county. Overnight, the house you "own" for one hundred dollars will have increased ten thousand dollars in value, but it's still yours to buy for sixty thousand dollars. Of course, should the state run that same highway right by your front door, your sixty-thousand-dollar house may lose half its value, at which point you'd be smart to walk away from the deal, having lost only one hundred dollars.

Stock options work exactly the same, except that instead of a sixty-thousand-dollar house, we are dealing with six thousand shares of Consolidated Widgets trading at ten dollars. And that highway could be any external factor that would affect the future of Consolidated Widgets.

Before the index options came along, investors had to determine where the market was heading, what industry group to bet on, and which stock to buy. The index option reduced the process to a single bet: the direction the market would take over the next few months. And, as already noted, it also offered some protection to large portfolio holders against wide swings in the market, while giving the program traders in New York and Chicago a new toy to play with.

| | | |

Good as it was, McMillan's book did not prepare me for what would face me in real life and in real time. For example, "trading" to me—late removed from the playgrounds of suburban Buffalo—still meant baseball cards from bubble-gum packs. I'm sure that, had I studied American frontier history in college, I'd have imagined old John Jacob Astor, the first furrier, paddling through the wild-rice swamps of Minnesota, swapping guns and firewater with the Ojibwas for freshly skinned pelts. Had I done any world traveling, I'd have thought of trading as haggling over rugs in Morocco or unstrung water pearls in Hong Kong.

If what was going on around me in the XAM and XMI pits was *real* trading, I'd sure need a lot more instruction from John Torres. He gave it, gladly and generously.

I began to wonder as the days passed, was there anything this savvy young guy *didn't* know? He must have been born right there, on the trading floor. The Force was definitely with him. As it was with Ant'ny, his assistant. Ant'ny played Lou Costello to J.T.'s Bud Abbot, the willing butt of his pal's good-natured insults, straight man to his sick jokes, and co-conspirator in many of his lord-and-master's stress-reducing fun and games.

Titularly, he was J.T.'s clerk; actually, "alter ego" would have been more like it. It was Ant'ny who, early on, reassured me that "whatever shit's gonna come down the road at you, don'tcha worry, you'll get the hang of it in a few months. And if you don't"—here a long, pregnant pause for effect—"then maybe

you should try out for food service upstairs [in the cafeteria]."
How reassuring.

Wise beyond his years—he was only twenty-four—and, like
J.T., Brooklynite Italian to the core, Ant'ny was everything a
trader could possibly want in his clerk. Above all, he was trust-
worthy and dependable. That this dependability also applied to
his chronic tardiness seemed to amuse more than anger J.T.

"I think he's got the most inventive excuses," J.T. said one
day, with a touch of admiration. "In my part of Brooklyn water
mains don't break, third rails don't short, and they don't have
hurricane watches. Why do these things always happen to him?"

Actually, Ant'ny would just oversleep and, according to J.T.,
on his way in would scour all three tabloids—the *Post*, *Daily
News*, and *Newsday*—hoping to find a disaster that somehow
could be linked to his area of Brooklyn. No natural or super-
natural phenomena escaped Ant'ny's eagle eye. But the one he
never used was a solar eclipse. I never did understand why he
was reluctant, since it's floor folklore that eclipses and snow-
storms are bullish indicators, whereas forest fires and tidal waves
signal the coming of bear markets.

| | | |

They were teaching me all the things that went into a single
trading decision—prompted by my question, "Are all these
screens necessary?"

I had seen some historic photos of the American Stock Exchange, back when they still had chandeliers hanging from the
ornate gilded ceiling 650 feet up, instead of spotlights, and when
the great hall still had a sense of elegance, grandeur, and majesty
about it. But the advent of computers and telecommunications
had changed all that.

A group of specialists were clustered around trading post 8, craning their necks this way and that, bobbing up and down like short people in a movie house trying to see around the big people sitting directly in front of them.

"What are they looking for?" I asked.

"Everything, and nothing," J.T. replied. "There's a lot of information that goes into making an informed buying decision that would never occur to the small investor—information that may in fact have nothing to do with finance. Which is why sometimes no news is good news. Go see for yourself."

Brokers and traders I ran into would invariably precede each remark with, "According to the broad tape," or "The ticker said . . ." I, of course, would look everywhere for one or the other, and I squirmed with embarrassment the first time someone pointed them out to me. I should not have been looking down for them but up.

Why people persist in using those old names mystifies me. Historically, Dow Jones used to distribute its news only on eight-inch-wide paper, or "tape," so you would think, logically, that the service conveying stock quotes on paper three-quarters of an inch wide would be called the thin tape. Humpty-Dumpty would have fit right in on Wall Street ("It means just what I choose it to mean, neither more nor less").

I wish I'd been around in the old days, just so I could see the ticker tape spooling out of those glass-domed contraptions that Joe Petta, Sr., used to keep in his office, and which gave Lower Manhattan its richly deserved reputation as the ticker-tape parade capital of the world. These days, homecoming heroes given the key-to-the-city treatment are more likely to be pelted by unspooled toilet paper and shredded documents, along with an occasional tuna-stained paper lunch plate.

| | | |

J.T. was right when he said that as long as I worked the floor I'd never need to buy a newspaper again—except maybe the tabloids for their gossip columns—because, sooner or later, everything I would need to know would be right there, moving across the electronic boards. For some of us, reading newspapers proved to be actually injurious to our financial health. At first it was hard to shake the habit, but once I began trading in earnest, I quickly stopped reading the papers. Some guys, I realized, couldn't trade before they'd digested every page, including the how-to-make-a-better-quiche section. I used to be that way, too.

Then, one fine day in 1986, the *Times* declared the financial markets to be in disarray and forecast a cataclysm by Monday—Tuesday, latest. I went short and the Dow went up forty points. I got killed. Just the opposite happened to Frankie Borenzo, a fellow trader at Spear Leeds. The day he read the *Times*, the paper's financial oracles forecast unlimited growth for at least the next millennium. Naturally, the market tanked and Frankie got a big haircut, as they say.

Afterward, Frankie and I agreed it would be smarter for us to talk about last night's sit-coms or baseball before trading; let the others read their papers. It only cost them fifty cents while it could cost us fifty grand.

I never ran out of questions. In high school back home, I remember our teachers egging us on. "Don't be afraid to ask. No one will think you're stupid. You're probably asking what they'd ask if they only had the nerve." True enough. Nobody snickered at Michigan and NYU whenever I played Statue of Liberty, one arm aloft, the other clutching a book. Any book.

So now, confidently, I asked J.T., "Why do I have to put a broker's badge number in our book?" figuring I'd get another history lesson. Looking back, not a stupid question, but J.T. thought it was. First he couldn't believe anyone would ask it. Then he broke up and laughed uproariously. "Are you kidding me? Yeah, you must be." When I primly assured him I wasn't, he asked, "How the hell are we gonna find the guy if the trade kicks out? Check for his fingerprints on the order ticket?"

As it happened, this colloquy was overheard by some of the other clerks, some of whom began cackling like hens—I suspect more out of relief that it was the new dodo and not them being publicly humiliated. J.T. wasn't going to shelter me like Gene had. "Hey, Artie!" he yelled across the post. "You wouldn't believe what your protégée wants to know—why we put badge numbers in the book. Ho-ho, that's rich."

I winced. Silently, I swore vengeance. But for now, all I could do was try to make myself invisible. So much for trying to play Miss Bright Eyes. What had I gotten myself into? How many NYU credits would I lose transferring now to the University of Buffalo?

The next day, J.T. seemed to have forgotten all about my gaffe. He handed me a take-out menu from the Greenwich Gourmet Deli.

" 'Flying Fingers,' time for lunch. Get me two cheeseburgers with everything and a couple of Cokes. See what Ant'ny wants."

Flying Fingers? It was nice to get a nickname. It meant I'd been accepted by the boys. I remember that in high school all the good soccer players got nicknames. But with J.T. you couldn't tell. I knew I was fast processing those little slips of paper marked BUY in black and SELL in red, but I didn't think I was setting any world records.

I was actually nervous about getting the lunch. I didn't know what had earned me the "Flying Fingers" name, and I didn't want to find out, nor did I want to be undeserving of my new moniker. But leave it to J.T. to bring me down to earth. "Screw this up, kiddo, and I won't be able to recommend you as a Girl Scout leader."

| | | |

I don't know why, but a small alarm bell went off inside my head. *How* could I screw up so simple a thing as picking up lunch? Then I remembered hearing about certain initiation rites J.T. and Ant'ny used to dream up to welcome the newest kids on the block. They especially went for clerks they found guileless. Had I set myself up with all those questions, I wondered.

One of their standards was to send a clerk to a nearby kosher restaurant and have him place a take-out order for a bacon cheeseburger, a Virginia ham sandwich, shrimp-salad plate, and a container of chocolate milk. The fact that the kid sped off with alacrity only proved the mark's unworldliness and gave them much glee.

I was relieved. My maiden voyage to the Greenwich Gourmet Deli came off without a hitch. When I returned to the floor, J.T. grabbed someone else's Perrier and, after opening the cap with a stapler, downed it in four gulps. I tried the same trick, only I wasn't adept enough: I cut my finger and broke the top of the bottle. J.T. looked over at the mess I'd made. "Get out your spiral notebook, kid. Rule four, don't try any mechanical stunts on the floor without first practicing at home."

9

Culture Shock

THE COMMUTE TO and from Grandpa's house in the 'burbs was a killer. By the time I would get through with classes at NYU, the earliest Long Island Railroad train I could catch would be the 11:23 P.M. out of Penn Station, which would get me to Huntington Station by 1:00 A.M. I wouldn't get to bed till 1:45.

It wasn't too bad at the very beginning, when I didn't have to be at work till 9:00. But once at Dritz, to make it to the AMEX by 7:30 at the latest, I had to rise at 4:15 A.M., which meant I averaged no more than two hours' sleep weeknights during most of the six months I stayed there. Somehow, Grandpa's bacon and eggs didn't look as appetizing that early in the morning, so I switched to Hostess cupcakes.

They didn't help much. After a while I felt like a walking zombie. The only thing that kept me going was the hope of making enough money eventually to live closer to the city.

The first time I dragged myself out there with all my suitcases turned me off forever to the idea of commuting by train—or to having anything ever to do with commuters. I'd made the mistake of going out at the height of the evening rush hour, with all my worldly goods packed into two large, heavy suitcases, both of which I carried with aching arms.

By an incredible stroke of luck I found, in the smoker, four empty seats facing each other. I sat down. Big mistake, because just then a man old enough to have started commuting before the Long Island Railroad was electrified slid in and told me I couldn't sit there because it was "reserved for the card players." *Reserved?* I stupidly got up just as two other men pushed their way up the aisle to claim their "reserved" seats. Too inexperienced to argue, I got up meekly and just stood there for ninety minutes, next to a very pregnant woman, while these four old farts played poker.

Grandpa suggested I find myself a roommate. Good idea. Thus I discovered the exciting new world of the personals in the classified ad pages of the *Village Voice*, New York's liberal weekly tabloid which, over the years, had switched from cheering on reform politics to reporting on every possible deviant act known to the three sexes.

I'd first encountered the *Voice* at the Tribeca apartment of my friend Suzie Benzinger. Also from upstate, she was a theatrical fashion designer who was sharing an apartment with her sister. She agreed to put me up several nights a week while I looked around the Village. Suzie also helped me decipher the apartment/ roommate ads in the personals. I learned, for example, that

Bi-TV doesn't mean two television sets but bisexual transvestite. That SBF stands for single black female, SJM for straight Jewish male, and so on.

Now, years later, I'm still sort of confused. Does the code tell what the advertiser is looking for in a roommate, or is it an open invitation to anyone caring to apply? As I didn't see any listings for BU—Buffalo Unitarian—I never bothered to find out. And so I stayed with Grandpa till June.

In May, I put my name on the waiting list for Suzie's building. I'd have done so sooner, but the manager asked for a fifty-dollar deposit, which was about forty-eight dollars more than I had to spare. Once he'd taken my fifty, he informed me I was four hundred and thirteen in line and that the list moved by about seventy a year. At that rate, I figured that would get me in by the middle of 1990.

I remembered Mike Dritz's line about having made my first bad trade when I came to work for him *after* Washington's Birthday. The fifty-buck bribe was clearly my second—the guy wouldn't refund my money. I felt like a first-class idiot. Again. Suzie told me that the only way to survive in New York is to look either dangerous or crazy so that nobody will want to tangle with you. I decided to be both. First I went to Herman's sporting goods and bought myself the meanest-looking basketball sneakers without metal toe plates I could find. I also took off the chrome tip of my umbrella and substituted an ice pick. I pulled it out after I stabbed myself twice in the palm, the first time while reaching for a subway token someone had dropped, the second while bending down for a newspaper.

I thought simulating a nervous tic would be nice. Crazies don't like to mess with other crazies. That night I practiced in the mirror till I got it down pat.

I taught myself other defensive techniques. I wasn't prepared to go so far as the subway vigilante, Bernhard H. Goetz, who that very December shot and wounded some black kids he thought were going to mug him.

Paranoia in New York City is pervasive. I heard about an options broker who rushed in late one morning, dragging part of a torn suit jacket—not his—looking like he'd just come off the New York Marathon and telling a typical Transit Authority horror story.

He was coming off the Times Square Shuttle and was heading for the Seventh Avenue IRT downtown platform when some guy pushed him from behind, then quickly started to move away. Instinctively he felt for his wallet. Sure enough, it was gone. He started to give chase, and almost had the "perpetrator" in his clutches, when the guy jumped into a downtown express just as the doors were sliding shut, catching his coat. As the train pulled out, the broker refused to let go and in fact ran alongside the subway as it gathered speed. Just before the train plunged into the pitch-black tunnel the coat ripped. Teetering on the edge of the platform, he was left with half a topcoat clutched firmly in his hands. He sought out a transit cop, who told him he was lucky not to have been killed. Just as he was telling his colleagues this harrowing tale, his clerk handed him a note to call his wife, it was *urgent*. He did. She told him he'd left his wallet on the dresser at home.

| | | |

On June 2, 1984—some dates stand out—Kim Schultze, a woman with whom I rode the Long Island Railroad and who was concerned about my slow demise due to exhaustion and lack of sleep, told me about a friend of hers who was off to Greece for a year and was looking to sublet her studio apartment on Jones Street in Greenwich Village, six blocks from NYU. The lease-holder wanted $525 a month.

By this time, I was willing to take it sight unseen, and I did. It turned out to be a dark, damp, and gloomy studio apartment with a kitchenette, and a radiator that worked sometimes but not often. I immediately named it the Mushroom Factory and on chilly autumn nights sought refuge at a nearby coffee shop. There I met an eccentric but rather loveable guy from the Middle East named Mike, who—after making me fried eggs and french fries every night for two weeks—quickly became my buddy, self-appointed bodyguard, and human alarm clock. He would call me every morning to make sure I'd get to work on schedule.

At the time I was making $175 a week with overtime. Back then, the rule of thumb in Manhattan was that if your monthly rent came to more than two weeks' net pay, you couldn't afford it. Tough. Even less could I afford to keep commuting to Hunt-ington. So I economized by unplugging the refrigerator and stor-ing my perishables on the fire escape and skateboarding to work and school to save on transit fares. Because I was an "illegal" tenant, I had to become an unperson. My name appeared no-where, as I could not take a chance on having mail, groceries, or dry cleaning delivered.

Precisely one year later, my benefactor came back from Greece and called me to say I had to move. She herself wouldn't be moving back, but a friend's uncle's brother-in-law or someone equally distant had agreed to take over the place, *legally*. Meaning he would be getting a new lease and paying a lot more than $525. I was given nine days in which to find a new place.

When I called Grandpa, he urged me to come back. I told him I'd rather throw myself on the train tracks. He understood it was nothing personal.

With two days to spare, I found new quarters in the West Village. There'd been a sign in a Seventh Avenue store window advertising for a roommate. The one-bedroom apartment's principal occupant was a twenty-three-year-old who, for reasons that will shortly become obvious, we'll call only by his first name, Alan. His roommate Tim, I was told when I rang the bell, had just left to return to his family's farm in Idaho.

The "room" for let turned out to be the kitchen. If I were into Tupperware parties or had an urge to snack in the middle of the night, I suppose it would have been a great find. That way I wouldn't have had to do more than roll over and open the fridge. On the other hand, the price was right—$575 a month—and the clock was ticking, so I said okay, I'd take it.

The sign hadn't read "unfurnished," but it was. I bought myself a dilapidated walnut desk-*cum*-bureau, a new lamp, and a mattress, put a divider between my "bed" and the stove, and, as there was no closet, hung a shower-curtain rod from the ceiling by using a couple of bike hooks and charmed a local dry cleaner into letting me buy one of those elongated dingamabobs with a claw at the end to get my clothes down. I prayed that the editors of *Architectural Digest* wouldn't want to do a story on the new urban lifestyles of wannabe yuppies in Greenwich Village.

Actually, Alan turned out to be a charmer. He had recently graduated from college and had just quit his job to do freelance work (what kind he declined to say).

It was weird, at first, having a male roommate; it was also tough explaining the setup to my family when they asked about Alan. My Aunt Sue called to ask whether I had to watch my Maybelline with Alan around. I didn't think he was gay. I did think, however, that his principal occupation was dealing in drugs, as I didn't know many people who kept triple-beam balance scales in their bedrooms next to the phone. There were other signs as well, like the fact that a lot of people would drop in unexpectedly, always late at night, never staying longer than five minutes. Phone conversations were always short, hushed, and punctuated by references to "pounds," "street price," and "harvests." The song "Stairway to Heaven" was blasting on his stereo—only backwards—which supposedly gives it some sort of satanic meaning. What finally convinced me was the day he came in from the market with what seemed like a gross of Baggies, and I had never seen him make a luncheon sandwich and bag it.

To pick up some pocket money, I decided to take a shot at becoming a stand-up comedienne. After standing on the trading floor all day long, with people angrily shouting at me from 9:30 A.M. to 4:15 P.M., it was nice to make people laugh. Well, at least *try*. People had always told me I was a card and that I should write down my "routines," though to me they were spontaneous. The most amazing things would come out of my mouth at the most improbable times. At least, that's what my high-school principal said when he suspended me.

The first gig I did was at Catch a Rising Star, one of a handful of improv nightclubs that were springing up all over town back then. I also "worked"—if that's the word—the Comic Strip, Mostly Magic, Comedy U., and the East Coast version of the famous Improv itself. As I was never "discovered" by one of Johnny Carson's talent scouts, you know I was less than a hit.

It was tough work with long hours. Sometimes I had to wait from nine at night until three in the morning to get on, and when I did, I might get paid all of ten bucks for a twenty-minute gig. It certainly didn't have the same career potential or cachet as being a Wall Street gofer; nor was it very confidence-building.

One of the guys who preceded me at the Comic Strip summed it up nicely when I asked him what it was like trying to make the audience laugh. "Horrible," he insisted. "You feel like an embryo holding a microphone."

|　|　|

I lived in the wretched apartment kitchen for exactly a year. Early one morning in May 1986—can't remember the date but I can the hour, around 2:00 A.M.—I awoke with a godawful itch. I thought at first I'd come down with hives—or perhaps had used the wrong detergent on washing the blanket. I got up and knocked on Alan's closed door, but he pointedly refused to let me in. He probably thought that after all these months, I could stand it no longer and would rape him. I ended up sleeping on the floor below the sink, with no blanket or pillows, my head resting on the dirty mat we stood on when doing the dishes. I dozed and woke up cranky and depressed.

Daylight provided the answer: The boric acid I'd sprinkled three inches deep around the mattress to discourage the cockroaches from their nocturnal rounds had gotten into the bedding.

I told my tales of woe to my ardent admirer, Mike the short-order king, who said he knew of an available studio down the block, above an Italian restaurant.

There was only one little hitch to getting the apartment: Mike would have to co-sign the lease, as I had no tenant history and no real bank account to speak of. "Fine," I replied. "As your husband," he added. "As my *what?*" I shrieked. "A mere formality," Mike assured me. "What the hell," I thought, with the Long Island Railroad in mind.

"What else haven't you told me?" I now asked. "The key money," he replied softly. "You know—*Baksheesh.*" "What's that?" I asked. "A bribe," he replied. "Oh," said I, getting wiser to the ways of the world.

And so, at 2:00 A.M. the next morning, Mike and I met with

a swarthy, pinstriped gentlemen named Paolo, who wore a snap-brim fedora, a black-onyx and diamond pinkie ring, and, for all I knew, was armed to the teeth. I don't remember now whether he was the owner or merely represented him. In any event, he had no trouble accepting the two thousand in unmarked bills. I was given no receipt, not that I expected one.

I moved in and remained there a year and a half, till the crash of 1987. I persuaded my best school chum, Mary Pyne, to come down from Buffalo as my roommate and split the rent. She would do so only if I could help her land a job at the Exchange, which I did.

She hadn't protested; after all, she owed me. I don't know how many times I had had to pull her out of scrapes. Back home, she was always having car trouble. Mary was the world's fastest driver, the scourge of the local SPCA, always jumping stop signs, making illegal U-turns, and running over dogs. One would have thought she hated pets. Not so, they just got in her—and harm's—way. She'd then offer to replace the dead dog. Her kill ratio seemed to be a consistent two-to-one—two purebreds for every mutt. We all decided that the only way to keep Mary from either eventually killing herself or gradually decimating the canine population of Erie County would be to get her out of there to a place where she would not have to drive.

Mary hung around for about two years, working for me as a clerk, then at Dean Witter Reynolds. After Carmine Street we upgraded our living conditions to an apartment over on East Ninth Street and then took a big loft on lower Broadway, but in August of 1988 Mary had had enough of the Big Apple and went back upstate. She claimed that it was to get married, but I think she missed the thrill of the canine kill.

How to describe the Carmine Street apartment? Just as I had

named the previous domicile the Mushroom Factory, this one became the Borgia Brothel.

If you were into Italian food, the place smelled divine. The elevator especially, as it doubled as the restaurant's dumbwaiter: Most of the time I would share the tiny cab with a garbage can overflowing with discarded spinach linguini with calamari, tricolor tortellini, and lobster Fra Diavolo. Not an empty jar of Paul Newman's industrial-strength spaghetti sauce to be seen.

It was similar in many respects to the apartment young Don Corleone grew up in during the flashbacks in *The Godfather II* and—what with those heavy brocaded curtains and the red-damask wallpaper—the one in the 1921 silent *The Sheik*, starring Rudolph Valentino. There was also a Murphy bed just like the one in TV's "The Honeymooners," which had to be lowered in a certain way if you valued keeping your head.

But what was really interesting about it was its location. There were nights I felt I was living above "Checkpoint Charlie," the old Berlin Wall border crossing that came down in 1990. The back-and-forth traffic was something fierce.

Then I remembered. On his way out of Mike's coffee shop, Paolo had turned and—somewhat inexplicably, I thought at the time—assured me that the building was quite secure and that there was no need to call the cops if I heard suspicious noises, or even to lock my doors. I now understood why.

Apparently, the restaurant doubled as a fencing operation, dispensing hot pasta during the day and evening and hotter electronic products early in the morning—stuff that, I was told, had "fallen off the truck." I hadn't been aware that there were so many delivery trucks with faulty tailgates running around New York, because there seemed to be no end to the number of television sets, VCRs, copying machines, camcorders, "ghetto blasters," and desktop computers that came and went in the middle of the night.

There was other excitement in the neighborhood, too. At least once a week, mysterious fires would gut various storefronts, and most of the time the fire brigades would get there too late. I was later told that most of the fires were "of suspicious origin," meaning arson, and were set by various miscreants who always went under the quaint name of Marvin the Torch. Mr. Torch, it seemed, worked for the equal-opportunity employers across the street.

I'm not sure whether they were Gambinos, Lucheses, Gigantes, Castigliones, or Gottis, not that it mattered. It was like being at the Oscar ceremonies. Nightly, these long gray and black stretch limousines would slide up to the curb, disgorging all sorts of Paolo-lookalikes, lawyers with bulging briefcases, go-go dancers, and other ladies-of-the-evening. There'd be no applause, of course, from adoring fans manning the bleachers, no flashes of Instamatics, none of that Hollywood folderol.

Every once in a while, a blue-and-white NYPD patrol car would come gliding by, slow down, and move on. "Our taxpayer dollars at work," Mary would say.

When I first moved in I found the cupboard fully loaded with mismatched dishes, and a toothbrush in the bathroom. Whoever said New Yorkers were cold and unfriendly, I thought. Here they left me their kitchenware! I threw out the toothbrush but kept the dishes. The pile of mail, addressed to a Charlie something-or-other, kept getting bigger, so after a couple of weeks I rang the doorbell of my neighbor, a woman I remember only as Linda. "Do you have Charlie's forwarding address?" I asked. She looked pained. "Oh, didn't you know? He died of AIDS."

Mike, who once offered to buy me my own coffee shop, had

planned to return to the land of the pharaohs but he stuck around to oversee his investments.

I always thought Mike was an astute businessman. I remember him telling me one night, after I'd made my first real trading money and had asked him about what sort of real estate to buy: "If you are interested in restaurants, first check the garbage." According to Mike, one should never trust the owner's books. "They are probably, how do you say it here in America? *Cooked.* Instead, wait until the place is closed, even if it's five in the morning, but before the garbage trucks arrive and go through the cans. The more garbage on the streets out front, the more potential customers."

Bet you they don't teach that at the Harvard B-school.

I finally packed my bags again when there was a shoot-out at the corner on my way to work in the morning.

10

"AMEX. Not Just a Job..."

SPECIALIST JOHN TORRES had the *New York Post* open to the racing pages as he chomped away on his cheeseburger. Ant'ny was doing a pretty good job of demolishing his.

Given my passion for the ponies, I leaned over J.T.'s shoulder to look for yesterday's Aqueduct Raceway results. He followed my finger, looked up at his pal, who had just taken a big bite. Examining his cheeseburger, he said, "Hey, it looks like we've both got Sandy's Pride here, last place in the last race. It's still warm..." Just then, Ant'ny opened his mouth. "You could have..." was about all he could get out before starting to gasp and choke uncontrollably.

J.T. jumped up, yelled "Heimlich!" and ran behind him. Ant'ny's arms shot up over his head and, as his friend expertly wrapped his arms around the victim's waist and yanked inward, a half-chewed chunk of cheeseburger flew out of his gullet to land with a soft thud on the *Post.*

The patient looked at his savior for confirmation. "Damn! Another piece of Aqueduct hoof." At that point, both started cackling hysterically. I'd been spared the kosher kitchen, but I'd nevertheless been had: One look at their carrying on convinced me the entire medical emergency had been staged for their enjoyment—and, of course, at my expense. Worse was to come.

| | | |

Down on the floor and in the pit, the common enemy was always boredom. Nothing so much eats at the innards of a trader as having to twiddle his thumbs while waiting for the market to come back to life. To paraphrase Hippocrates, "Idleness and lack of occupation are dragged toward mischief."

There was plenty of idleness to spare, and much of the mischief unfolded during the noon to 2:00 P.M. stretch when most of the "suits"—the nontrading stiffs who worked at the big investment-banking and brokerage houses—were having their two-martini lunches at fancy restaurants.

"Pit entertainment," as these extracurricular activities came to be called, fell into two categories—the cerebral and the visceral. The latter usually came in the form of contests of will and endurance, sweetened by wagers—admittedly childish, frat-house stuff that would probably be cause for immediate dismissal in the comparatively sedate trading rooms of Salomon, Shearson Lehman, and Goldman, Sachs.

In the former category were those pranks that required more than a little imagination to be carried off.

Two traders—let's call them Barry and Roy—were somewhat fed up with having to hear their cohort Sam carry on about his knee operation. So, after breakfast, Barry went down to Whitehall Hardware on Greenwich Street, a block from the Exchange, and bought a small hacksaw. Whenever Sam sat down—which, it being a slow day, was often—either Barry or Roy would cut an inch off Sam's aluminum cane. By two that afternoon, they noticed Sam looking slightly panicked and stooped; by three he was on his way back to New Jersey, convinced the operation had gone awry. The next morning he hobbled into Harry's, steaming. "I'm gonna kill you assholes! I felt like I was going down on the fucking *Titanic!*"

The same hardware store also sold some coiled wire to a group of bored quote reporters. They used it, along with two rolls of pennies, the digital face of a plastic watch, and a few strips of electrical tape, to rig the most absurd-looking "bomb" that I have ever seen. After tossing it at various traders during the noon lull, none of whom were very impressed, the boys abandoned it under some trash near the employees' lounge. It was such a pathetic-looking device that it would have been laughed out of the Fisher-Price boardroom, had any toy designer presented it. The following morning, a Saturday, one of the janitors discovered the "bomb" while sweeping the floor. Being a responsible citizen, he immediately called "911," which in turn called out the NYC Police Department's bomb-disposal unit. For the first Saturday in memory, there was a lot of floor activity. The entire six-block area surrounding the Exchange was closed off; the janitor got his fifteen minutes of Warholesque fame. They even shut down the Brooklyn-Battery Tunnel for part of the morning. The stunt probably cost taxpayers two hundred thousand dollars, but it gave the *New York Post* a great headline about the "explosiveness" of the options market.

The most eager participants in these stunts seemed to be the transaction reporters, because if the market was slow they would have absolutely *nothing* to do all day, and the Exchange wouldn't allow them to read books or magazines for fear they would miss the few trades that took place. So there in front of the trading post they would *stand*, hours at a stretch, and watch the big digital clocks.

Jerry, a twenty-four-year-old transaction reporter with a family to feed, was our egg-and-water man. He'd be offered a hundred dollars to drink a gallon of water in twenty minutes, no big deal for a chugalugger. The kicker was that Jerry wouldn't be allowed to throw up for at least twenty-five minutes. The traders and clerks would have up to three thousand dollars in side bets riding on his ability to sit tight. There was a lot riding on Jerry the day he doubled over and ran out of the pit, with a couple of the bettors right behind him to make sure that he didn't throw up for another seven minutes.

Jerry never had as much luck with the gallon of water as he did with the raw eggs. He could easily down a dozen raw eggs without tossing them for at least fifteen minutes.

Some of these food flights even proved instructive for those interested in natural phenomena. For example, I had no idea how difficult it could be to swallow two slices of fresh Wonder Bread ("builds better bodies twelve ways!") in sixty seconds without washing them down. Many in the pit have attempted this feat and as yet have not managed to succeed.

Things really got messy whenever one of the boys in the pit, about to get married, was given his bachelor's party. I vividly remember Bobby Duffy's send-off into married bliss.

First off, some of the clerks were sent to the Greenwich Gourmet Deli in back of the Exchange to stock up on the stickiest edibles one hundred dollars could buy—eggs, mayo, mustard, custard pie, yogurt, tapioca, and rice pudding. While they were out, four burly guys suddenly pounced on Bobby, trussed him, and bodily carried him out the back door to Greenwich Street, where he was handcuffed to a parking meter. Someone thoughtfully removed his wallet and watch. "Wouldn't want to see you get needlessly mugged," Bobby was told.

Then the barrage began. As in the old days when the clerks hung out the windows taking their cues from the brokers on the street below, their latter-day descendants, sitting astride the window ledges, began pelting the helpless Duffy with all the goodies. Everybody got into the spirit of the occasion, including the female clerks (one of whom tiptoed down the street and deftly slid a smoked mackerel down Bobby's back). The bombardiers on the sixth floor weren't very accurate, laughing so hard their projectiles landed on innocent bystanders. And the cops, when they came by, sized up the odds against their uniform allowance and decided to hell with it, they'd rather redirect traffic than try to break things up.

Duffy, of course, knew he was due and had made preparations by bringing in some clean clothes and stowing them in his locker. "I just didn't know when, that's all." Finally unshackled, he went up to the thirteenth floor, cleaned up, changed into fresh attire, and went back to work.

Few were spared such indignities. The Exchange's leadership was utterly helpless to put a stop to these antics and spent an inordinate amount of time apologizing to first-time visitors, writing warning memos, and collecting fines. It was a fruitless proposition, much like the proper and church-going widow Douglas trying to reform the irreverent and slothful ways of Huck Finn.

When the traders had been on good behavior for a few weeks, the Exchange would go back to harassing them about coming to work sockless or in collarless shirts. After a while, it seemed pointless to act respectable, as the governors were bound to find some other reason to issue reprimands.

They *were* right in one regard: We not only acted but *looked* slovenly. So much so that after one state visit, the head of one of Europe's most prestigious bourses took me aside and asked, "Why do you need all these janitors on the floor?"—pointing to our stately brokers and millionaire traders.

Thereafter, every few weeks an Arthur Levitt*gram* would come shooting down from the eleventh floor, reminding the men to wear shirts with ties, the women to wear skirts or pantsuits but no jeans. These upstairs missives from the Dress Police would invariably be followed by visits from some of the floor governors. I remember the day one of them stormed into the XMI pit to grab the mike right out of the hands of one of our ranting and raving lunatics. In his Sunday-school best, he intoned, "May I remind you, sirs, that we are today hosting the chief of a very important new listed company, his family, and the media, so (pause) *watch* (pause) *your* (pause) *fuckin'* (pause) *language!*"

One favorite prank was to tape or pin objects to unsuspecting visitors while their backs were turned or they were otherwise too preoccupied to notice some guy stealthily approaching on all fours, cutout cardboard spurs clenched in his teeth, which he would then tape to the back of his victim's six-hundred-dollar pair of John Lobb boots.

I wasn't there when that particular gag got started. According to my fellow horseflesh lover, Michael Pascuma, who came to the AMEX during President Franklin D. Roosevelt's second term, it must have begun back in the mid-1970s, when there was still a visitors' gallery and "those J. R. Ewing types from the Texas oil patch in their ten-gallon hats and alligator boots flew up to see their exploration companies listed." Most of these had been transferred from over-the-counter (OTC) status, giving them a new legitimacy that demanded celebrating. When the miniskirt made its comeback in the 1980s, long after the visitors' gallery had been replaced by the trading posts, the visiting company men would ask to give their families a bird's-eye view of the floor. AMEX floor personnel noticed that some visiting media photographers would seem strangely distracted when this happened, preoccupied in peeking up at the trading posts closest to the railing. It didn't take management long to figure out that what the cameramen were really doing was looking up the skirts of the wives and daughters of the VIP guests. Shortly thereafter, the house carpenters arrived to hang sheets of plywood from the mezzanine railing.

|　 |　 |　 |

During my tenure at the AMEX, total stock listings rose from 791 to 860 companies, well below the 1,215 listings recorded for 1975. These days, to qualify for AMEX listing, a company must report a pretax income of $750,000 for the latest fiscal year, or two out of the last three years; have at least 800 shareholders; and have a public-float market value of at least $3 million (at a minimum of $3 a share), with stockholder equity of at least $4 million. New York State and California account for 34.9 percent of all the AMEX listed companies (314).

The average AMEX-listed company in 1989 posted a pretax income of $13.8 million on $235.5 million sales, had assets of $341.8 million, shareholders' equity of $86.9 million, and a market value of $176.4 million. Among the better known and most active AMEX companies during my last year were BAT Industries (Saks Fifth Avenue, Marshall Field's), Texas Air (Continental Airlines), Wang Laboratories and Amdahl (both computers), Fruit of the Loom (underwear), and Hasbro (toys).

|　 |　 |　 |

The day the new Hershey Foods option was listed, no one from Hershey, Pennsylvania, came down, but Hershey bars did. It happened to be "triple witching day"—that time, four times a year, when index options, index futures, and stock options all expire at the same time. The PR people arranged to have the specialist assigned to run the Hershey option pose for a *New York Post* photographer. To record the event for posterity, the specialist climbed up on the narrow balcony overlooking the trading post and began tossing down hundreds of Hershey Special Dark, Mr. Goodbar, and Krackle bars. Pandemonium broke out when the four-ounce bars, dropped from a height of twenty-five feet, hit the unsuspecting traders on the head like lead sinkers. The traders were not amused.

Granted, taping fake spurs onto fancy custom-made shoes would appear to be a rather boring form of entertainment for a group of professional financial hotshots, but when you throw in the Indian war dance around the victim, and of course the cowboy whooping, it's actually more fun than playing King of the Castle. At least it's not as unkind a cut as pinning crude, hand-lettered signs to the backs of particularly handsome visitors, proclaiming, "I Got Mine at the Ramrod"—a notorious Greenwich Village leather bar. That stupid trick went into quick disuse the day the *New York Times* belatedly announced the existence of AIDS.

| | | |

When I first looked over the great hall from the mezzanine, I had just turned fourteen. I remember Joe Petta, Jr., my guide, telling me that, from the floor to the gilt-paneled ceiling, it was larger than a five-story building. To someone down for the day from Buffalo—even with Niagara Falls next door—that meant a lot more than if Petta had said the distance from top to bottom was so many feet and so many inches.

Clearly unimpressed by the immense size was a young specialist named Evan Lovett, who worked with his father, Joel, in one of the mezzanine trading firms and who occasionally came in to trade in the XMI pit.

I hadn't been there very long when word got around that, before the afternoon was up, young Lovett, while standing on the main floor, would attempt to throw a softball all the way up to the ceiling. He would not be satisfied with anything less than a direct hit.

News traveled across the floor faster than word of Vice-President Dan Quayle's latest gaffe. Traders and brokers ran into the pit yelling, "Two thousand dollars for," "Five hundred against," "I'll give odds—two to one against." Seconds later, bets began pouring in by phone from traders as far away as California.

Clerks were signaling down from the balcony with phones pressed to their ears: "Softball or baseball?" There seemed to be as much money riding on the throw than had been traded in stocks all day. Meantime, a clerk was sent to Herman's sporting goods over on Nassau Street to buy the softball.

A couple of traders had called the Exchange building department for the exact height of the trading floor because, if the probability of completing the throw was to be mathematically determined, the measurements would have to be exact. Did the 650-foot figure reflect true floor-to-ceiling height or the distance from the floor after it had been raised to accommodate those thousands of miles of computer cable?

The Big Throw had been scheduled for 2:00 P.M. that day. At 1:50 P.M., the odds had changed to three-to-one that Evan would make good after word got out that, before his clerk internship, he'd tried out for the New York Yankees.

Suddenly Evan's father, a formidable-looking gentleman who also happens to be an Exchange governor, entered the XMI pit and whispered angrily in his son's ear.

The throw had been canceled. His father stalked out, after which some bets were called off while others pleaded with Evan to stand his ground.

At 4:17 P.M., two minutes after the closing bell, Evan looked up at the mezzanine and did not see his father. He phoned up and learned that his father had gone upstairs to an executive meeting. On hearing this, he walked out to the center of the pit, kneeled down on one knee, and side-armed the ball skyward. It ricocheted off the ceiling into a booth on the balcony. Up there, one of Evan's partisans claimed that the ball had chipped the ceiling fresco. As there was no way to prove it, he just may have been exaggerating, as did those on the floor who insisted that if he'd wanted to, Evan could have doubled the distance.

Then the floor fights erupted. The winners said that the bets were still on. The losers said that the bets had all been canceled. There were some threats of bloody noses. The arbitrators were called in to adjudicate each wager on a one-by-one basis. What Lovett *pere* said to *fils* remained a family secret.

One day, J.T. sidled up to me and whispered, "Hey, Flying Fingers, see that tall guy coming this way? He once stapled his clerk's hand to the side of the post. Accidentally, of course. I think."

"Hey, Clem!" J.T. called out. "You look like a million bucks. All green and wrinkled."

At that, Clem veered off course and headed toward us. Continuing to scribble in his palm-size order pad and without looking up, he gave as good as he got: "Hey, old buddy, I was gonna get a suit like that, but my grandfather wouldn't tell me where he got it." Put-down comic Don Rickles would have nothing to worry about, I thought to myself, these guys are bad, *real bad*.

"Making any money?" asked J.T.

"Sure, gold stocks are easy these days. Just read the papers," replied Clem, explaining he'd just done a straddle in ASA Limited, a gold company. Thanks to Larry McMillan's book, I knew that meant he'd bought an equal number of puts and calls on ASA at the same strike price and maturity date. "When the Afrikaners kill black folks, gold stocks move up; when the blacks kill whites, the stocks go down."

What a brilliant synthesis of a very tangled situation! Imagine the kind of future he'd have had if only he'd gone to work for the State Department.

J.T.'s and Clem's exchange struck me as so typical of a place that has given the expression "friendly enemies" a bad name. You remain visible not because you want to but because you *have* to. In this business, out of sight most assuredly means out of mind.

| | | |

"It's game time!" The market was going nowhere and trading seemed to be the last thing on people's minds. J.T. dug deep in his smock and produced a set of dice. As if on cue, Ant'ny reached up to the shelf where we stowed office supplies and record books to extract a peculiar-looking shoe box. One of its sides was missing. "You staying, Clem?" asked J.T.

Clem extracted a roll of bills and peeled off a hundred. "Gentlemen, let us play," he deadpanned.

I was about to get lesson 5, shooting craps on company time. Now my gambling education would be complete. But on my pay I could only watch, as the stakes started at one hundred dollars a throw. The clerks and reporters assigned to post 13 drifted into place.

What were the Exchange's visitors to think, walking by the post and hearing the stewards of capitalism rally their troops with, "Holy shit . . . snake eyes!" "Box cars!" "Who loaded the dice?" or "Next time we'll play with my shoe box"?

I caught Ant'ny looking up at the big Quotron overhead, when out of nowhere he yelled, "Get the keys!" As if on command, the game dissolved. Was this a password for "Cheeze it, the cops," or what?

Everyone at the post hopped to. Even Clem looked panicked. "Flying Fingers, quick!" yelled Ant'ny, becoming very familiar with the nickname J.T. had bestowed on me a few weeks before. "Need you to get the keys to the clearinghouse! This is not a test but an emergency. *Run!"*

I ran, in which direction I no longer recall. All I remember is I couldn't let them know that I was totally discombobulated, that I didn't know what they meant by *clearinghouse*, where I was supposed to be going, and what I was expected to do once I got there. My mind raced. Was this something Sheila had told us about, which I'd somehow missed or forgotten? Just what was in the clearinghouse that had to be locked?

By the time I got to post 8, I was beside myself with anxiety, close to hyperventilating. What the hell was I doing and why? I braked. And started running back to post 1.

"Where do I go?" I gasped, stumbling in. Ant'ny grabbed me by the shoulders and violently spun me around and pushed me back out. "Upstairs on the mezzanine, hurry!"

I was on the escalator, jumping two moving stairs at a clip, when I ran into the first broker whose face was familiar. "Quick, Herb, tell me who's got the keys to the clearinghouse." I panted. He was truly sympathetic. "Try Jesse Greenwald over by Texaco," he said, pointing the way. I slammed into Greenwald and screamed, "Keys, I need the keys!"

He knew precisely what I was talking about. Yet he took his

sweet time: "Attention everyone, this young lady needs the keys to the clearinghouse . . ." The fact that trading didn't stop should have tipped me off. But, no, I kept going, a woman possessed.

The guys were wonderful; couldn't have been more helpful, if they'd only had better recall.

"Jesse, I gave them back to you, dontcha remember?" Jesse didn't. Another piped up, "C'mon Jesse, *think.*" He thought, clapped his forehead, "Of course, how stupid of me. Billy's got them, I'm positive."

Jesse told me to run down to post 11 and ask for Jimmy Daly. He'd know Billy's whereabouts. Off I went. I could see Dritz, Goldring losing millions as each precious second ticked by. When I got there, Daly was eating lunch. He gave me the most dazzling smile. "Oh, hello, you must be the new Dritz girl who needs the keys. Jesse just phoned."

Oh, wow, I thought, now we're getting somewhere.

Just then, from the far side of the post, "Is that her?"

I suddenly felt very important. Billy pulled out a key ring. "Damn, wrong ones." At this he stood up, put a set of fatherly hands on my shoulders, and turned me in the direction of the elevators. "Go on up to Artie Levitt's office. He's got a spare set of keys."

Did I hear him say Levitt, the Exchange chairman? Tears began to well up. Shit, I said to myself, now I've blown it. This was taking much too long. Dritz was probably on the ropes by now, all because I didn't do my job. I'm going to get expelled, I know, then fired.

The respite in the slow-moving elevator gave me pause to reflect. Clearinghouse. Isn't that where all the trades are processed? It's got to be a big room, since it takes a big computer to kick out mismatched trades. But where's the sign? After all, this isn't CIA headquarters.

I began smelling a rat. Something didn't seem quite right. For an emergency, there seemed to be a lot of smiling guys. The inner voice of reason spoke: "Laura, you asshole, they've done it to you again." I waited for a contradiction and got none.

When the elevator reached the executive floor, I didn't bother to get off. I couldn't imagine Arthur Levitt being part of this sophomoric trick. I pushed the DOWN button. I'd never show my face at post 13 again. Better to go back upstate and sell snow shovels. I would never, but never, be able to live this down. It had to be worse than the day in junior high when my mother brought my lunch to the bus stop with her bathrobe on.

Striding back to my post, jaw grimly set, I ignored the sideline calls, "Hey, Laura, did you find the keys?" As I neared the post, I heard spontaneous applause. Everyone was outside the post. J.T. made a production of looking at his watch. "Hmmmm, seventeen minutes, thirty-eight seconds. Not bad, kid, not bad at all . . ."

I whirled around, shrieking, "You bastards!" They'd been tracking me all along, as if I were some criminal walking into a police stakeout. "Aww, c'mon," said Ant'ny, "don't be sore. They had me spend two hours looking for odd-lot stretchers down in the basement." Bobby, one of the other clerks, volunteered that he'd fallen for trying to locate a bag of plus-ticks, while Terri allowed that she'd been "dumb enough to fall for the kosher-deli routine."

"Aww, that's nothing," bragged J.T. "Mere child's play. The night before my friend got married, they got him drunk and put him on a TWA to Heathrow. Couldn't get back for the wedding. Had to postpone it a day." Didn't sound too bad to me; he got to go abroad, I only got to go upstairs.

Months later, when I had become a full-fledged trader, I met this clerk who told me he'd been sent over to 11 Broad Street to bail out the basement of the New York Stock Exchange "with a bucket on a rainy day." He got as far as the service elevator when he realized this was all wrong: Why would the AMEX care whether the NYSE sank or swam?

I couldn't stay mad and I couldn't get even. At least not yet. So I did the next best thing. I reached for a Perrier and deftly flipped open the lid with a stapler. Naturally, I sliced open my palm, but at least the bottle didn't break this time. Apparently word had gotten around fast. As I walked through the tube room to retrieve my coat, one of the maintenance workers pointed to me and whispered to her friend, "Yep, I think that's her." Whereupon they both broke into hysterical laughter.

11

Surviving Wall Street on Less Than Five Dollars a Day

ANT'NY WAS RIGHT; after three months, I did become a pretty good clerk. Not that I didn't make plenty of mistakes, like the day I misplaced a cancellation order, leaving the janitorial crew that night to put back all the trash I'd dumped on the floor in the process of retrieving it. Had it not shown up, I'd have lost the equivalent of my first ten weeks' salary. I knew I would find it; I'd had excellent childhood training foraging through garbage cans in the school cafeteria upstate for those two-hundred-dollar orthodontic retainers I somehow always managed to leave on my lunch tray.

More important, J.T. taught me how to make markets and keep the positions updated, skills that could actually only be imparted by trial and error, as there were certain things not even Larry McMillan's book covered. In any event, the more time I spent observing the options traders, the more determined I was to become one of them. As J.T. once explained it to me, "The course they teach here [at the Exchange] won't make you a trader any more than an auto school will make you a driver. You'll learn the rules of the road and how to signal, but not how to remove your jacket or retrieve a lit cigarette from the back seat while doing sixty miles per hour on the New York State Thruway."

He also made me aware that, in this business, it's not so much what you know, but how *fast* you can absorb and process incoming data from many different directions, and that the more you can retain, the better.

"The average person," he told me, "can do twenty things well, but no more than five at one time. The *above*-average person can do seven, eight, or more. Which means that if your brain can handle no more than five or six bits of information, you'll probably remain a clerk."

| | | |

That was the summer the Exchange moved the Dritz, Goldring trading post next to Spear Leeds's. As anyone could have foreseen, the Bentley did not materialize, and the XAM Ford Pinto—by then operated by a different driver—ran out of gas the following year.

J.T. and his ever-faithful Sancho Panza, Ant'ny, were shifted back to trading stocks, which they didn't seem to mind at all. Clerks like myself who couldn't be readily absorbed, now that Dritz's personnel needs had been pared after selling XAM, were advised to cast about for new connections.

I didn't have far to throw out my line. With XMI next door becoming more popular with each passing day, Ron Shear and his partners realized they would need additional support troops.

I began making myself more conspicuous to the voluble Mr. Shear, who had been pointed out to me earlier as the man of the moment.

One day I decided to confront him. Around lunchtime, I saw him come in. I looked clean and pressed in a white-linen suit. There was no way he could miss me. I wormed my way into the XMI pit and climbed the raised steps until I was right next to him. As I hadn't come to make small talk, I contrived to bump into him, excusing myself. He looked up from whatever he was reading and scowled. "Why aren't you handing out perfume samples in Bloomingdale's?"

I hadn't expected *that* for an opening gambit. What a nasty SOB, I thought. I decided to forget about the job and said, "I didn't get a fourteen hundred score on my SAT's to work at Bloomie's," adding, "By the way, why aren't *you* selling second-hand cars in Paramus, New Jersey?"

He didn't expect that. Putting down his papers, he now gave me the once-over. His expression left no doubt: Nobody talked to him that way, least of all a *clerk*, and a *girl*-clerk, to boot. When he saw I didn't blink, he broke into a big grin and asked, "Hey, you want a job? Write down how much you want and give the paper to Jeff Feins, over there." He pointed to a tall man in his mid-thirties, thin as a rail, who was at that moment arguing loudly with a broker about an order that hadn't been canceled.

"That's it?" I asked. "That's it," he said.

Thinking back, how typical of Shear. Everything had to be some kind of trade or it wouldn't be fun.

This was an even more bizarre interview than the one I'd had back in February with Mike Dritz. I tacked fifty dollars onto what that firm had been paying me, walked over to Feins and handed him a folded paper, and made my way back down to catch up to J.T., who was on his way back to the Dritz post. "So, how did it go?" he asked. "Dunno. I *think* I've got a job but I think this is one of those 'don't-call-us-we'll-call-you' kind of things."

Jeff Feins called the next day.

| | | |

I didn't know it at the time, but, in his way, Ron Shear would have as profound an influence on my professional life as Pete Heffley, up in Buffalo, had on my adolescence. I suppose I'll always be indebted to Ron for giving me more than enough money and rope with which to go hang myself. My throat may still be sore, but at least my neck bears no rope burns.

Like so many eccentric savants, Ron Shear would trip over his own brilliance and turned out to be an inept tutor. Ron couldn't teach himself out of a paper bag. Instead, he led masterfully through wit and intimidation, and not always in that order. When angry—his large, six-foot-one frame erect, swept-back hair bristling like a cat's, granny glasses dangling precariously from his nose—Ron would resemble a mean Ben Franklin. Brilliant to a fault, arrogant, and loud-mouthed, Ron possessed a perfectly compartmentalized brain that he could tap into effortlessly, switching seamlessly back and forth and never sounding in the least muddled. I might approach him and say, "Hey, Ron, Reuters says Gorby has been overthrown by a cabal of former KGB guys headed by General Viktor Chebrikov, who apparently has launched a preemptive missile strike right at North America. NORAD confirms." At hearing this, he'd think for a second and say, "Well, they say war is bullish. Go and raise the markets (*click*). By the way, I need to see the mail, *now* (*click*). Someone get me a Diet Coke!"

His idea of breaking you in was to give you an assigned spot and for the next year or so ignore your existence. Much later on I learned that he really was watching but didn't bother you as long as for the most part you stayed out of trouble. I learned fast and, because of it, was promoted fast.

Most of the clerks were scared to death of him. He knew it and took shameless advantage of it. On more than one occasion, when I had to ask him a question on a specific trade, he would look at me wordlessly, quickly scribble down some numbers on the empty back of a reporter's transaction card, and plug them into some formula—not bothering to explain the formula to me or jot it down. I would try my damndest to follow the swift movement of his pen, but he went much too fast. Then, looking up, he would ask, "See?" knowing damn well I didn't.

The trouble was that I was too nervous to do anything but nod my head vigorously, which he naturally interpreted as assent. And with that, he'd rip up the card with a flourish, toss the scraps on the floor, and walk away, leaving me to fall on my knees to retrieve the paper shards and bundle them up. In the ladies' room I'd attempt to Scotch tape them together, and that night, on my kitchen table with my trusty McMillan open beside me, I'd try to reconstruct what Ron had done. This went on time and again until I felt confident enough to challenge him.

He would test me. He'd look at the S&P 500 displayed on a monitor behind us and catch me taking a furtive look at the moving jiggles. "You don't even know what the hell you're look-ing at," he'd say with mock exasperation, sounding just like Mrs. DiCenzo, my high-school biology teacher, during frog dissec-tions. "Yes, I do," I'd retort. "Don't think you're the only one around here who reads the Edwards and McGee book on stock charting. That graph there means the index is in an uptrend and, as you never tire of telling us, 'the trend is your friend.'" We then proceeded to argue.

"The trend is your friend" and other Shearisms got to be like the daily catechism, to be recited almost at command if you wanted (a) to appear to know what was going on when you were actually clueless and (b) to impress Ron with how much you'd absorbed. Naturally, just to be properly perverse, from time to time Ron liked to set his specialists-in-training up for a fall. He didn't want us to suffer from swelled heads. I fell more times than I now care to admit.

Finally convinced I wasn't just some "bimbette" (as he'd call them) out for something to do between college and marriage, he agreed to become my Wall Street mentor. Of course, he never said so. He just gave me a hard time regarding my performance, because he knew that I could learn more.

Back in my clerk days, when I still worshipped the skidproof rubber matting he bounced up and down on when taking part in the trading, I used to go to sleep with his rubber ID stamp next to my bed as a talisman. I kept hoping that osmosis would make me as smart and successful as he.

When he got mad, which was often, he would roar like a lion, sometimes loud enough to wake up the dead in the mezzanine. When the action slowed to a crawl, he would fall asleep right on the microphone at his trading podium, standing up like a race horse. What most amused me about this forty-four-year-old hotshot was that, for all his trading prowess, he was Mr. Klutz when it came to running so simple a machine as a calculator. Repeatedly he'd pick one up off the console and attempt to calculate a formula. He seldom could. He could never get it right whether to enter the plus or minus before or after the principal, and, easily frustrated, he would toss it behind the post, muttering something obscene about dead batteries. Nobody dared to mention that they were solar-powered calculators, although I think he knew that.

| | | |

On my first day as a Spear Leeds Kellogg/Investors Company employee, I was notified that there was to be an auction that afternoon and that I was to be the prize. At the time, there were only two girl clerks in the XMI pit, and Karen was married, so lucky me got to be taken out to dinner by one of the boys.

Normally I'm not into white slavery, but what I had left over after paying the rent on my illegal sublet did not allow me to stand up to everybody and yell, "What sort of young lady do you take me for, anyway?"

Peanut-butter sandwiches with an occasional Twinkie for dessert do not add up to balanced meals, so I agreed to play. I'd been supplementing my involuntary diet by going down to Harry's after work and chomping on their "sodium balls." J.T. had informed me that chemical analysis had revealed four of them to contain as much nutrition as a Quarter Pounder from Burger King.

All the guys wanting in on the Laura Pedersen drawing had to initial a time-stamped piece of trading stationery. The winner was a nice guy named Nicky. He took me to a Lucullan spread at the Water Club but never got around to making a pass. He was too busy listening to his Walkman for any bulletins on President Reagan's health—not that he had been shot at again or was between cancer operations. Nicky's problem was that he'd taken a huge position on a Star Wars subcontractor and just didn't want to jeopardize his investment. What a way to live!

| | | |

I don't think there was enough left in my food budget to take care of the cockroaches in the Jones Street apartment because, soon after moving in, they left me. So scrounging for food freebies became a necessity for a while.

The month I switched from Dritz to Spear Leeds, I got wind of a reception the Exchange was holding for new members. I hung around the post pretending to do cleanup paperwork. Nobody paid any attention to me. The food came out fifteen minutes into the slide presentation, so I filled the side pockets of my green smock with some finger sandwiches, several fistfuls of unshelled shrimp, cold asparagus, and clams on the half shell. Then I tiptoed out of there and headed up to NYU and school. It was a little messy, with the cocktail sauce for the shrimp, and it was a little embarrassing slurping down clams in class, but night-school faculty are a lot more tolerant of such things (the finance professor opined that "shrimp are sure signs of success," after I shared some with him). Until I came down to New York, the only time I'd gotten to eat shrimp was at wedding receptions.

| | |

On December 3, 1984, someone at the Union Carbide pesticide plant in Bhopal, India, forgot to turn off the spigot on his way home, and that night forty-five metric tons of methyl isocyanate blanketed the area, killing over thirty-three hundred and maiming as many as a hundred thousand.

The next day, Monday, all hell broke out next door to us at the Dritz, Goldring post, which held the Union Carbide options. Before the opening bell, the UK specialists were nowhere to be seen; I was told they were all downstairs at Harry's having a war council. What would they be talking about? I wondered. Would they buy, sell, *dump?* I pictured the heavy deliberations going on in some smoke-filled, closed-door room, waiters scurrying in with fresh pots of coffee. I thought of all that collected market wisdom gathered around the table, hammering out a strategy for survival. Why, it was probably like a papal conclave. When would we see the puff of white smoke signaling that a decision had been reached?

About an hour later, the specialists came up and took their respective places. They looked exhausted. I walked over and asked J.T., who had been there, "Hey, what was decided?"

He looked at me gravely. "It's not good, Flying Fingers, not good at all."

"What else can you tell me, huh?"

"When it's not good, you get short [sell]. When it's good, you get long [buy]."

"Is that *it?*" I asked, completely puzzled. There had to be something more secret or mathematical to it. "That's all?"

"That's it. You've got to be in it to win it, you know that," he stated, walking away.

Throughout the morning, I looked over at Dritz, Goldring, and everytime I did, their short position got bigger and bigger. During lunch break, J.T. confided in me: "Today's lesson—when in doubt, double up your position." I swear, the guy was beginning to sound like some kind of fortune-cookie machine. I didn't know what the hell he was talking about, and said so. Well, he explained, as each new wire-service report upped the body count, the Dritz traders made more and more money. By the end of the day, J.T. told me, without embarrassment, they'd made over a million dollars. So backed up was the paperwork that the clerks stayed late and were either put up overnight at the Vista Hotel or sent home by limousine. Everyone got double paychecks the following week.

Seen through the prism of traders going berserk, of computers going down, the piles of paper that would take days to sort out—and the money made on their misery—the Indians of Bhopal didn't seem very real. They were discussed in terms usually used in context with the trade deficit or rate of inflation. It was all too surrealistic. J.T.'s spectral words, "It's not good," echoed in my head.

Hey, I can do this, I thought. It was all much less scientific than I had expected. I wouldn't need an MBA from Wharton, after all.

12

Frankie and Johnny—and Larry

ROM THE FIRST, the action was so frantic, the noise so deafening, the fractions spewing out so fast—and so *wet*—that a few enterprising transaction reporters who stood underneath the specialists made themselves cardboard "spit guards"—helmets, actually—which kept them relatively dry. Those who decided to brave the elements risked being showered with spittle and frequently came down with colds and throat infections. By now, standing on the platform, I was above the spray. My worry was whether I'd ever be able to keep up. I was even afraid to sneeze, cough, or blow my nose in case I'd miss hearing a trade that would cost half my salary.

I'd been assigned to two veteran traders, Frankie Borenzo and John Mulroy, an Italian and an Irishman as different as one could imagine in physique, looks, and general outlook; yet, when it came to business, birds of a feather.

Dark-haired Frankie, two inches taller than me and twice my age, had been on the floor for about twenty years and had started as a transaction reporter. His daily intake of cholesterol was prodigious, but you wouldn't know it from looking at him. Orange-haired Johnny, about ten years younger than Frankie and three inches shorter, like me began as a data clerk or, as he said, "came in through the back door." He was a great believer in physical exercise and in the luck o' the Irish and would always be seen sporting four-leaf clovers or claddagh rings or other lucky charms. I noticed, for example, that at the newsstand, Mulroy would never pick up pennies that were face down.

One day, shortly after I'd ceased clerking for him, Mulroy had to run to the men's room. "Watch my spot for a minute, will ya? But don't trade thirteen contracts"—referring to the options which he was in charge of trading. By then I should have known better than to ask why, but I did, anyway. "Bad luck. Haven't you noticed?"

Hadn't I noticed *what?* I had to wait for his return to learn why no one used red pens or why Mike Schwartz always wore the same "lucky" tie or why Kenny always stood on the same set of floor tiles.

The luck of the Irish was being tested by computers. Trading was becoming more scientific by the minute, and it seemed to trouble the guys who operated on instinct because, by its very nature, trading isn't entirely quantifiable the way corporate finance is. Most traders depend on "feel," so whenever they have to take contrarian positions—whenever the trend *isn't* their friend—they reach out for whatever extra assurance they think can be squeezed out of talismans.

Frankie made it all seem so easy, so effortless, and it used to drive me wild trying to figure out his knack. "I understand how options are priced mathematically with dividends, stock price, interest rates, etcetera, but what I *can't* understand is how you price them while all hell is breaking loose around you. Just what's your secret?"

He scrunched up his face, as if this were the first time anyone had asked him that. "Hmmm, instinct, I guess. It's like driving a car or bicycling. You *know*, you can't *explain*, you just *do* it."

That simile gave me pause: For months after I got my driver's license I felt unable to go through toll booths on the thruway—too narrow—or even to pull up next to a gas pump, as I'd probably knock it down and cause a massive explosion. Was I really cut out for this line of work? Could I hack it? But of course I did it; I just had to convince myself I could.

He saw my troubled look. He pointed to the two moving tapes and looked thoughtful. "Take a look at those prices; it's all there. You just have to know how to put it all together. Become a walking encyclopedia but don't get hung up on details."

Easier said than done, I thought. Not only would I have to understand what all these crazy people were screaming about and what these numbers meant; I would also have to know by how much to move the options and what the economy was up to (how the members of the Federal Reserve Bank were voting, who was In and Out of favor in the Reagan Administration), and what every broker on the AMEX and NYSE had on their order tickets at that precise moment. Small order. Who dreamed up this job, anyway? Who wants it?

But the self-doubt and self-pity didn't last. Not against the promise of what I could make in this business if I only set my mind to it. Over the next few days I thought about Frankie's line: "You just do it." Then I put away McMillan, as well as other books on options, stopped being scared, and tried to learn what the market was showing me.

I told Frankie of my recurring dream, in which I was being parachuted into Saint Peter's Square in Rome, not speaking a word of Italian or in any way conversant with Catholic dogma. But everyone in the dream was screaming fractions and trading XMI. He liked that: "Very Freudian." He smiled. "Tell me, was I the pope or just another cardinal?"

It was a lot easier once I decided to learn the "Italian" of options trading and to recite the Father Borenza's catechism. I even tossed out my trusty spiral notebook, left over from my days with J.T. In my mind's eye, the market was one of those remarkable books that has to be read over and over again to be fully understood and appreciated, which gives new meaning every time. I came to accept the fact that the "book" served up its secrets at its own pace: Just because I was ready to learn something on a Tuesday did not mean the market was ready, that day, to teach it. I savored and quickly came to appreciate the subtlety and nuances of each new word or descriptive phrase, even the euphemisms Wall Street came up with to rationalize its occasional free-falls.

Frankie was right. The only way to learn was to keep your ears and eyes open and not to be embarrassed to ask stupid questions—but to hope that someone else would ask them instead, as you just happened to be standing by.

| | | |

In the autumn of 1984, the Major Market Index was getting all sorts of press as the "hot" product of the moment. The business press played XMI as a "tail-wags-dog" story, with the index leading the market, rather than the other way around.

At times, we got so incredibly busy we had no time to eat. Or think. This also was true of the floor brokers, like Bobby, who, like the pink rabbit in the Eveready battery commercial, just kept going and going and going. As a broker he impressed me with his computerlike mind. While dashing around the floor, he'd figure out $\%_{64} + 3 - \frac{7}{16} + 4\frac{7}{8} - 22\frac{3}{4} + \frac{78}{32}$ and shout out the answer like a contestant at a 4-H math bee. Meanwhile, the trader would still be fumbling with his calculator's ON switch. To say Bobby was all business would be an understatement. The week before, he'd hand signaled a confirmation to one of the booths on the balcony. The hand signal for "Your order is completed" looks like a sideways salute right up to the face. Bobby had forgotten about the pencil in his hand and stabbed himself, splitting open his lip. With blood running down his chin and staining his smock, he kept on trading—stopping only long enough to stanch the flow by slapping masking tape over his top lip.

My job was rudimentary: As Borenzo and/or Mulroy screamed out the same number as their oppositions, I had to write them down. Then, as best I could, I'd enter the details of the trade into the book I was clutching. I couldn't help but learn. It wasn't that I was just inundated with trading rules and strategies but *bombarded* by them.

| | | |

Before switching from Dritz, I was told by my friend Pete LaBadia, the floor broker, that in the options pit the guys are so competitive that "when somebody has a heart attack, they'll just grab the orders right out of the dying man's hands." I never saw that happening, which doesn't mean it couldn't or wouldn't happen.

Neither Frankie nor Johnny had the killer instinct. On the contrary, I found them to be extraordinarily kind, friendly, and, above all, generous to a fault. I couldn't say that about everyone I worked with, but for the majority, yes. Whenever Frankie wasn't trading, he'd be hustling for some charity or needy individuals—such as a young girl he met while vacationing up in Lake George, who needed a costly operation on her spine. Or for something he read about in the *Daily News*, such as a center for homeless people in Newark, New Jersey, that had lost its funding. Frankie is just a guy who *can't* say no, an easy mark for whatever charity needs big bucks fast. When I worked next to him, he always carried pocketsful of pens that didn't work, because he'd clean out the curbside handicapped who'd proffered them (grabbing their brochures as well and passing them out to us during breakfast down at Harry's). He would draw the line at the cults, especially the Hare Krishnas, because during one encounter at an airport somewhere, as the guy put an arm on Frankie, he spotted a gold Rolex under his saffron-colored sleeve. "I give to the needy, not the greedy," Frankie explained. But for every other street beggar, Frankie was fair game. A good thing he was so good at making money as a trader, so he would have some left over after all that he gave away.

In that sense, Borenzo was typical of guys who had never made big bucks until they came down to the Exchange, free of the sort of insecurities that would drive better-polished and educated arrivistes to turn their backs on the less fortunate and indulge themselves.

The traders liked to refer to the benevolent ones among themselves as "stand-up guys," men expected to do the right thing. Indeed they would. Once, a data clerk's infant girl needed a bone-marrow transplant, and hundred-dollar bills came flying out of every pocket. A few even offered to donate their own marrow. Then there was the time one of the floor brokers, in less than an hour of putting the squeeze on his colleagues, raised enough to ensure that the kids of a transaction reporter who had died of cancer, without leaving enough insurance, could complete their parochial-school educations.

On my first day I'd hoped to prove my usefulness by showing the boys what I'd learned at my previous posting. Unfortunately, nobody drank Perrier, so I couldn't demonstrate my bottle-opening trick. I had to learn a new one.

Frankie was a caffeine freak, and a klutzy one. At the opening bell, each morning, reaching for his position card, he'd knock over a freshly poured container of coffee. I would dutifully clean up the mess, run out to get a replacement cup, and hope for the best. That kept up for two days, the Ten O'Clock Spill. But on day three, I was ready. I caught the cup in mid-air with one hand, so artlessly—sort of like that lady in the DuPont rug commercial—that I actually heard applause. As time went on, I perfected my technique and on visits home would demonstrate my newfound skill as art—"full-cup coffee catching"—to church groups and other interested parties. Should they ever bring back TV's "Gong Show," will someone have emcee Chuck Barris call me?

Why, I asked myself the first time I looked, were the tops of Larry Trainor's shoes marked "right" and "left" with white mailing labels lettered in black magic marker? Was he eccentric? I would say so. Out of his briefcase he pulled a strange-looking object, which he now carefully placed before him on the counter. It was a block of wood to which a thick layer of green rubber had been nailed.

Then the trading began and I saw Larry ranting and raving and furiously banging his tightly closed fist against the "anger-banger."

The clerks had given it to him as a Christmas present because he was one of those guys constantly throwing telephones, smash-

ing the Quotrons, and pounding on his clerk's shoulders. From
time to time, he'd miss the anger-banger and connect with someone's jaw or outstretched arm. That would cause some unpleas-
antness and lead Larry to apologize—something he found difficult
to do, as he saw this as an act not of contriteness but weakness.

When the action subsided, a bored Larry would stare at his
anger-banger and start thumping on it like a village elder calling
the tribe in for supper. Soon the thumping would spread beyond
the pit—*dumm-ta-dumm-ta-dumm*—as others picked up the nearest object on which to bang. Within minutes, the beat would
start to reverberate throughout the great hall, building to a cres-
cendo, sometimes punctuated by fake jungle calls.

Invariably, we'd hear the yodeling of a Johnny ("Tarzan")
Weissmuller fan. Needless to say, the Exchange executives who
worked upstairs in offices, or the "decorum patrol," as I called
them, were mortified and asked, "What the hell is wrong with
them? Why can't they snap rubber bands like every other professional under stress?" As there was nothing they could do about
it, they would just go back to the elevators.

That, at least, was to be preferred over Larry's customary use
of the anger-banger as a speech enhancer. To emphasize that he
meant business at all times, he would scream, "Where *(bang)*
the hell *(bang)* is fuckin' George *(bang)?*" At this, our heavyset,
green-jacketed pit supervisor, obviously named George, would
come huffing and puffing around the corner, obsequiously asking,
"Yes, Larry?"

George was our majordomo and head housekeeper. He'd held
this job for two years when I joined XMI, and nothing seemed
to faze him. I suspect he got paid very well: He seemed *meant*
to be abused by guys like Larry, who were tyrannical traders. He
once confided to a fellow supervisor, Richie Thomas, "I've been

called 'fuckin' George' so long that I've begun to sign my pay-checks that way."

| | |

For women who prided themselves on being individuals rather than objects to be put down, the Exchange must have seemed like a benign Gulag, work a sentence to be endured until something better came along. For distaff brokers and traders, the conditions have improved markedly, as more of them have entered the profession and fought their way to the top. En route, they were even given a bathroom below the third floor of the fourteen-story AMEX. Still, machismo remains the order of the day. One time when I told one of the specialists next to me to cover for me because I needed to go to the bathroom, without thinking he amiably growled, "Go put a rubber band around it."

Typical of the culture was Larry ("Anger-Banger") Trainor, who never felt very comfortable working alongside women. It wasn't that he was a misogynist; it was just that no one had prepared him for feminism. "Women shouldn't be allowed on the floor," he said over a staff breakfast one day, at which point I slid back my chair and started to get up. "In that case I might as well go back home, as I have a lot of baking to do today."

Another time, at another "power breakfast," Larry took out his stress-fracture pills and popped one, insisting for the umpteenth time he couldn't figure out how his wrist had received a stress fracture. (I visualized the two-inch-thick plywood anger-banger, which just yesterday had cracked and flown into pieces under Larry's fist). Bruce Baker, an XMI specialist, looked at the bottle and said, "This is Midol!" Larry got so angry at that he threw the pills and gave the table a hard *Bang!* with his good fist.

It was no secret that he was very much opposed to making me a partner in the firm. It wasn't the money, so I wondered what had set him off. He was too good at what he did to be threatened by the likes of me. I know he thought I was too theoretical and methodical in my trading; he more or less went by the seat of his pants and took huge positions; yet, because of his uncanny instinct for reading the market, he made the firm a great deal of money.

Actually, the die had been cast early on. One day I had to clerk for him, and his ceaseless use of the anger-banger had made me so nervous I goofed up on my addition. I somehow made 35 plus 85 add up to 20 instead of 120. He got on the microphone and, in front of the entire crowd, yelled, "You're (*bang*) stupid!" He looked at me as if for confirmation, and, like a fool, I agreed, vigorously nodding my head and mouthing, "I'm stupid, incredibly stupid." And I *was* stupid. That was how you learned to be careful when working in the pit.

| | | |

As I write this, there are about thirty women traders on the floor; still a minority, of course. While some strive earnestly to be buddies with the men, others hold themselves aloof because they *know* they are just tolerated and they don't want to expose themselves to insult more than is absolutely necessary. The prejudice is deeply ingrained and will take a long time to work its way out of the system.

It was even picked up from the floor by the waiters down at Harry's. To get properly served, one usually had to get up and give chase to the waiters. Down at Harry's, as upstairs, chivalry wasn't just dead but long interred. But I figured that if I wanted to be treated as "one of the boys," then I shouldn't expect preferential treatment anywhere else.

ı   ı   ı

One Monday in the spring of 1986 I had to come in earlier than usual—I distinctly recall that it was just after the weekend of the Chernobyl nuclear meltdown in the Soviet Union—and was surprised to see Anthony Spina, Ronnie's clerk, pawing through boxes of trading slips.

"What brings you in at the crack of dawn?" I asked. His dark expression made it clear he was not happy to be there at that ungodly hour. "I got a call at home this morning," he said. "There's been a major fuck-up." Seems there were some "irregularities" on one of his big trades on Friday, which needed to be fixed before the market opened. Ron had been trading Pennwalt Corporation—PSM—most of the day, "and this broad who was the specialist kept ticking him off so much that he wrote PMS on all the tickets. None of them cleared. *Damn!*"

I suggested to Elisa Fromm, the other female specialist in the pit, that we go into the perfume business, like Cher and Elizabeth Taylor had done. Only we could feature shots taken on busy days in the XMI pit when we're sweating, our clothes are torn, and we're fighting with a hundred primitive males. We'd name the product "Naked Aggression—For the Woman Who Is Clawing Her Way to the Top." She said that my NYU marketing classes were obviously using outdated textbooks.

13

Getting Seated

E ARLY IN JUNE 1984, after I'd been working on the Exchange
for about five months, I finally got to execute my first
trade.

It had been a very slow trading day. Senior management was
off somewhere in the building at a meeting, and J.T. was nom-
inally in charge of the store.

At around eleven o'clock, J.T. said he was "going out for a
smoke" and told me to keep an eye on the screens. At that
point, I'd been under his tutelage for about four months, had
pretty much overdosed on McMillan, and had been going at him
like a fourteen-year-old pestering Dad for a crack at the wheel
before her legs could reach the floor pedals.

There was, of course, no way J.T. could really let me do a
trade because I didn't have a seat, and, short of robbing a bank,

there was no way I could even afford to rent one. So I'd more or less given up, had stopped bothering him.

Now, suddenly, J.T. turned and said, "As the duty officer I'm giving you complete fiduciary responsibility over what happens here while I'm gone." Before that had time to sink in, he bent over and whispered in my ear, "But whatever you do, don't fuck up."

Lightning had struck. Did I hear right? He couldn't have been clearer had he posted instructions in moving lights on the broad tape. And so it was that I got to make six trades that day in the Market Value Index. I must have done okay, because J.T. never said another word about it. The following week, during another of his nicotine fits, I executed my first "scalp"—selling ten XAM options at 5⅝ and, seconds later, buying them back at 5½ for a total profit of an ⅛ ($125). I remember it scared the hell out of me, especially after seeing the trade crawling along on the ticker. Upon returning, J.T. just glanced at my trading sheets and said, "Way to go, Flying Fingers! Nobody ever went broke ringing their cash register."

| | | |

As the aspiring star Eve Harrington discovered in Joseph L. Mankiewicz's *All About Eve*, before you can get ahead, there first has to be an opening, and if no opening exists, *make* one. Only, on macho Wall Street, be more subtle about it than Eve was on Broadway. In a pit full of male vipers, best you tread lightly. Over a year had passed since my first trade. I'd been working in the XMI pit long enough, I figured, to win a battlefield promotion. But that's not how these things worked, I was told. For me to get in, someone had to leave, preferably standing up, on two feet.

It was the week of Yom Kippur, the Day of Atonement, the

holiest of Jewish holidays. I was taking a break down in the cafeteria with two of the floor brokers, Donny and Steve.

The left side of Steve's jacket was soaking wet, as if he'd just been caught in the rain. So were half his trousers. I knew better than to ask. The previous weekend he'd torn a muscle on his side playing tennis. As he couldn't afford to stay home and nurse his wound, he came to work wearing an ice bag inside his jacket. To make sure no one would bump into him there, he had drawn a red cross on a piece of paper and pinned it to the outside of the jacket. He should have known better. By two o'clock the ice had melted and, sure enough, by two-fifteen a PaineWebber broker in the next booth had come up to him with a pushpin and pierced the ice bag.

"You think it'll be busy tomorrow," asked Steve, "it being Yom Kippur and all?"

"Why do you pronounce it like a herring?" Donny asked. "It's kip-*poor*, isn't it, not kipper? You're Jewish, ain't you?"

"I'm assimilated," replied Steve, standing up and removing the empty ice bag.

"Oh, you coulda fooled me," replied Donny. "As to your question, yeah, I think it will be busy as hell, 'cause all the *goyim* will come in to trade so as to prove that we Jews don't run Wall Street."

It suddenly hit me that I was working for an outfit where all the specialists save for Frankie and Johnny were Jewish. That would mean they'd be short of traders. " 'Scuse me, guys, I gotta go study," I said, making a beeline for the door.

That night, I skipped classes at NYU and boned up on McMillan instead. *This* time I'd make it.

Once before I had thought the Big Break had come. Six months earlier, the opening bell had rung and none of the traders had shown up. There was a blizzard raging outside and only a few of the Long Island guys had managed to make it to work. The New Jersey trains had all ground to a halt, so Frankie wouldn't be in till noon, if then. Ronnie came by and told me to open John's options. I thought of a million excuses not to, but Ronnie had already disappeared and at least fifty traders were looking up at me expectantly for prices and public-order imbalances. I grabbed the mike tightly, more for support than for volume, and opened the first three options. Just then Mulroy ran up, out of breath, and tore the mike away from me. "You're not old enough," he said, laughing.

Mulroy, who lived in the Bronx, depended on the subway to get to work, so a snowstorm didn't hold him up very often. Guys had been known to do almost anything to get to the AMEX, especially if they had a big position to worry about. Once Ronnie actually got his milkman to drive him through the Holland Tunnel from New Jersey because it was closed to automobiles. A trader named Gary was stuck on the ice in his car on a side street and had to pull out the urn in his trunk conveniently housing his grandmother's ashes. Slightly wincing while scattering them under the tires, he reminded himself aloud, "She always said for me to do everything I possibly could to get ahead in the business world because that's where the money is." And the car shot out into the middle of the road.

Sure enough, Yom Kippur turned into a holiday for me as I began trading like a maniac. Looking back, I didn't do spectacularly well, but I made thirty thousand dollars for the firm—not bad, considering that the guys I was trading against used every dirty trick in their book to one-up me. Their favorite that day was to play a variation of the old kids' games, Freeze Tag and Red Light–Green Light. Only this entailed more than making physical contact ("I touched you!" "No way, you only touched my clothes!" "I'm on home base"). Here it involved money.

They'd try to purchase options from an offer I might have made five minutes earlier when the market was lower, petulantly insisting, "Hey! you didn't cancel, I got witnesses to prove it," demanding I *had* to sell them at the lower price. They really behaved like a bunch of rotten little kids from the neighborhood, right down to the childish "Gotcha!" "Did/Did not!" "Cheater!"—even a variation of "I'm telling on you!"—only instead of Mom, they'd tell the governors.

I wasn't worried. I had Frankie and Johnny in my corner of the playground. At least they wouldn't let the other kids beat me up.

At the end of the day, Michael Gann, a pit broker, ran over all frazzled. "Laura," he asked hurriedly, "I'm in a bind. Can you check a sale for me?"

"Sure, Mike," said I, all business, "just let me get a report on some futures I sold."

I should have known better.

"Run over to Macy's and see if they've got any flannel sheets left from their last white sale," at which he ran off, giggling.

But then, a minute or so later, he paid me the supreme compliment. "Hey, kid!" he yelled from across the trading room floor. "You did a good job today!"

From that moment on, having proven to Ron and the partners that I could trade without losing the house, it was only a matter of time until they let me fill in regularly for absent specialists. Then, as the market got more volatile, turning from a yo-yo into a runaway roller coaster, I became a regular trader, if not a legitimate one in the eyes of the Exchange.

I remained apprehensive. I wasn't yet convinced that it wasn't just market momentum and blind luck. On a Thursday morning, a week or so after I began trading full time, the alarm went off and I dreamed that I was doing a trade—buying XMI options at 6:15 A.M. They were cheap, so I pushed the snooze button— as if to buy them. Then the alarm went off again and, looking at the digital display—6:32—I thought that I was selling the options at a higher price and hit it again. I was losing my mind.

I tried to get out of my trance by turning on the early-morning business report. It never ceased to surprise me how little the Wall Street "experts" knew. If you want to know how easy it is to sound profound without having to be, just tune in "Wall Street Week" on PBS any Friday. "When would you switch from stocks to cash?" asked the always-unctuous Louis Rukeyser of an analyst from Prudential-Bache. "If a recession got under way," she said.

"And what indications are you looking for?" he then posed. "A rise in interest rates," his guest replied. On such information, stock-buying decisions are made all over America. It is frightening. How did this marketwise lady get her job? Rock solid, all right, in the head.

| | | |

At the end of December 1985, my star twinkled brighter than usual. A genuine opening occurred when Jeff Feins—the guy Ron Shear had turned me over to after our first meeting/interview—resigned after seeing the size of his bonus check.

He wasn't happy. He'd expected a lot more. Bonuses are management's way of separating the goats from the sheep. They can be as high as ten times one's base salary. Traders wait all year to find out, in just five seconds flat, whether they made $75,000 or $750,000. If the firm has had a good year and the bonus doesn't reflect it, the message is clear: Move on.

The weeks leading up to bonus time are fraught with nervousness and anxiety. Those who never work out are at the gym every night. Guys who don't smoke are buying crates of Havana cigars. I tended to keep lots of M&M's within reach.

The question was, did you *already* spend $400,000 this year when you should have spent only $75,000?

Due to the tremendous overhead of operating a specialist firm, salaries are usually kept low for Wall Street—$35,000 to $80,000. This way the company doesn't have to lay people off during a bad year.

Those who are supremely confident of scoring big will take the ultimate gamble by borrowing against anticipated earnings. It's not the smartest thing to do, unless, like so many yuppies, they overspent during the previous eleven months and are hearing the world knocking on their door. One guy who did just that went for his bonus but, after overhead and expenses were factored in, ended up *owing* his employers money.

The 1987 crash really came home to a lot of guys who'd bought weekend houses and BMWs on the strength of their anticipated bonuses. It gave rise to the saying "At E F Hutton the road to success is always being repaved."

| | | |

On January 8, 1986, I was given Jeff's seat. Actually, my employers went out and rented it for me for about four thousand dollars a month. So, to celebrate I made forty thousand dollars for the firm while the market dropped forty-three points. Now there were seven of us who held trading seats—Ron, Larry, Frankie, Johnny, Doug, Ralph, and me. The word "seat" is actually an irony, because when you finally sit down to sign the contract, it's probably the last time you're off your feet.

I sort of expected it, even before Jeff quit. At the Christmas party, Ron had come up to me and said, "I made a New Year's resolution. You're going to have breakfast with us every morning." No more coming in early with the other clerks to go over rejected trades.

I'd only asked about getting a seat about twenty times, and each time Ron had walked away, saying, "I'll think about it." Of course, Ron was so smart that he never had to think about anything in his life. Par for the course at a firm where it's a cold day in hell when someone pats you on the back. That's why Michael Gann's comment about my doing well meant so much. Compliments from the trenches were as rare as having lunch out.

It was a good thing they'd come through. If they hadn't given me the seat, I'd have threatened to quit. In reality, I wouldn't have. I loved working in the pit too much. But then, I had been one of those kids who skateboarded forty-five miles per hour while hanging on to car bumpers and had gone on the Crystal Beach amusement park's "Comet" roller coaster twenty-seven times in a row.

Promises, promises. I'd believe it once I saw the white of their papers. Back in 1984, when Ron made me his Galatea, he grandly offered to pick up my NYU tuition for the next two years. It wasn't entirely altruistic, he explained, as he could take most of it as a corporate tax deduction. I didn't care one way or the other; I was glad to get the subsidy. But now, less than a year later, I was told the firm no longer wanted to pay for my schooling, because they figured that with what I was making off trades I no longer needed to be subsidized. I hit the roof. A deal is a deal, I insisted, and stalked off the floor.

I spent the next hour aimlessly walking around the financial district. Two blocks from the Exchange, on Pine Street, I passed the New York Institute of Finance. I walked in and asked to see the head of the school. On a whim, I asked if they needed someone to teach options-trading strategies. As luck would have it, they did. And they would pay! And so it was that I began with a class of six students, which within a year grew to forty, and more than made up for the loss of Spear Leeds's NYU subsidy.

I was still harboring a grudge toward Spear Leeds when I heard that there were various openings at Goldman, Sachs, so in November I called. They sent a messenger over to pick up my skimpy résumé. It must have interested them because a day or so later there was a message on my home answering machine asking me to come down and discuss filling a vacancy as a foreign-currency trader. That sounded new and offbeat, so I went over to the Deak International office at 29 Broadway to pick up whatever brochures they had on the subject. But when I returned for my second interview at Goldman, a strange feeling overcame me. As I got off at the twentieth floor at 85 Broad Street and was escorted past rows of uncluttered desks manned by people who didn't shout, didn't sweat, and seemed oh-so-polite to one another, I suddenly got cold feet. This was not the right sort of environment for me. It would be like working in some giant insurance company. Much too quiet. I could die there and nobody would ever rip the trades out of my clammy hands.

Before I could actually wave my AMEX membership certificate, I would have to qualify by taking a battery of tests upstairs—not so much to prove I knew how to trade, but that I knew the rules of the game. That Wednesday morning, Ron came over to the pit after the partners had voted me in and beamed: "Congratulations, kid. Of course, you understand that if you fail the tests, you're fired. Good luck!"

How typical. He thought he was being funny. I was suddenly petrified. What *if* I flunked? Would he really toss me out? Stress, always stress. On the best day of my life he had to go and make me a nervous wreck.

Out of curiosity, more than anything else, I called the membership department and asked how old one had to be to have a seat on the Exchange. Seems they hadn't ever been asked that question, because the woman on the other end put down the phone and said, "Just a moment." In the background I heard people talking softly and some papers rustling. She came back on the line. "Nineteen." I breathed easier. Two months earlier, I'd turned twenty.

Someone in the AMEX public-relations department must have gotten out a release, because I got a call from business reporter Dan Cuff at the *New York Times*. I asked Ron if it would be okay to be interviewed. He seemed perplexed. "Why would the *Times* want to interview you?" I told him I thought my age might have something to do with it. "Age?" he asked. "How old *are* you?" Now it was my turn to be perplexed. He really had no idea how old I was, so I told him. He looked at me in disbelief. "Sonofabitch, you're younger than my daughter! Sure, go do your interview," he said, laughing and going over to the phone to call the office and see if Ralph Fogel, the partner representing Spear Leeds & Kellogg, had heard about *this!*

| | | |

The schedule for qualifying me as a seat holder called for three days of seminars—once a month—followed by three tests. A few days after Ron's announcement I got a call from Ralph Fogel. "Ron and I," he began, "are not happy. We really can't afford to have you off the floor all that time."

I was taken aback. Hadn't they known of the rules when they got me the seat? There'd been no reason to know, he explained, as most of the principal traders already held seats when the company was formed. I was a "special case." (So my parents had always said, but in a somewhat different tone.) I told Ralph I didn't think I was in the position of asking for a waiver and said I had to do whatever was expected of me.

I have no way of knowing whether Fogel and Shear ever appealed, but, if so, they apparently got nowhere. An hour after I'd started my first seminar I was called out to the phone. It was Ron and he was flipping out. "The place is falling apart! Get your ass down here!" Ron slammed down the phone. Either that or he tore it off the wall. I apologized to everyone and ran out of the room to the elevator.

He'd have really freaked out had he come upstairs and monitored the seminar. The first three-hour session reminded me of those tedious, mind-numbing, and totally humorless driving courses where they make you sit through movies of monkeys driving cars and have you calculate blood-alcohol content after three bottles of Bartles & Jaymes. They're not really meant to make you a better driver, or in this case, trader. I think they just want to put a little bit of the fear of God into you, to remind you a license is a privilege, not a right.

Another time Ron tried pulling me out of the seminars, the instructor—a woman named Linda Clark who was in charge of new membership—took the phone and told him calmly but assertively that Ms. Pedersen *had* to finish the course, that this was the fourth time he had tried something like this, and to please go away.

Ron does not gladly suffer being dressed down by anyone, especially one of "the suits" or "upstairs people," as traders refer to anyone in AMEX administration, and so he let fly. He was screaming so loud the entire class heard his diatribe come through the phone: "Dammit to hell, lady," he was screaming at Linda, "I'm not gonna lose fifty thousand dollars because of some lousy slide show. You tell Pedersen that if she doesn't get her ass down here *now*, she's fired."

Getting Seated

Linda dropped the phone as if it had suddenly become radio-active. She was clearly not used to being addressed in such a crude fashion by one of the downstairs philistines. She waved me out with a nod of the head. I picked up my knapsack and tiptoed out, at once relieved to be out of there and secretly flattered that Ron needed me badly enough to give Linda a sleepless night. Not that I had anything against her personally. I didn't even know the woman. But I so identified with the traders that she represented "them." They *were* different, like the pod people in the *Invasion of the Body Snatchers*. They were calmer, didn't play practical jokes, their clothes looked better on them than ours did on us, and they always spoke well, in modulated tones, and appeared so, well, *neat* and clean. No food fights for these folks. And doubtless they were different from us off the job, as well. They probably drove within proscribed speed limits, got fewer tickets, kept neater apartments . . . and played gin rummy. They probably planned for retirement the year after they came to work here and made out their wills in their thirties. We traders didn't. We figured someone else would get stuck with our funerals and that VISA could whistle for its money.

Ron may have won the initial skirmish, but Linda Clark won in the end. As head of membership, she held all the cards: I would not get my membership until the requirements had been met, period. When I reappeared upstairs, I felt like adding the letters PG—postgraduate—to my name tag. Linda came over during the slide show (which I'd now seen whole or in part at least four times) and snatched away my *MAD* magazine. What now, *detention?*—as in high school when I was punished for reading *Batman* during an earth-sciences a/v show? Dammit, why didn't he call?

In retrospect, it was a good thing Ron didn't call, otherwise I wouldn't have been there the second day when a guy from the

AMEX marketing department named Jay Baker came in to do an interesting presentation on options strategies. He recognized me from the floor and had heard about my Institute of Finance courses. He invited me for coffee downstairs. He had an idea: How would I like to go on the road for the Exchange to talk up the index options program? I said I'd think about it; I had to first get through this Mickey Mouse stuff.

I did get through it, no thanks to the impatient Ron Shear. On my first official trading day, the boys took me downstairs to Harry's and handed me the big blue plastic badge that carried my name, that of Spear Leeds Kellogg/Investors Company, and my number—885–F. I'd become so accustomed to having Ron bark at me that at first I thought it was another order. "No," he said, "this is the only advice you'll ever get from me: Yell first, think later." It would serve me well for the next four years.

I was so thrilled to have that badge that I wore it to bed, clipped to an extralarge T-shirt. I stopped doing that two weeks later, after Mulroy asked, "What's that white stuff on your badge?" and peering closer: "Why, it looks like toothpaste!" This is silly, I told myself a few nights later when, on the eleven o'clock news on channel 7, I saw this report about a family that had been burned out of their house in Bayside, Queens. They were all huddling around in their pajamas, looking distraught. I was still living with the friendly pusher on Barrow Street. What if . . . ? I could see myself running out the door, smack into a crew from "Eyewitness News," wearing that AMEX badge and little more. I'd never hear the end of it.

I was assigned a "spot" on the podium and assigned three October options in which to make markets. Also a microphone that screeched whenever I touched its base, and two clerks.

No sooner was I screaming and trading than I was called upon to arbitrate a dispute between two traders, Mark and Davy. They were going at each other with hammer and tongs.

"Tell him!" Davy yelled. "Tell him that you don't split eights or twos."

I looked perplexed, so Mark yelled, "Blackjack, dammit!"

I screamed back, "Not when the dealer has ten, *assholes!*" and resumed trading.

My response had solved nothing. Mark was still fuming, so later that afternoon, during a lull, as Davy leaned against the back of the pit scanning the *New York Times*, Mark snuck underneath him and held a match to the paper and ran.

Whoosh! We thought it was pretty funny--Davy's shocked expression when inexplicably the newspaper caught fire. "Hot story, eh?" someone asked as he dropped the paper and stomped out the .fire. He *knew* who'd done this to him and he looked from side to side, but no Mark was in sight. He let loose with a series of expletives-deleted. "I'll get you for this, you sonofabitch, you can run but you can't hide."

Maybe it was just a coincidence that in that particular *New York Times* there had been an article leading off with "Anyone who wears an ID name tag in the workplace after the age of twenty-five has serious vocational problems."

14

On the Road

THE DAY I ARRIVED at the American Stock Exchange, the Dow stood at 1086.57; the day I left, it was 2791.41—slightly above the precrash pinnacle of 2722.42. More to the point, AMEX options volume—individual stocks and the immensely popular stock index options—had risen from a little over 40 million contracts in 1984 to nearly 71 million by the time of the first October meltdown. And of all the new AMEX products introduced over the past forty years, the Major Market Index (XMI) was the most successful, bar none.

Ever since anyone could remember, the AMEX had played second banana to the Big Board, the all-powerful New York Stock Exchange, giving its management and many of its members a massive inferiority complex. The one area in which the American clearly excelled was in options trading, but outside of the few city blocks surrounding both exchanges in lower Manhattan, few knew, fewer cared. To the average small investor, options were far too esoteric to understand. And too many brokers didn't know how to sell them.

But once the stock-options indexes were created, with their appeal of letting the small investor follow the DJIA up or down, indexes started taking off like gangbusters. At that point, someone upstairs had the astute idea of using the XMI to get the AMEX better press.

Though XMI was not designed for the fainthearted, there were plenty of rich investors bored with the products their brokers were offering and looking for new action. Getting the brokers behind XMI would almost certainly reduce their incessant sniping at the AMEX for not being innovative enough to get new listings, doomed forever to play second fiddle to the New York Stock Exchange, as far as stocks went.

But who would explain it all to them? Who else but the specialists who knew the options index product better than anyone else? (In 1989, specialists accounted for over eleven percent of trading volume on the American Stock Exchange and were involved in nearly ninety-two percent of the trades, and they were thus able to stabilize prices by their intervention.)

There was only one hitch, delicately stated privately by a stalwart in the AMEX options marketing department to one of the governors: "The specialists most knowledgeable about the workings of XMI should not be let out of their cages after the closing bell." Apparently the floor antics referred to earlier were being closely watched upstairs by the Levitt morals squad. They must have felt very antsy about unleashing the animals downstairs.

"That's a nice way of putting it, Laura," my new friend Jay Baker told me when we had coffee after the seminar. "I'd just say they were nervous about it."

Which is why Jay had sought me out in Linda's classroom upstairs and what now brought him around to his mission of recruiting me as new product-pusher. As he explained it, I was "presentable," meaning I was not seen upstairs as either a troublemaker or too disheveled. At least I started out each day dressed well. Jay also said it was difficult to keep using the same floor people over and over because the quiet, sedate marketing presentations had none of the action of trading, and the brokers soon tired of the PR rigmarole. My after-hours work at the Institute of Finance on Pine Street had also not gone unnoticed, and, being female, I symbolized the Exchange's slavish devotion to the nation's equal-opportunity employment laws.

So, asked Baker, how would I like to go on the road as a marketing rep for the AMEX?

While I pondered the question, Jay went on to say that, in exchange for my time, the Exchange would pick up all expenses, would fly me business class if I chose, let me keep whatever frequent-flyer miles I might rack up, put me up in four-star hotels, and provide limos and all the other trappings of executive privilege. I wouldn't get paid but, as he so shrewdly saw, it would give my voice box and my ear drums a needed respite. "And you'd even get to see daylight again"—an insider reference to the heavy-mesh curtains covering the unwashed windows that mainly served to trap paper airplanes sent up from the floor.

Thus began my three-year-long stint as XMI spokesperson, which began auspiciously in Washington, D.C., one spring evening in 1986, when one of the brokers in the audience afterward insisted on walking me back to the Mayflower Hotel. At the elevator he said he wanted to kiss me. "Why?" I asked, somewhat perplexed. "We've barely met."

"You don't understand," he replied. "I want to kiss you not because I find you beautiful, which I do; not because I admire what you've done or your intelligence, both of which I do; but because kissing you would be like kissing the American Stock Exchange, which I have always held in the highest esteem."

I squirmed out of his halfhearted embrace by promising to send him the 1985 AMEX annual report so he could lick the cover to his heart's content.

The next morning I had breakfast with Howard Baker, the Exchange's options-department lawyer. "What do I talk about?" I asked him. "Whatever you want," said he. "Just explain what you do, answer their questions, and don't tell Reagan or Communist jokes."

I probably needed looking after. Turning me loose in America's better hotels may not have been the smartest thing the AMEX ever did. The only hotels I'd ever stayed in before were all Howard Johnson's; in fact, I'd never even had a hotel room to myself, and these had two beds from which to choose! Like Goldilocks, I slept in both, and the first night went slightly nuts jumping from one to the other, doing flips trampoline-style.

At first I didn't trust a place that did not have an ice-making machine down the hall. I'd never before used a plastic card in place of a room key. I was tempted to raid the fridge until I remembered Pete Heffley, up in Buffalo, telling me about this friend of his who had cleaned out the entire contents of a Hilton Hotel's fridge, believing them to be giveaway samples, only to be billed months later on his credit card for something like three hundred dollars for little bottles of booze, candy bars, and assorted nibblies, all of it worth maybe fifty dollars—if that much.

But, once I called home while reclining in the bathtub and used those deep-pile towels I swore were a new invention, I was determined to make at least one of these trips a month.

After breakfast I crossed Connecticut Avenue mid-block, dodging traffic just as I do in New York, and promptly was given a summons for jaywalking. I never paid. Someday the Washington police will probably come and try to take my feet away.

When I flew to Long Beach, California, with Joe Stefanelli, head of AMEX options marketing, the Exchange's travel department booked us on coach class. Just as well, as I was bone tired and the plane was more than half empty, which meant I could stretch out across three seats in the middle section of the wide-body jet. Before I went to sleep, I brought out "Porkchop," my trusty little stuffed pig I had been carrying around since childhood, and propped him next to a pair of those pillowettes the airlines give you. When one of the flight attendants came by, she told Joe what a cute daughter he had. He looked over and asked if I would like some cookies and milk when I awoke.

When I was out promoting XMI in Oklahoma City, where all the taxi drivers claim to be between oil strikes (as opposed to New York, where they are either Iranian exiles or former Drexel Burnham brokers waiting for Mike Milken's parole), I was approached by one of the Stetson-hatted, Justin-booted, and silver-buckled brokerage-house managers who must have seen one-too-many "Dallas" reruns. "Honey," he cooed in a feeble attempt to sound like Larry Hagman, "you look more like a Barbie Doll than a specialist. Are there any pictures of you in the slide show?" What a smoothie! "Yup," I lied, "just in my bikini." "Hubba-hubba," he said. *Hubba-hubba?* He must have been older than he looked.

Unfortunately, this guy was all too typical of the sort of people we had to win over. The following week Joe and I had been scheduled to give a presentation to Thomson McKinnon in New York City, but just before leaving the Exchange we were told that the presentation had been scratched. Seems a Thomson McKinnon manager had fled the country after being indicted for embezzlement. *Some* people in this business do get to fly first class; it was reported widely on the rumor circuit that he skipped by Concorde, once again proving that if you don't ask, you don't get. It reminds me of what Ron Shear told me about a trader sent to jail for parking stock—the crime for which the Feds got some of Ivan Boesky's pals. Seemed the broker had paid the bail of a couple of small-town crooks so that he could have a private room in the Monmouth County jail house. That's what I call *class*.

What I remember best are all the trips I took with Jay Baker, who had recruited me. He was a crime buff, loved TV's "America's Most Wanted"—a show he viewed weekly with all the passion of Dustin Hoffman's Raymond in *Rain Man*, who needed his daily fix of Judge Wapner. One time, driving up from Seattle to Vancouver, B.C., Jay told me hair-raising tales of the SEA/TAC murderer—so-called because all the killings took place in or around the Seattle/Tacoma Airport. Driving from Palm Beach to Orlando, I learned all about the notorious serial killer Ted Bundy, then awaiting execution at Stark. It was just a hobby of Jay's, but I always felt safer back at my Mafia-owned apartment on Carmine Street, with the rickety fire escape and the loose hinges on the front door.

| | | |

In 1987 the XMI began trading on the European Options Exchange (EOE) in Amsterdam, the first international trading link for an American index option.

The idea was to give Dutch traders, six hours ahead of us, a place to lay off risk during the early-morning hours when America was still asleep. The European Options Exchange had invited Morgan Stanley and Salomon Brothers to come talk about trading some sort of market basket of stocks all night long, which would operate as a sort of futures contract so the Dutch traders could protect their positions.

I had never before been out of the country, other than on those bicycle runs across the Canadian frontier to play the ponies at Fort Erie. I knew this was going to be a memorable trip when the usually punctilious Dutch apologized for a six-minute delay in airline KLM's takeoff. By then a frequent flyer on People's Express and US Scare, I never knew delays could be that short.

After landing at Schiphol, we took a Mercedes taxicab to the Hotel L'Europe on Nieuwe Doelenstraat in the heart of Old Amsterdam. I had just come out of the shower naked, when in strode a uniformed bellhop bearing a huge basket of fruit, compliments of the EOE. I grabbed for the bedspread and screamed, "Hey, don't you guys knock?" He looked me up and down and nonchalantly replied, "Oh, we're used to it." From behind the slammed bathroom door I yelled, "Well, I'm *not!*" Clearly, I would have to adjust.

The Dutch are certainly different from us Americans. For one, they don't flaunt their wealth; for another, they gladly pay their taxes—about sixty-five percent—and accept that as the price of a society that cares for its unfortunates. Read their lips. Our counterparts working the Amsterdam financial markets were, for the most part, far wealthier than any of us, but they were careful not to let it show. One of our EOE tour guides, Sem Van Berkel, explained that there's no place to spend all that money, and, being historically frugal folks who live somewhat precariously twelve feet below sea level and who have known some real natural calamities, as well as "*de Moffen*" (as they call the Germans next door), they're not into blowing it all on conspicuous consumption.

The word "efficiency" got a good workout during our stay. Whereas the quintessential American entrepreneur starts his space-age business while still in college, then sells it for a couple of million after graduation before retiring and landing on the cover of *Industry Week* at twenty-seven, in Holland you don't do that. And if you do, you don't hire a PR firm to tell the world how wonderful you are. And you certainly don't go around strutting and preening, throwing around your wealth, and bullying critics just because you've got bundles stashed away (or have the public believing you do when, in fact, you may be in hock to the banks and your creditors).

Open as they are to all sorts of eccentric behavior, when it comes to business, the Dutch can be hard-nosed and scornful of childish behavior. Which is how they viewed the "negotiations" conducted by some of the Morgan Stanley and Salomon Brothers representatives. At one of the business dinners, our competitors sauntered in as if they were doing the Amsterdam financial community a favor by just showing up, and then rather arrogantly "talked Dutch uncle" to the Dutch. What these city slickers didn't know was that far from dealing with country bumpkins, they were in fact addressing a bunch of multimillionaires. The way these guys talked down, one would think they were the rich ones, instead of just working for the multimillionaires.

Our hosts just smiled and said nothing. The Dutch are very tolerant of fools, and they are experts in the theory and practice of risk and reward. Had the Americans from Salomon Brothers and Morgan Stanley done their homework, they'd have remembered that the Dutch formed the world's *first* stock exchange (in 1611) and, as the world's first great mercantile power, have seen and probably instigated more financial scams than anyone. They tend to be skittish about propositions that smell of tulips in bloom. In this instance, they liked our XMI package and the American Stock Exchange better than anything Salomon and Morgan Stanley brought to the table.

After we made our deal, the Dutch insisted we celebrate, so we headed for the red-light district, not far from the Beurs, between the Oude Zijds Voorburgwal and Achterburgwal—hence the name *Walletjes*, or "Little Walls." We came to gape, though the women plying the world's oldest profession hoped we were in a buying mood.

Like Times Square, only cleaner, Amsterdam's red-light district is a prime tourist attraction; only here the commerce is a lot brisker, more open. Men line the street and hawk sex paraphernalia, cassettes of X-rated films, tickets to live sex shows, while the women, looking bored in their skimpy dresses, sit in open windows, reading, knitting, beckoning, and encouraging the browsers to sample the goods. At the edge of the district is a small brick building identified by a large sign reading "VD Clinic." How thoughtful of the authorities.

On one trip Ron and I were walking past some of the better "window shopping," along with three guys from the Exchange's operations department. Ron went up to one of the girls and started negotiating a deal for all four of the guys loudly enough so that they could hear. Not knowing that Ron was playing a joke on them, they were halfway back to the hotel before Ron came up with an agreeable price. He's a tough trader, even in flesh.

Eventually, our group shrank to six—four Dutchmen from EOE and two of us from the AMEX. We tried to make excuses to go back to the hotel, but the Dutch were determined that we should have more fun. My colleague was dedicated to his AMEX job and determined to keep up with his clients. After a blurry tour of discos and sawdust-on-the-floor pubs, we ended up in a very old house on one of the inner-city canals. We congregated around a beautiful mahogany bar, near some tall, lissome blondes, all of whom claimed to be students. At first I took them at their word.

The place had all the trappings of a private men's club, with plush leather chairs, wainscoted walls, fine art on the walls. Soft music was piped in to a small mirrored dance floor on which two or three couples—the women blonde, of course—swayed to the music and held each other tight.

My colleague stood off at the edge of the bar, puffing on a Dutch cigar, sniffing brandy, flanked by a couple of blondes. He seemed to be having the time of his life but was actually trying to steal a glance at his watch. He was obviously tired and wanted to go back to his hotel.

I now took another look around the place, observed more closely the way the girls were dressed—no pesky buttons to slow things down—and said to myself, Laura, you are in a whore-house!

I signaled to my colleague off at the far side of the bar; he began to work his way over. The dialogue ran something like this:

ME: Listen, I don't mind if you stay but I . . .

HE: Laura, no problem. I'll meet you for breakfast but I'm going back to the hotel . . .

ME: Sure you are. Look, it's no problem for me, either. I'll just grab a taxi and see you later (*pause*). By the way, don't worry. I'll forget I even saw you.

HE: What d'you mean by that? Hey! They're real nice but it's just not me, y'know what I mean? (*Turning to his Dutch companions*) Listen, you guys have fun now, y'hear?

At that precise moment, we both realized we had no business there and ought to get out, but fast. How would we explain our expense-account entry—"drinks for escort service"? How to beg leave of our hosts without insulting them? Who could tell? Perhaps it's a native custom to follow up dinner with visits to the nearest brothel to talk about Kierkegaard and NATO. Now that we had just established the first international link with the EOE, why risk offending them?

We mumbled our farewells and dashed out the back door, our integrity intact. I swore that had we hung around another five minutes, somebody's pants would have come down to the ankles. Some of the girls had even been eyeing me.

I regret now having left so abruptly. It really was one of the nicest "nightclubs" I've ever seen, and what I'm sorriest about is that I never got to take a bath in a heart-shaped tub. Knowing what I know of Dutch marine engineering, the tub probably would have vibrated but the bathwater would not have come sluicing over the top. It would have been more exciting than vacationing in the Poconos.

15

Triple Witching Day

I N THE INDEX options trading pit, Halloween came four times a year, always on the third Friday of March, June, September, and December. That's when floor traders or specialists like me would wake up and go to work not knowing whether we would make our big score—or be annihilated. While stock index options expire every month, it is only four times a year that they expire along with stock options and stock index futures—the three witches that have caused these days to become known as "triple witching expirations."

Compared to the triple witching days, all the other option expirations added up to no more than dress rehearsals. Sure, one could make money whenever options expired, but the real heavy, serious bucks came to us—or slipped through our fingers—on those third Fridays in March, June, September, and December.

Everything that took place on those days seemed magnified: Trading volume, price swings, spreads, profits, losses, whatever, were either the biggest, greatest, widest, deepest, tallest, fattest—or all of the above.

Obviously, those of us who scored stuck around for the next one; those who were wiped out, at once or incrementally, left the game forever. They are just blurs in my memory bank. I don't even remember most of their names; that's how fast they came and went.

Because of the way Spear Leeds Kellogg/Investors Company was set up by this time—eight specialists in eight positions with eight microphones and sixteen clerks—it was nearly impossible to take a day off from work. When you trade in stock index options, you can't very well put orders aside and take care of them the next day. It's not plumbing supplies that are being bought and sold. Finding people to sit in for you is out; I've never heard of an office temp trained as a specialist. Perhaps if full job automation comes, there will be options specialists trained as office temps.

The only legitimate way of taking time off is to Find God, but even that's likely to be challenged on grounds that God has Infinite Patience and can damn well wait till the closing bell. A death in the family is immediately suspected to be a lie, and a request to take off must be accompanied by documentation such as the relative's obituary, a note from the undertaker, a mass card, or funeral-service program. I once witnessed a clerk trying to use two dead flowers as evidence that he had been absent for a funeral.

Being hard-nosed wasn't limited only to Spear Leeds; it extended to all the other specialist firms as well. Some could be real bastards about it. In one case, a friend's employer called TWA to make sure the individual was on the manifest of a plane, which had landed too late for her to make it down to the Exchange, and wasn't just squeezing out an extra vacation day.

Floor legends have sprung up as a result of this Spartan policy. The latest version has a Bear Stearns options trader called Marty finally getting his boss to give him ten days for needed R and R. The proviso is that Marty's got to call in every day to make sure he's not needed. So Marty goes to Club Med in Fiji, about as far away as possible, but true to his word, on day one he trudges ten miles through the tropical jungle to get to the nearest public phone center. It is 3:00 A.M. in Fiji. He waits another thirty minutes for the call to be put through. It's hot, humid, and Marty's bones hurt. Finally, the connection is made. At that precise moment, his boss is putting up a very important trade: "Hiya, Marty here. What's up?" "Busy!" his boss snaps. "Call me back in an hour," and hangs up.

Once when I wanted a couple of days to attend my stepsister's wedding in California, Ron Shear asked, "What day is the wedding?" I said, "Friday," to which he replied, "Then you can have Friday off." I said, "But I'm in the wedding party; there's a rehearsal Thursday." But Ron was already miles ahead of me. "Shit outta luck, if you can be a whizbang options trader at age twenty, I'm sure you're smart enough to figure out how to be in a wedding in less than a day." Friday only, take it or leave it, appeal denied.

Ron felt that to lessen his resolve would only invite anarchy. He hadn't banked on the specialist's innate ability to spot a trade in any situation. Frankie Borenzo one day asked for a Friday off, but Ron refused, saying John Mulroy had first dibs. It happened that John's throat was so bad, not even the microphone helped. He looked so dreadful, so anemic, that some of us were seriously considering taking him over to Beekman Downtown Hospital for a blood transfusion. Frankie rushed over to John and offered him a hundred dollars not to take the day. Mulroy turned him down flat. "Two hundred?" countered Frankie. "Two-fifty," John whispered. "Sold!" yelled Frankie. The next week Mulroy was sore, not because all Frankie wanted was a long weekend in Florida, but because he probably could have held out for five hundred.

The story is told of a broker who ran up to the specialist in Spectra-Physics and tried to get a better price for his customer. The specialist refused to budge. "No discounts today. Full price or nothing." Noticing that the specialist looked stressed out, the broker tried again: "I'll throw in some of my Valium." At this, the specialist called over to a reporter, "Print this trade!"

I don't know who first came up with the phrase "triple witching," but whoever did had to know something of the occult. There was no way not to get spooked, and the spookiest in my mind were the arbitragers, the program traders.

Faced with having to close out their stock/futures positions— with their futures turning into cash, they'd have nothing to hedge their stocks with—the arbs on those four days would go on a spree, buying and selling millions of shares of stock, roiling the waters, and setting off those violent swings that some experts claim led to the crash of 1987.

Typical during my time as an AMEX trader was the triple witching day of March 21, 1986. What happened then was characteristic of what transpired on other TWDs, and an exaggerated version of life on "normal" trading days.

That morning I walked into the coatroom to change into my Reeboks. It was freezing outside. Two traders came in together, coatless and shivering. They were locked into playing a kind of "chicken" game with each other.

Every winter they'd see who could go the longest without an

overcoat before coming down with bronchitis, flu, or worse. They'd try to trick each other by calling the night before, one of them saying something like, "Okay, I give up. It's supposed to be twenty below zero tomorrow with the wind-chill factor," whereupon both would pledge to wear a coat. Of course, neither would, figuring that the other guy would show up coatless. Finally, just as their lungs were set to collapse, their wives would blow the whistle and the game would be up till next year.

I went up to the rejected-trade room to try and correct a grievous mistake I made the day before when I effectively blew one hundred thousand dollars. My mood lightened somewhat when I saw a Merrill Lynch clerk standing on the edge of his booth, valiantly trying to subdue a marauding pigeon that somehow had gotten inside the building. Panicked, the bird kept dive-bombing the Merrill Lynch clerks, while they stood swatting away at the pigeon with a broom handle. As I left, the clerk yelled out, "Don't eat the chicken fricassee in the cafeteria today!"

I next walked down the stairs to Harry's to join the unofficial breakfast club of all the specialists. Most were dressed for the occasion, in their most comfortable work clothes. They'd never make *GQ*, *M.Inc*, or *Esquire*. Never stylish to begin with, on expiration day they would revert to utter garishness. I had long ago switched to disposable clothing. For some of the guys, triple witching was like Mardi Gras in New Orleans. They could dress down with impunity and no one would bat an eyelash. For example, Bruce and Duffy both happened to wear Day-Glo ties emblazoned with witches. John Mulroy wore a Jackson Pollock–style hand-painted tie on a shiny satin turquoise shirt and two-toned wing-tipped shoes that must have been the rage of Wall Street in 1927.

Elisa Fromm, a serious, thirtyish specialist, opted for clothing more suitable for desert warfare. All that was missing was the camouflage netting. *Tres chic.*

As I arrived, Dominick and Bruce had their usual expiration-breakfast battle over what to eat. One ordered a rare hamburger ("Gotta get a protein fix!") and a chocolate Yoo-Hoo, while the other asked for fresh fruit. This prompted the first to arbitrarily cancel the fruit, without asking the guy's permission, and tell the waiter, "Bring my friend here some bacon and eggs, instead."

The "friend" howled, "No way, asshole, I'm on a diet!"

"Not while you're standing next to me, you're not," Bruce said. "Listen, pal, fruit makes you piss a lot, and I'm not gonna cover for you while you trot off to the john every half hour. Fruit's wimpy. You gotta get yourself some male hormones."

This led to a round-robin discussion on nutrition and how best to get through another expiration day. Everyone claimed to be an expert and, of course, had a surefire formula. They ranged from breakfast cocktails (vodka with fruit juices) and chili dogs and omelettes drenched in Tabasco sauce, to Milky Ways washed down by Orange Crush and Dick Gregory's Bahamian liquid diet. Elisa always ended the food discussions with some totally disgusting fact she had just read in the "Science" section of the *New York Times*, saying such things as, "Did you know that chickens are packed in their own urine?"

With the topic of food pretty much exhausted, talk switched to the trader's second-favorite subject, sleep, or lack thereof. Another pit trader, Mike, sat down at our table for a few minutes with his bottle of Flintstone vitamins and was doling them out. I asked for two Dinos and a Barney; Mike would never give anyone his Freds.

Traders have to hit the line running at precisely 9:30 A.M.

With so much money at stake, it's just not possible to sit out the first couple of rounds or take a couple of trades just to get warmed up. If sleep could be traded as a commodity, I have no doubt it would command over a hundred dollars an hour if it were offered right before the opening, when traders display most of their accumulated exhaustion. Paradoxically, they will leave the floor at the end of trading exhilarated.

As a clerk new to the Exchange, I'd once asked Arthur Hartigan—a floor broker who is seen weekly during the opening sequence of Louis Rukeyser's "Wall Street Week"—why he crammed sixty pens and sharpened pencils into his jacket's breast pocket.

"I've had this recurring nightmare over the past twenty years that my clerk hollers down from the balcony with the biggest order of my life. I reach for a pen to write it down and there aren't any. I lose the account."

I said to myself, "This guy is really nuts."

A year later, I no longer thought so. Not after hearing the crew recount some of their nightmares. Mulroy had a doozie: "I jumped out of bed and in my half sleep thought the TV set was the market minder and I couldn't see anything, but everyone else could and was trading against me." This prompted Davy's "I heard the alarm clock go off and picked up my Tensor light like a phone, trying to get a futures report form Chicago." "Big deal," said Walter, "what's so unusual about that? Suppose I told you I actually wrote trades on the phone pad on our night table?" *That* impressed them.

"Tell you how to get rid of nightmares," Donny volunteered, while continuing to do the crossword puzzle. "Before you go to sleep, think of ten parts of the human anatomy with three letters . . ."

"Like A-R-M?" I volunteered.

"Yeah, but don't start now or you won't have any parts left for tonight."

Predictably, that set us off. By the start of trading, we'd gotten the other nine—leg, hip, toe, lip, rib, jaw, gum, eye, and ear.

Back upstairs, this day, on my way to the XMI pit, as I walked past post 11, I noticed what at first looked to me like a dead beaver hanging off the top market minder. "Hey, Richie, whose cat died?" Without looking up from his note pad, the quote reporter said, "That's no cat, it's Jack's toupee. His partners offered a thousand dollars to whoever captured it first."

Richie asked me if I had heard that Al Abbate had announced his retirement but that he had set no date for his departure. Nice guy. No, I hadn't heard. I liked Al, one of the long-time "two-dollar brokers," like my pal LaBadia. "Yeah," Richie went on, "some guys say it's the end of an era. I say it's the end of an earache"—a dig at Abbate's constant bantering. "Yesterday was his last official trading day, and the boys sent him telegrams from all the dead presidents, wishing him luck and all that crap. He shuffled through a stack of these things and asked, "Where's Reagan's? He died five years ago, didn't he?""

Abbate *was* an institution, no doubt about that. He had been the butt of many a practical joke—but he told me about one played on someone else that is already part of the folklore and will be told and retold whenever old traders get together. To fully savor the careful planning and execution that went into this caper, bear in mind that this particular trader had taken only one personal day off in twenty-five years of loyal service to his customers.

So on this, his *second* day off, the trader decided to sleep late. At 8:00 A.M., the phone rang. It was a realtor inquiring what time the open house began. He jumped out of bed, opened the curtain, and saw a big "For Sale" sign on his front lawn. At nine sharp, the front door bell rang and there stood the upholsterer with a crew of five to pick up all the furniture. Over their burly shoulders, he espied a used-car dealer sizing up his Audi 5000. In pajamas, he ran out the door in time to see his hedges being trimmed to knee height. It kept getting worse. A dozen roses arrived for his wife, no card enclosed, and then the aluminum siding people drove up.

His buddies on the floor made sure the poor victim got the bills for everything, and he never took another day off after that. Understandably.

As I rounded the corner of post 11, I spied a sign-up sheet for a seal-clubbing outing. How sick, I thought. Just then Andy Schwarz of American Specialists, Inc., came heading in the opposite direction. "You like it?" he giggled. Then I remembered Andy had this running feud with one of his clerks, Diane, an ardent environmentalist who would drive people crazy by slapping Greenpeace stickers onto anything that moved, including traders. Lately she'd been on a "save the whales" kick, distributing petitions. That clearly demanded a Schwarzian response, and so he came up with the seal-clubbing orgy. The ads asked for signatures and "choice of weapon." Most were predictably crude: sledgehammers, pick axes, crowbars, meat cleavers, and so forth. Only one person was witty enough to write in, "Cafeteria food, a slow but sure death."

As I made my way into the pit, past the sign reading "Move It or Lose It," a new one had gone up overnight: "More Hugging, Less Mugging." Over where Larry Trainor would shortly be wielding his new makeshift anger-banger, the clerks had adjusted the hostility index, a cardboard half-moon-shaped dial with a moveable red arrow the clerks had designed to register tension levels. The market opening was still fifteen minutes away, but already someone had moved the dial to the number 10, for expiration Friday.

I checked the clocks. The futures markets had opened up ten minutes before, at 9:15 A.M.—an hour earlier in Chicago. The news was not good.

Overnight trading around the world was going to give us a bad day. Tokyo and London were both down. There was renewed talk in Washington about rising interest rates and the growing trade deficit. Companies that were worried about junk-bond-financed takeovers were hunkering down, all of which worked against the Dow.

With five minutes to go till the opening of the market, futures were down four, indicating there'd be a gap opening—translated, stocks would open considerably lower than yesterday's close, with the Dow down as much as fifteen to twenty at opening.

What made it worse was that we had to wait. As an index based on averages, XMI couldn't start trading until fifteen of its twenty stocks were open. The oat-bran muffin I'd just finished minutes earlier sat in my stomach like a chunk of concrete. I was beginning to feel slightly nauseated just watching the futures bouncing around like Ping-Pong balls, while the order slips kept dropping on my podium. The pressure kept mounting. All we could do was wait while our order imbalances increased. The sells were outrunning the buys two to one.

I glanced over at Mulroy and he was wringing his hands, as if to crank up a little heat. I reached out; they felt cold and clammy. He was beginning to sweat, as was I. Given the fact that I was still trying to account for a hundred-thousand-dollar error from the day before, I was now losing twenty thousand dollars with every ticking second. I tried not to think about it and instead tried concentrating on some small stupid task like sharpening my pencil.

Finally, seven minutes later, I heard Ronnie yell, "Go! Go! Open!"—and suddenly, the place exploded with the roar of two hundred wild, starving pit-bull terriers—tethered far too long—in angry pursuit of their next four-legged meal. It was a fearsome sound that would send chills down the spine of anyone foolish enough to pick this day to visit the floor of the Exchange. There would be no letup, no lull, for the next six and a half hours. In the midst of this cacophony, amplified by the primordial screams of the mob facing us, it was my job to determine the price of millions of dollars' worth of options.

Upon entering the pit I had started with a mathematic model in my head that had to be scrapped the minute Chicago "spoke." Now I was doing my Flying Wallendas act on the high wire—without a safety net. I looked over at Ronnie. He was mouthing his favorite mantras: "The trend is your friend" and "Go with the flow." While I didn't know which way the trend was going, I sure knew the flow had turned into a flood.

There are more floor fights during expiration day than during normal trading days:

RON:　　Hey, Ralph, look at those two guys fighting. Shouldn't we call a floor official?
RALPH:　Stay out of it. Worry about your positions. (*Looking at fight*) But I'll put a hundred bucks on Glenn.
RON:　　Make it two and you've got a bet.
RALPH:　Deal! I gotta go and sell some futures. (*To clerk*) Chris, keep watching that fight and let me know who wins.

Eleven o'clock. No letup in trading. Suddenly Elisa was standing one step below me in the pit. Handing me a pair of scissors, she pointed at a set of stitches in her hand, which she had gotten from an injury in her kitchen the previous week, and commanded me, "Take out my stitches." "You gotta be kidding," said I, looking at the ugly red welt of ten stitches in the palm of her hand. "They're itching like hell and I've got no time to go to the doctor. Just do it!" My clerk, Julie, poured some Perrier over it as I snipped away. As an afterthought, I called on a trader, a former M.D. who had been the head of kidney dialysis at Mount Sinai Hospital, and had him come over and inspect the surgery. He approved and trading continued.

The first line of defense against flagging energy is a quick sugar fix. If your clerk so much as appears sluggish on expiration day, the unwritten rule of the house is: "Get down to Stanley's— *quick!*"

Stanley is the candy man Sammy Davis, Jr., *didn't* have in mind. He runs the cigar stand with complete candy counter. It's just down the steps at the edge of the floor, so a round trip takes only a minute. It's well worth the seventy cents (Stanley has a bit of a markup problem) because one wrong entry on the trading sheets can cost upward of ten thousand dollars, one subtraction error can lose you a month's profits.

On a day like this I once blew ten thousand dollars by going to the bathroom. I'd left the pit for thirty seconds and my clerk duplicated a trade after failing to take an order off the rack.

It's a rough business. There's no "error account" in which you can bury your mistakes. Even if your clerk is a perfect screw-up, the Exchange rules allow no exceptions: It's your mistake, so you eat it. Your only recourse is to keep trading and hope to make your money back on someone else's loss.

On my clerk Julie's first triple witching day, she was sent out for a chocolate bar but came back with a granola chew. I sent her back for a couple of Three Musketeers. They seem to give the quickest jolt. Hershey bars aren't bad, but Nestle's Crunch and M&Ms take forever. Trouble with subsisting on candy bars and experiencing those sugar highs all day is that, come evening, you're likely to go into insulin shock and pass out.

Speaking of nourishment, Ron got a call during that crazed day from George, the owner of Towers Deli restaurant on Greenwich Street, where the firm orders take-out food. Seems somebody up at Spear Leeds had forgotten to pay last month's five-thousand-dollar lunch bill, and he was given the old runaround. In turning to pick up the phone, Ron missed participating in a big trade that could have made him a couple grand. Understandably pissed, he canceled the charge account, called George some names, and slammed the phone into the side of the pit.

"No one's getting burgers today," he roared, "you're on your own." Then, sensing a growl of dissension rising from the floor of the pit, he backtracked: "Maryanne, order twenty pizzas." Perhaps it was just as well that Ron was in a snit.

On another Bad Day at Black Rock, months earlier, when the market dropped twenty points in the first half hour and I was out fifty thousand dollars, then another twenty by 11:00 A.M., triggering the program traders, my forgetting to order lunch almost landed me in the hospital with food poisoning.

With the firm buying all our members lunch, we usually would write out our selections by 10:15 on index cards and hand them to the clerks. But on that morning, things got so busy so fast that we forgot all about ordering food.

By 1:00 P.M. that day, we were starving. Suddenly, "Devo," Bobby Schneider's clerk, who was with another firm, showed up with a huge steaming container of white-clam-sauce linguine— and a couple of forks. He had felt sorry for us. We were so famished by then, we didn't think twice about using other people's eating utensils or drinking out of used straws.

We slurped down what we could before getting back into the trenches. The pit was redolent of sweat, and people were tripping over each other and making a holy mess out of the place and themselves. The market closed down sixty-five points. Everybody lost money except for Frankie, who somehow managed to come out ahead. "He is the Amazing Kreskin, while you little people are only human," another specialist announced.

At five that afternoon, on the IRT local heading uptown, I suddenly felt this excruciating pain in my abdomen. I doubled over and had to be helped off the subway at Astor Place. I don't remember how I made it up to my apartment. I was sure I was coming down with appendicitis. On my way to the bathroom I switched on my answering machine. It was Mark, calling from the hospital. He had food poisoning. There were other calls that night. Everybody in the pit who'd dipped into the linguine was down over the next two days. Next time Devo came around proffering food, I ran the other way.

At 4:15 the closing bell rang, but on this day nobody heard it over the rush to close out positions. Time tends to get distorted when you are working under such incredible stress and pressure. On slow days it seemed the morning would never end; on days like this I'd open the options at 9:30 A.M., look up, and find it was time to close.

It was so chaotic that at one point near the end, Larry Trainor and I were both tethered to the same phone line, he selling and me buying the same futures. Steve, the wire clerk, was on an open line, placing the orders with the CBOE in Chicago, and was even more addled than the two of us. He also got himself snarled up in the phone cords. He was our third wire clerk in four months and would not be the last. The first wire clerk that year, Fred, lasted forty-eight hours, having run out of the pit sobbing after being verbally abused by three specialists. The second, Randy, really wanted to succeed but by the third week had developed a speech impediment. I didn't know whether we'd been the cause of it or if it was a childhood affliction he thought he had conquered. In any event, I know he didn't stutter when I hired him.

Finally it was over. We assessed the gains and losses—more of the latter. If only trading were a board game, the rules would be so simple:

1. Let your profits run.
2. Cut short your losses.
3. Buy your options cheaply.
4. Sell them high.
5. Don't be afraid to go ballistic trying to accomplish 3 and 4.
6. Whoever ends up with the most money by 4:15 wins.
7. If you lose all your money and owe others, you can't play again till you make good.
8. If you break even, come back tomorrow.

I dragged my tired bones down to Harry's to find Ron. I wanted a raise. I was getting a base salary of only forty thousand dollars, and bonus time was still nine months off and I couldn't wait. I was making a million bucks a year for the firm. "How much do you want?" he asked, stirring his drink. I hadn't thought about that. I blurted out, "Sixty!"

"Done," he said, sliding back his chair and getting up to join friends at the bar. "Have a good weekend."

"Dammit," I said to myself, "that was too easy. Why does everything happen so fast around here?"

I should have asked for twice as much.

16

The Day the Carousel Broke Down

FUNNY HOW, AFTERWARD, you remember where you were at what time and what you said, to whom you said it, and in what context.

For me, the moment of truth arrived at precisely 4:21 P.M., EST, Monday, October 19, 1987—"Black Monday." The futures market had been closed six minutes when I turned to Frankie Borenzo: "Do you think I can get Aetna to cover some of these losses? Surely they'll consider losing a million bucks in less than two hours an act of God."

Up until then, it had been a terrific year. Ten months earlier, XMI had become the American Stock Exchange's flagship product. We were trading an average of thirty-five-thousand contracts a day, well above any of the Exchange's stock-option contracts.

My firm had gone from eight to ten specialists. Clerks were promoted as quickly as they could be moved up the ladder. In one week alone, I hired eight of them. It was like the Battle of the Bulge in World War II, when cooks were handed M-1 rifles and told to kill.

Going to NYU at night gave me a leg up on other recruiters. As I was starting to nod off in class after a hectic day on the floor, I'd keep half an eye cocked, talent spotting for students who always had their hands up. After class I'd come up to them: "Give the questions a rest. Wanna work on Wall Street?" About twenty of my clerical recruits went on to get seats on the Exchange; not having been there long enough to get clobbered by the crash, they are all still there, as specialists, traders, and brokers.

One day we ran so short of clerks that I went next door on Trinity Place to the NYU Stern Graduate School of Business, stood on a table in the cafeteria, and announced, "Who wants a job on the floor of the AMEX and can start now, this instant?"

Two students followed me out the door. On the short walk over, I asked each, "Are you a lefty or a righty?" Both righties, they would work down at Larry's end. And: "By the way, you ever been in jail?" They hadn't, meaning they could be bonded. By the end of the day the two greenhorns were well into their new jobs of sending out reports. The only setback was when one of the students got splattered after a tinfoil ketchup packet found its way under Larry's anger-banger and exploded to the refrain of "Where (bang) is the goddamn (bang) lunch (bang)?" I told the guy to go to Macy's, buy their most expensive suit, and we'd reimburse him.

Another sign of how high we were riding was the rising divorce rate. The old bromide "for richer or poorer" was obviously written by someone poorer: Every week, a new name would be added to the unofficial roster of the "Vista Hotel Party Club," as we referred to guys who'd been thrown out of their homes.

They weren't bad guys; they just came into too much money too fast, and stayed out too long after the close of trading. "It's not that I didn't ask my wife to come in, but . . ." replaced the more banal "My wife doesn't understand me."

Overheard at Harry's: "You shoulda stayed in the house. My lawyer told me to move into the rec room in the basement . . ." and "My accountant told me to file this year to get a deduction," and "Mine told me to wait till next year, that I'm making too much this year." (Oh, how prophetic!)

Crazy Harry (no relation to Harry's Bar) had gotten tossed out of his house in Port Jefferson and had taken an apartment in midtown. One night he and his buddy were pub-crawling all over town until 2:00 A.M., when Harry dragged himself out of his favorite, the Kit Kat Club, and plopped down in the back of his regular limo out front. He went out like a light. The driver—not apprised of Harry's nonmarital status—dutifully drove the two hours out to the north shore of Long Island. He helped Harry to the front door and even tried opening the door for him with the keys Harry handed him. None worked. The ensuing racket brought Harry's estranged wife downstairs. She had to remind him that he'd been living in the city for the past three months. I told him the next day that it was a good thing he hadn't brought along his "date."

They say it's not history that repeats itself but historians who do. Insofar as the crash of 1987 goes, the historians are already wrong when they say it began on "Black Monday." It actually got underway four days earlier, Thursday the fifteenth. With less than an hour remaining in the trading day, none of us were alert enough to see what was really coming down.

At 3:30, the Dow began to slip, up to then having been down only four points. I looked at the clock, slightly apprehensive. Ron Shear turned to me. "Those bastard 'suits' are gonna slam 'em before we get outta here." I knew who he meant—the young guys in the uptown trading rooms who liked to wile away slow afternoons playing PacMan on their PCs. Were they about to play with our lives?

Ron was right. The market that Thursday closed down 57.61. Not too bad; it could have been worse. As I said, at the time none of us gave the drop much thought. It was a yo-yo world and besides, you couldn't go too far wrong sticking to the maxim "Buy low, sell high." Yet . . .

Yet, with Wednesday's drop factored in, Ron reminded me, we were now down 152 points since Tuesday. So on Thursday afternoon, as I left the floor, I remember telling him, "Some days you're the bird and some days you're the windshield."

On Friday, the Dow dropped another 130 points, but a buying flurry at the end of the day narrowed the loss to "only" 108, before the weekend. We all breathed a little easier. We shouldn't have.

Because it mirrors the overall performance of the market, the XMI option is not only an excellent portfolio-insurance tool but, if used properly, an early-warning detection device as well. Had we been more alert, less stressed-out, maybe we would have seen the tsunami starting to build that would come crashing down on us the following week. During that last half hour on Friday I screamed for Ron to come and help me with all the orders. We were both trading December XMI call options now, and I heard him trading the same option series at 11¼—$1,250 for one contract—while I was trading with Bear Stearns at 8½—$850.

Something didn't click. I leaned over to him and hoarsely yelled, "What the hell . . . which option is *that?*" It might as well have been a whisper; he could hardly hear me over all the hollering and fighting. He whipped around and screamed, "The 25's!"—meaning the December 425 calls. That's what I was afraid was happening. We were both trading the *same* option, $275 apart. I screamed back, "This isn't fucking Chicago! We can't trade this option at two different prices!" Clearly, things had gotten completely out of control. "So you buy 'em and I'll sell 'em! I dunno anymore, just trade!" he hollered right into my ear.

Afterward, a bunch of us headed down to Harry's Bar. It was time for the drinking hour. I've never figured out whether traders behave more obnoxiously when tanked up than do the "suits" because their work is more stressful or because they've had a three-hour head start cranking up their blood-alcohol levels. Traders usually hit the bar soon after the closing bell, unlike the suits, who, because of all that research, usually don't get off work till seven or eight.

The biggest difference that I've noticed is that traders make it home, to a hotel, or to a friend's house, generally in one piece. They're much tougher and more concerned about keeping in shape for tomorrow's battles. Because they're not into floor combat the way we were, the suits aren't as careful and tend to be more accident prone. From time to time when walking through the World Trade Center before 6:00 A.M., I'd noticed a couple of well-dressed dudes passed out on the floor of the concourse with their eight-hundred-dollar shoes missing and their pockets cut out.

That Friday, at about 8:00 A.M., EST, Reuters had reported that Iranian gunboats attacked a U.S.-flagged oil tanker in the Persian Gulf. By the time the markets opened, the incident had escalated to the point where there was a likelihood of war breaking out any minute.

Pete LaBadia, frenzied as usual, came rushing into the pit clutching a fistful of sell orders, quip at the ready as always.

"How do you fight guys on camels wearing something from Macy's White Sale? With tanks or slingshots?" Before I could answer, he was swallowed up by the swarm of traders.

He didn't know it then, but the events of October 1987 would be the beginning of the end of his long career as a "two-dollar broker." It would drive out of the market, perhaps for good this time, the so-called small investor and make LaBadia more dependent than ever on large-bloc trades. But with more institutional orders being rerouted to autopilot, program trading, and automatic-order execution systems, the LaBadias were beginning to be irrelevant. For many, the collapse of the junk-bond market in 1989 would be the final straw. By early 1990, Pete and many others like him weren't making enough to cover their business and living expenses.

"Did you know," he asked me around the time he quit the AMEX, "that the word *broker* is derived from the Saxon word *broc,* or misfortune?"

Wall Street can cope with wars—indeed, it seems to positively thrive on them—because military showdowns bring out both the panic sellers and the buyers of opportunity. Everybody wins. Rumors pose a problem because there's so much uncertainty attached and refutation or confirmation is often slow in coming.

The Reuters report that Friday was just that, a report. No confirmation from the White House or Teheran. Wall Street did not take it too seriously because, by eleven o'clock, the Dow was off only seven points. Clearly, no one was yet running for cover on the strength of a hit-and-run naval action in the Strait of Hormuz.

During my years on the floor, I figured Ronald Reagan had died no fewer than thirty-seven times, not counting assassinations, bouts of pneumonia, and acute memory loss. Bush had died five or six times; former Federal Reserve head Paul Volcker had had several fatal heart attacks. Wall Street kills off U.S. presidents at least once a month. The character assassins are usually the foreign-currency traders on the COMEX, two blocks away at the World Trade Center.

A really smart independent trader, Michael Schwartz, taught me how to check out these rumors. He runs to the nearest phone, calls his mother, and asks her to turn on the radio. Used to her son's frequent calls, she no longer asks why. She tells him what songs are playing, and if he's a good boy and promises to come over for dinner, she'll probably throw in a ski report. Mike figures that if the president were *really* dead, they'd be playing a funeral dirge and doing nonstop remotes all over the world.

Otherwise, we would have to wait for a confirmation on the broad tape, which might take as long as a half hour. In those thirty minutes, a person can lose his shirt trading, under the assumption "dead until proven alive." The news confirmations are models of deadpan brevity: "President Bush was just seen petting Millie on the way to the Oval Office." Then the market comes roaring back.

If Reagan so much as sniffled, the market would start dropping and the boys at the COMEX would have turned it into pleurisy before you could holler "Sold!" But when he was diagnosed for colon cancer, they were a great deal more circumspect. It took Bethesda *three* days to make sure. Unbelievable. We're a country that can develop film in one hour, but we need three days to do a biopsy on the most important American.

Those were just little ten- and fifteen-point dips for Reagan catastrophes. Of course, Bush is worth twenty-five to fifty points because of Vice-President Dan Quayle. (Floor joke: "What are the Secret Service's standing orders in case Bush is assassinated?" "Shoot Quayle.")

It got so bad that you had to be skeptical even about actual news reports. The pool reporters at Reuters—the Kelly Girls of pack journalism, as we sometimes referred to them—were not always on top of things, and as the week slogged toward Friday, they would sometimes oversimplify the news. Such as the day "Fried-Foods Frankie" (Borenzo), having taken a huge bite of his usual light lunch—bacon-cheeseburger, fries, potato chips, and onion rings with enough grease to lift the pencil marks from the Formica podium—looked up and saw moving across the tape: . . . THE U.S. FIRED A NUCLEAR WAR MISSILE . . . He spit half his burger at me, choked on the other half, grabbed my shoulder, and began pointing at the broad tape. I read the report and grabbed all the position books—a record of who owned how much of what and at what price—and reached for the phone, ready to sell every future in Chicago. Seconds later, Reuters corrected itself by explaining the missile firing was part of a successful test.

With the market in decline and apocalyptic rumors abounding, it was the portfolio insurers who began, at 11:00 A M. on that fateful Friday, to dump the first load of S&P 500 futures, valued at $265 million. I didn't have to look at the clock. Michael Gann, the spread broker, was into holistic medicine and always stashed his one-liter plastic bottle of Evian underneath my podium. Just like I was taught in eighth grade to tell the age of a tree by its rings, I could tell the time by the level of the water in Michael's Evian bottle. The sixth ring meant eleven o'clock.

That afternoon, the portfolio insurers' dump truck collided with the large orders of the program traders, who automatically reacted to wild swings in the marketplace. The collision marked the start of the meltdown. By 3:00 that Friday afternoon, the XMI pit resembled the stands at a British soccer field gone mad. Julie said it reminded her of that night of the Who concert at Cincinnati's Riverfront Stadium, when several fans were trampled to death. I told her that was a bit of an exaggeration, as no one here was killed. Still, the physically smaller guys didn't have a prayer. They were simply run over. Some were actually swept out of the pit by this human tide and deposited like flotsam on the main floor, where they picked themselves up and charged in for a second pass. By the third pass, they had learned to grab at my shirt, even my leg, to make sure they had a trade before the tsunami dragged them out again. A few traders kept raising their arms, prompting broker Mark Meade to yell, "Put your hands down, we're not in school!"

Standing five clerks away from me was my co-worker Elisa Fromm, who'd come to the AMEX five years before from New York University, where she'd been a laboratory biologist. Luckily she was acquainted with animal behavior, but nothing had prepared her for this day. She was handling so many orders that she couldn't keep up with the volume and was too conscientious an employee to walk off the job. Buried by paper, verbally assaulted by a bunch of screaming lunatics, poor Elisa couldn't even turn around to grab the phone. Her computer order screen was beeping and flashing like one of those penny-arcade Space Invader machines. I knew she'd reached the breaking point when I heard this piercing scream, "I quit!" I saw her throw up her hands as if she were surrendering to some unseen enemy. "Enough! I can't take it anymore!" she yelled, tears forming, saying over and over, "I don't care anymore, I can't do this anymore." But in the incredible din, nobody could hear her resignation, much less accept it.

A broker ran through the pit. "Elisa, how are the January forty calls? Sell five hundred." She replied that she'd buy a hundred and fifty contracts on her bid, and was about to tell him where he could sell the rest when he disappeared through the crowd, signaling to his clerk that he had sold all five hundred.

Yelling at the top of her lungs, she finally got the broker back, one minute and thirty DJIA points later. "You only sold a hundred and fifty!" she shrieked over the microphone. The broker became so enraged that he grabbed the microphone, pulling Elisa across a Plexiglas table. Her feet dangling in the air, she kept trying to tell him that he was not complete on his order. Larry Trainor saw the situation and jumped off the specialist platform. He grabbed the broker and threw him five feet backward into fifteen preoccupied traders. "Don't you know she's pregnant?" he bellowed. That area of the pit went silent, and Elisa knew her secret was out.

Trying to collect herself, she turned around and immediately collided with Frankie Borenzo, who was racing down the aisle trying to get to the futures wire. Splayed on the floor, she was gasping for air.

"Get her out of here!" another specialist hollered, and two clerks promptly carried her out of the pit—but not before some of them prudently removed from her clutches the position card and public order slips. Business first. The clerks dumped her on a bench in the Members' Lounge, yelling, "Someone get her a doctor!" on their way back to the pit. Hyperventilating and heading toward a state of shock, she couldn't speak. A member of the Exchange called the health services agency located on the tenth floor of the building—"Life Extension," also jokingly referred to by many of us as "Life Extermination." Diagnosing the situation incorrectly, he explained, "There is a lady down here having an asthma attack; send someone quick."

A physician and a nurse came rushing down to their "asthma" patient. While Elisa was trying to muster up enough air in her lungs to breathe, her arm was being prepped for a needle. "It's only adrenaline for your asthma, honey," the nurse explained. In absolute horror, Elisa gathered what she thought was her last breath, and blurted out, "Stop—I don't have asthma; I'm pregnant!"

They immediately switched gears, putting away the needle and other paraphernalia. What followed was perhaps Life Extermination's most sensible treatment ever: They walked her outside, put her in a cab, and sent her to the obstetrician. A Sonogram and three hundred dollars later, the doctor told her that no permanent damage had been done; however, she should cut out the roughhousing at work or find another job.

Back in the pit, push-and-shove had come to knock-'em-down/drag-'em-out fistfights between ordinarily civilized brokers, who were just trying to work their way through the frenzied throng. One sight I'll long remember was that of Peter Orloff, AKA "Grandpa Executioner." He was called that either because of his advanced age (fifty-two) and his adroit handling of difficult trades, or because of his skill at cutting down with his left hook anyone standing in his way. I felt a tug on my sleeve. One of the newer clerks, Bob, whispered in all seriousness, "Can people get rabies?" When I asked why, he pointed at Peter foaming at the mouth. I said no, "But stay out of his way. He'll kill you."

When the 4:15 closing bell rang, as on triple witching day, nobody heard it over all the noise and confusion. Finally, a floor official had to run up the steps of the pit, screaming, "Stop trading! Next trade I hear gets a hundred-dollar fine!"

Damned if he didn't start doing just that, pointing at a couple of violators and screaming, "That's it! One hundred dollars! Illegal trade. Cancel it and get it off the tape!"

Finally, things began quieting down. I looked up at the clock. It was 4:25 and I burst into tears. It was the first time I'd ever cried on the floor. But I was so relieved that it was over. On a normal day, I'd trade about five thousand contracts. This day,

I traded twenty thousand just in the last forty-five minutes. And had made about two hundred thousand dollars.

I literally staggered out of the pit, soaked with sweat, my throat so raw I could barely whisper. As I was leaning over a table under the broad tape, trying to pull myself together, one of the brokers came up to me and laid a sympathetic hand on my shoulder. "Don't worry," he said, "it's only money." I looked up and smiled wanly. I hadn't the heart to tell him I had just had the best financial day of my life.

I joined the rest of the walking wounded downstairs at Harry's, which resembled a first-aid station that had run out of plasma, morphine, and bandages and was down to dispensing hootch to deaden the pain. Today, they weren't telling big-fish stories; too many had gotten away—and pulled the dock down with them.

Veteran traders and brokers said it was the worst day in Wall Street history—worse even, we were told by a couple of old brokers, than 1929. The difference between then and now was that, this time, the entire floor had pulled together and put aside all their differences and worked with the zeal and near-suicidal determination of warrior ants protecting their nest.

We told ourselves we had prevailed. There was nothing we could not do. We'd handled a record $1.37 billion in sell programs and we had survived to tell the tale.

Had we only known what lay in store the following week.

17

Black Monday

AFTER THAT TERRIFYING Friday, Monday morning started out bleakly. At 9:15, the XMI futures in Chicago opened down fourteen points, equivalent to seventy on the Dow. When the New York Stock Exchange specialists in the underlying stocks did not start trading their stocks at the market's 9:30 opening bell, rumors flew that they wanted to sell their own listings. That told us the market was headed south to the boneyard. By 10:30, a total of 175 NYSE stocks, including IBM, Sears, Exxon, and eight other Dow blue chips, still hadn't opened. This meant the specialists were either stalling or that there was a monumental sell-order imbalance for more people wanting to sell than buy. Soon after the opening of what would go down in history as "Black Monday," every firm on the floor was in way over its head. On the floor, we specialists only needed to keep one hundred thousand dollars on deposit in order to support our inventory. Actually, that was just a drop in the bucket, given the millions of dollars in options contracts we normally traded every day. The Federal Reserve Bank didn't allow us to finance any more than seventy-five percent with borrowed money. By mid-morning, we'd broken every rule regarding size of position, quote spreads, and capital requirements.

By 11:00 the Dow was down 206 points. As the market went into free-fall, an independent trader from Larchmont, New York, stood in front of me watching the screens and, as the tears streamed down his blood-drained face, continued to make transactions. With each downward tick of the XMI future, he was losing his house, cars, and all the money he'd put away for his kids' college education.

Inexplicably, trading slowed around noontime, even as the Dow continued to sink. It was during this lull that an attitudinal shift of seismic proportions was first detected. Index options trading clearly had been a young person's game. Many of us had become not just tough but arrogant and disrespectful of anybody over the age of thirty-five. With money coming out of every pore, we know-it-alls fancied ourselves invincible. Nothing could hurt us. A breed apart from the uptown traders, we may not have qualified as Masters of the Universe, but on the trading floor we were every inch as cocky and arrogant as Tom Wolfe's bonfire burners. "Take your cane and get outta here, old man!" we'd shout derisively at brokers in their forties and early fifties who were trying their hand in the XMI pit. "Go trade stocks out on the floor, where you're not gonna make any big mistakes." To a nice guy who wouldn't have hurt the proverbial flea: "Nice toupee, but you're too fuckin' slow, gimme your order!"

Now, on the big screens above us, that perfect world was disintegrating before our very eyes. The "old-timers" who had taken all our abuse didn't say anything; they didn't have to. It was all in their eyes. The Wall Street brats were getting theirs. What goes around, comes around. What the Lord giveth... Only we didn't know it yet. The idea of being wiped out was utterly foreign to us; our generation had never experienced, could not even envision, such a cataclysmic shift. We'd come of age at a curious time of post-Vietnam peace and prosperity. Reagan had told us the merits of supply-side economics, and we had reelected him to ensure the day would never end. In Chicago, insurance magnate W. Clement Stone, the arch-druid of PMA ("Positive Mental Attitude"), was going around saying, "See, you guys thought I was only blowing smoke." Hubris, no longer a pejorative, had become a quality much to be admired.

Continuing to avert the vacant-eyed stares of the hungry and homeless huddled atop steam grates, we whistled our way to work on the trading floors and in the counting rooms. Life *was* a cabaret, after all, and nothing succeeds like excess. From time to time, we'd meet with the Elders and talk about the market's cyclical behavior in purely academic and philosophic terms. Months of unbroken record growth in the bull market made us fat and complacent. From time to time a pessimist or two would surface in the business press to warn us that, unlike 1974, it's not the empty gas tank we should worry about but the overheating engine. We dismissed them as spoilsports.

Now, with the sky falling, we saw these veterans of past meltdowns walking around, concerned but not alarmed. They appeared to be in far better shape than we were. At the first sign that the market was unraveling, they instinctively hunkered down. No panic selling for them; no headlong rush into Krugerrands—gold stocks, maybe.

Some of them had seen it coming and invoked the law of probability by selling just in time. Others *said* they did, but not many of them were believed to be telling the truth. Among them was the irrepressible Donald Trump, whose inflated ego carried him a long way to best-sellerdom and served him so well until he, too, was brought down by Milkenomics, commonly known as debt.

So while the elders sat tight, we traders didn't. We *couldn't*. Given the ephemeral nature of the product and the tough rules governing options trading, we were so much more exposed, far more vulnerable to a quick wipeout. Unprepared for a reversal of this magnitude—no one yet called it a "debacle"—many of us that day simply caved in. We'd hoped the weekend would cool things down enough for the market to recover. No such luck. Now, a little over ninety hours later, it occurred to many of us that we actually might not survive. We sought out the Elders, and the questions we asked probably sounded awfully naive to people who really weren't that much older than we were.

"Does this kind of thing happen a lot?" "Is this what it's like when war breaks out or they shoot a president?" "Can't the Feds do anything?" "Is there an end to this sort of thing?" "When will we know it's finally over?"

They couldn't offer words of either wisdom or encouragement because, they said, "We haven't seen anything like this before." Small comfort. We grasped at the straws of moral support. "Relax, this is not the end of the world. Things will be normal again."

Relax? Tell that to a twenty-eight-year-old, Single White Male who has been pulling down over $400,000 a year, has to maintain a $750,000 six-room duplex on the Upper East Side, $800 monthly garage for his Porsche, a weekend "farmhouse" in Columbia County, and has just put a down payment on a thirty-foot sailboat docked at City Island. It would take some time before the disbelief of this day gave way to the reality that we would be nouveaux riches no more.

Never having known "bad times" on Wall Street, I couldn't imagine what they could be like. A good thing I didn't have time to ponder the question. With every twenty points the Dow sank, I lost another hundred thousand dollars. And it was dropping with the speed of a skydiver who'd forgotten to pack his parachute. My options position was enormous, and there was no way I could get out of it.

At 1:45 P.M., I called the Chicago Board of Options Exchange to check the futures market. I was told the traders had walked out, left the pit. As an AMEX specialist I wasn't allowed to leave. According to the rules, we are the "buyer and seller of last resort." I found myself sliding down behind my podium, slipping out of sight, *hiding*. Normally I would have been aggressively leaning over the top, signaling frantically, hollering, and *trading*; now I didn't want to trade. I wanted to do nothing, to be swallowed up by the floor. I wanted to disappear. There was no place to unload my inventory. I just had to watch and wait.

At 2:00 P.M., I couldn't take it anymore. The rumor mill was working overtime. Some of what was going around was bound to be true; too many people were spreading the exact same stories. Supposedly, L. F. Rothschild, E. F. Hutton, and Drexel were bankrupt. That didn't affect me as much as word that there was, at that moment, a bank run on Manny Hanny (Manufacturers Hanover Trust Company) and that customers were lining up around the block.

Dropping everything, I ran out of the pit and across the street to the Bank of New York and withdrew twenty thousand dollars. Grandpa had often told me that in a depression, cash is king.

I felt guilty about taking out the money. I didn't want to look in the security camera. It was as if the electronic eye were accusing me of not having confidence in the capitalist system, of which I was an integral part. But at that point it was beginning to seem more like every woman for herself. Camaraderie was being subsumed by personal survival. I caught myself wondering if there was any canned food in my apartment.

Back on the floor, I wasn't quite sure what to do with the money. Two hundred bills is a big stack and I didn't want to just plop it in my briefcase, which sits in the coat room. I tried my pocket, but the money was too heavy. Finally I turned and stapled the whole envelope to the inside of my jacket. My clerk asked, "Did you lose a button?" Putting the stapler down, I replied, "Something like that."

In the last half hour, the market plunged another 180 points. We were beyond the point of panic. Pain had given way to numbness. We stood in pairs trying to decipher the prices-turned-gibberish flashing on the Quotrons and market minders.

In order to save space on the digital computer screen, only the last digits of the stock or future are printed. I asked Frankie, "Do you think that International Paper is 64½ or 54½?" Frankie looked and said, "No, it's 34½ now." We didn't know what we were looking at anymore. Nothing made sense. You couldn't trust the Dow average because, back at noon, the ticker had already been over an hour behind. By the end of the day, when asked at what price an option could be bought or sold, the specialists were shaking their heads in confusion, muttering something like, "I really don't know," or "Beats the hell outta me." We were all open to suggestions.

It was all so bizarre. It wasn't like when the film breaks during the movie and everyone screams and curses while storming the projection booth. It was more like going to Madison Square Garden, expecting to see Wrestlemania starring Hulk Hogan when, suddenly, the Ice Capades comes on instead. You don't know what to make of it because you're too surprised to be angry. You ask the people sitting next to you for their opinion. Maybe you got the day or the time mixed up . . .

By the 4:00 P.M. stock-market close, there was no way to finance the staggering paper losses. I made my last trade of the day saying, "Sure, I'll buy it. I don't know if I can pay for it." As a specialist, I had to buy it at some price. It was particularly horrendous for those who had ridden the market down with long positions. The volume finally landed at 604.3 million shares. We no longer cared about breaking records.

Instead, we wondered if our employers were still in business. The fact that stocks didn't have to be settled for five business days scared the hell out of us, because million-dollar mistakes could be hidden in back-office computers for almost a week. More losses than reported were bound to continue showing up.

When I stumbled into the daylight that Monday afternoon, there were reporters waiting to get interviews and rack up dev-astation reports. I couldn't believe that they actually wanted suicide stories, but there were news photographers and TV cam-eramen strategically positioned throughout the area, hoping to see a distraught investor climb out onto a ledge, so they could tape his swan dive.

The only suicide I knew about was a guy who used to work at my old firm, who blew his brains out. He probably only lost one million dollars, a drop in the bucket, and on top of that, he was born rich. His friends say it wasn't the money but a terminal illness of some kind. The *Wall Street Journal* carried it in a one-paragraph note but, for once, the scandal-sniffing *New York Post* was out to lunch. A good thing, too.

The floor governors had barred the press from coming onto the floor. Somehow, a "60 Minutes" reporter had snuck in to record the chaos of desperate traders. It led to a postcrash policy change in the way guest badges were distributed.

By Monday's close, everyone on Wall Street had been affected by the 508.30-point market drop. Normally when a stock goes crazy it's because of a reported takeover or some type of reorganization rumor that results in large losses. At such times, only the partners and the traders worry about the solvency of their firm.

The floor clerks don't worry because, in the worst case, they can get a job with another firm, should theirs go belly-up. That happens more often than one would think. The Exchange employees just move from one post to the next as supervisors, reporters, and data clerks. The Exchange keeps paying salaries and providing benefits. They aren't affected by the fortunes or failures of the member firms. But on *that* day, everyone—down to the janitor—was wondering whether he still had a job. Over hot dogs at the Sabrett stand after work, a floor supervisor wondered if the Exchange was going to be in business the following day or if it would be restructed as downtown Manhattan's largest bowling alley.

Ironically, all that money really hadn't disappeared, regardless of what the *New York Post* headlined in its late edition. What nobody talked about was that a lot of guys made millions that day. For every trade that has a loser, there's got to be a winner. Compounding the losses for some member firms and specialists was human error resulting from people being overwhelmed by the sheer volume alone. Many trades never made it into the books; clerks backing up three trades in their heads would forget to post them; scraps of paper floated away into the heating system. Some hurried entries were so illegible and indecipherable they were simply tossed out.

The firms with large amounts of inventory in stocks would

have to wait several days to even determine the profits or losses, while those carrying options on their books would wait weeks and even months for prices to come back into line.

The only winners on the floor were some independent traders who had no responsibilities other than to their own accounts. Knee-deep in the carnage, those who did make out all right wouldn't admit it or else didn't stick around long enough to gloat.

Most of the guys who would still be around to fight the next day went down to Harry's. Those who were out of business went up to their clearing firms to see how much money they owed and if they would be able to close out their positions. The clerks remained on the floor, along with the sweepers, confirming trades and trying to clean up mistakes.

That night, half of Wall Street, it seems, was pulled over by cops on every major artery leading out of the city. After the first couple of hours of writing tickets, the cops gave up and went full time into accident prevention. If the guy was wearing a suit and had a vacant look on his face, eyes glazed, the officer would lean into the window and ask, "Stockbroker?" When the offender blankly looked up, the officer would cite his speed: "Sir, did you know you were going ninety in a fifty-five-mile-per-hour zone?" The broker would just say, "Oh," and the cop would warn him to slow down because there was black ice (a veneer of frost) on the roads. If they'd wanted to, they could have ticketed every other car coming out of the New Jersey end of the Holland Tunnel.

I figured I'd lost about $1.3 million of the firm's money because I'd been locked in, unable to move any of my inventory. Worse, I had to buy from everybody who wanted to sell, whether I wanted to or not. Up to then, the worst loss I'd ever sustained was $80,000.

I walked home from the AMEX in a zombielike state. I was so stupefied I walked right past the subway. I stopped at the local deli and picked up a quart of milk. Standing in line at the register, I stared at the one-dollar-bill in my hand. It looked strange to me, as if I was seeing it for the first time. I even thought, can I afford this?

The people in the store appeared distant and blurred, as if I were watching an Ingmar Bergman movie of someone else's life. I walked through Washington Square Park. People were walking their dogs. They appeared to be living the same lives as they had the day before. It didn't seem fair, when everything had gone so wrong in my world.

My street was blocked off with police cars. Hundreds of on-lookers were gathered around, trying to push through the barrier to get a better look. I asked a bystander, "Heart attack?" The guy answered, "Naw, sniper. Machine gun." Talk about a bad day!

I got to my apartment and turned on the TV. "Gilligan's Island" was on channel 5. It was almost comforting. It took me back to my childhood days, when I used to watch sitcoms after school. I got undressed and climbed into bed with a bowl of cereal. I spilled the bowl, and the milk ran all over the bed. I didn't care. I went to sleep.

It was 5:30 P.M.

18

Bring Out Your Dead

I WOKE UP AT four in the morning. I dimly recalled hearing the phone ring the night before, so I punched in the answering machine. There were a number of messages, the first of which was from Spear Leeds & Kellogg's Ralph Fogel, who sounded in pain. "Laura. I'll either be back in the pit tomorrow morning or in intensive care at Beekman Downtown Hospital." *Click.* That's what I love about traders. They get right to the point. There's nothing wishy-washy about them. They don't waste time on preliminaries or the social graces. You either buy or sell. You're either dead or alive. Only wimps call in sick. Ralph was no wimp.

An hour later I stumbled into the subway. I wasn't the only one going to work this early. Too spaced out to be my usual wary self—even though the gold-chain snatchers of the summer were long gone to Florida for R and R—I got taken by a token sucker, another one of the Reagan/Bush Administration's contributions to the quality of New York life.

I should have seen him standing there, outside the gate next to the turnstiles but out of the change clerk's sight line. One of the city's hungry and homeless, he did not look like a transit worker, but I couldn't be sure, given the city's quixotic minority-hiring policies. I entered the turnstile, put in my token, and waited for it to drop. It didn't. Just then the gum-chewer ambled over. "Stuck turnstile, ma'am. Use the gate instead." He held it open, and in my semicomatose condition I dropped another token in the bucket by his feet. As I walked down the platform, out of the corner of my eye I saw him bending down as if to kiss the turnstile. What he was actually doing was *sucking out* the first token, which was resting on the wad of gum he'd shoved into the slot earlier. I'd never seen a token sucker in action.

I suppose that if you're into communicable diseases, it's as good a way as any to earn some tax-free income. Beats pickpocketing for small change, as you'll never earn less than a dollar. In 1990, the Metropolitan Transportation Authority reported that the token suckers pocketed ten million dollars from unsuspecting New Yorkers, some of whom—like me—got taken twice. They'd sell the tokens at discount to subway riders waiting in line to buy tokens, or to unscrupulous newsstand owners (who would sell them at retail), or use them as currency to buy crack.

ı ı ı

Sometimes, after you've had too much to drink the night before, you wake up in the morning feeling terribly introspective. It was like that on that particular Tuesday, even though the strongest thing I had had was milk. I'm sure I wasn't the only one "thinking things over." For some time I'd been struck by the sharp contrast between the gleaming skyscrapers, the fancy cars, and the human misery of the street people I encountered on my way to work. This feeling only got worse once I entered the pit.

It was clear that the events of the past twenty-four hours had afflicted the comfortable, like me. I began to ask myself, what were we all *really* doing? Were we producing anything *useful*, delivering a value-added service that would benefit humanity? If I were a stock trader, I'd at least be generating *something*, at least a certificate that could be tucked away in someone's safety deposit box as part ownership in corporate America. But I was only trading money back and forth. For the first time, probably since the age of twelve, I began to feel that maybe, just maybe, I'd made a mistake. Maybe going to Hollywood and wanting to have my palm prints embedded in concrete at Mann's Chinese Theater would have made more sense. What if, instead, I *had* stuck it out at the University of Michigan?

Back I went to the killing fields. How many of these bleary-eyed people, I wondered, were carrying freshly minted résumés in their attaché cases? Had any of them lost as much as I had the day before? Aside from the grim, tired faces I encountered the minute I stepped inside the Exchange, what made this Tuesday different from other Tuesdays was that everybody seemed to be walking in slow motion. That, and the suspension of niceties. Not the usual, cheery "Good morning, how are ya?" but just a plain, unadorned grunt, "'Morn." Anyone saying anything different was met with hostile looks.

The only ones who seemed to know what they were doing that early in the morning were those clerks who knew, without having to be told, that they were now unemployed, or at least would be between employers. Like the true-blue hessians they were, they weren't going to let any grass grow between their toes or waste precious time commiserating with one another. There was work to be done. They strode purposefully from pillar to post, looking to reconnect. Many of them did, especially those who'd been around a long time and gone through earlier sudden bloodlettings, although never one as bad as Monday's.

I headed for what we called the D.K. room—*D.K.* meaning "Don't Know"—the repository of orphan trades, those thrown out by the computers as mismatched. On a normal day, sorting out these "orphans" might take, at most, twenty minutes and cost those responsible a couple of thousand dollars, a mere pittance. The carnage Monday afternoon must have been awful. By the time I got there, others had been at it for an hour or so. They'd still be there long after the opening bell rang, pawing through stacks of paper. We'd later be told that the cost of mistakes that day alone had totaled over five hundred thousand dollars.

Around 7:30, Elisa Fromm and Frankie Borenzo joined me. Elisa had made a miraculous recovery from her collapse on Friday. By pooling what we knew, we began tallying up the number of dead, wounded, and MIA's who'd be in or out of business at the opening. We questioned whether our firm would still be a player. I wondered whether I still had a job.

We asked each other what we were going to do if this were indeed our last day. Elisa said she was going to start a wallpapering business in New Jersey. I thought that was a smashing idea. "Why not start right now by gathering up all these unresolved trading notices? There are enough here to do a three-bedroom condo." "No," she shot back. "I'm going to hold out for junk-bond certificates. They're prettier; also made of better paper."

I said I thought I'd try teaching. Since I was already giving classes in portfolio hedging at the New York Institute of Finance four blocks away, I wouldn't even have to change subway stations. As for "Fried Foods" Frankie, well, he said he'd have to think about it. After all, he had been on Wall Street for over twenty years and knew no other profession. I told him he could always go into magic—an "in" joke. He had such an incredible knack for knocking off the smartest trades, consistently, that I told him I wouldn't be a bit surprised to see him turn his order books into fluttering doves.

At our daily breakfast meeting downstairs at Harry's, I pulled out my calculator and did some fast number-crunching, looking at today's opening positions and yesterday's devastation. "We're still in the game," I concluded. But for how long, I couldn't say. I figured we'd have to make back a couple of million by lunchtime.

I kept looking across the table at one of the traders. He looked different. Maybe it was a new suit. Then I narrowed it down to a haircut. Then I realized his hair had turned silver-gray *overnight!* Honest to God. I had heard that in combat, some people's hair has the equivalent of a heart attack; something weird happens to the follicles.

Most of the regulars filed in and sat down. Our usually tactless waiter knew well enough not to press food on us, and kept the coffee cups filled. We all got a little giddy comparing superlatives. Our costliest trading error, the widest market, the most violent floor fight, the fastest bankruptcy, biggest fistful of Tylenols consumed in a single gulp—that sort of thing. To the people at the next tables, we must have sounded like we were trying out submissions for the next *Guinness Book of Records*.

Next, we shifted to telling postwar stories. Who got drunk, who tried but couldn't, who slept the longest, who got the most heart-wrenching phone calls from well-meaning family members the night before. Especially the calls. Most of them came from Middle America, west of Hoboken. Either the media was doing a shoddy job explaining what triggered the debacle or there must have been a lot of people Out There who just couldn't fathom what sort of stupid fix their city-slicker cousins had gotten themselves into *now*.

We all seemed to have the same relatives because, in virtually every case, they proffered us tide-over money—a hundred dollars, five hundred dollars, even a thousand—money we knew they could scarcely afford to give away. They would not take no for an answer. We wouldn't accept. A standoff. How do you tell people you see perhaps once or twice a year that they'd be helping to pay the five-thousand-dollar-a-month apartment rent, or covering the lease on a BMW, let alone putting a dent in the firm's million-dollar losses?

Instead, we all lied: "Things will be fine, Mom. Sure, I'm okay." Strange. You wanted *them* to feel better, and now, after hearing it from you, they did.

"Don't believe what you see or read in the news media," the relatives now told their next-door neighbors, who told theirs, and so on. "We've got it straight from so-and-so, who's got an important job on Wall Street. It's just a 'correction.' Don't sweat it." (The farther one moved from the original point of contact, the more important so-and-so's job became). Herbert Hoover couldn't have been more convincing.

On our way up the stairs from Harry's, Frankie suddenly turned around and, out of nowhere, uttered a single word: "Barbecuing." Nonplussed, I looked at Elisa. Before I could ask what he meant by that, Frankie continued. "Hey, I can always barbecue for a living. I've had years of practice." Sure, said we, but how would he keep himself from eating up all the profits? "Oh, well," he added, "I'm sure I can think of something else by the end of the day."

At the XMI pit, our clerks were without illusions. The scales had fallen swiftly from their eyes. Some even talked of not waiting to be fired but quitting to go back to school. One clerk who habitually filched my *Wall Street Journal* before I had a chance to read it, now couldn't be less interested in the markets. Exuding charm from every pore, he clearly wanted something from me. Money? No, he wanted me to write a letter of recommendation to the admissions director of Fordham University.

In the faces of the new and inexperienced traders could still be seen the elation (or pain) of every trade. They hadn't yet developed a thick skin to disguise their feelings when they screwed up. Their faces were walking billboards for the other, older guys, to take advantage of—and did they ever! Those who survived the basic training did so because they learned how to keep a poker face.

But nothing had prepared them for this. I truly felt for them. The Trading Class of 1987 had arrived at the wrong time. Overnight, like hot air seeping out of a *Forbes*—Capitalist Tool balloon, all the glamor had gone out of working on Wall Street. Life had suddenly turned ugly. Why hadn't anyone warned them that what goes up must inexorably come down? One of them actually told me, "It seems so . . . *unfair!*"

As we assumed our battle stations on that grim Tuesday morning, I heard a doleful call on my left, "Bring out your dead! Bring out your dead!" More black humor from one of our resident pixies, Marvin, an independent trader whose morbid preoccupation with life and death—particularly death—was manifested by his carrying around a dog-eared paperback copy of Barbara Tuchman's *A Distant Mirror*, which offers a vivid account of the bubonic plague. He even *looked* like a funeral director. "Gee," he said, "if I only had a wheelbarrow today. Just think of the photo opportunity! Bodies stacked like cordwood . . ."

"Get lost, creep!" snarled Anthony Spina.

Just then, the opening bell sounded. Our expectations for a

turnaround were practically nil. Ralph Fogel sidled up to me. "No room at Beekman," he said laconically.

Thinking only of how I'd ever make up for that $1.3-million loss the day before, I leaned down to Frankie and said I felt like a prisoner up for heavy sentencing. No matter what came down now, it couldn't be good. Then, out of the corner of my eye, I saw them, the grim reapers. "Vultures at two o'clock," Frankie called out, having seen one too many World War II movies on the "Late Late Show," "check your gun sights."

Whenever the market got itself caught in the wringer, these ghouls in their Armani sharkskins (apt) and Turnbull & Asser shirts would show up, right at the trading post, checkbooks in hand, specialists in a new kind of LBO—the Large Bankruptcy Opportunity. All you had to do to become whole was to assign them a piece of your business.

"Does anyone need money?" they would go around silkily asking principals whose trading firms were teetering on the brink of insolvency. "Don't worry about paying us back, we're here to help." Sure.

Frankie Borenzo knew many of them well. They were former traders, some of them even ex-partners. They had been friends. Unlike Frankie, they'd packed it in, taken their money out (or cashed in the inheritance) to retire at forty. But as one of them told me, "Retirement sucks." So they came back in, this time to trade on the misfortunes of their former colleagues. They'd buy them out or broker them to other firms.

"Isn't it sort of early for these guys to show up?" Frankie asked Ron. "Do they know something we don't?"

"Remember," Ronnie said at the market's opening, leading the charge up San Juan Hill, "buy low and sell high!" So everyone started selling at the opening. Naturally, perversity triumphed as the market began a two-hundred-point rally.

We stood there, slack-jawed, not quite believing what we were seeing. We weren't alone. Up in the balcony, the cliché experts from the media—the reporters, pundits, and photographers who'd come to record the end of the financial world—now were scribbling fast and furiously about "the largest, fastest rally in financial history."

Scrambling, we went from being sellers to buyers, loading up on options contracts. Then, no sooner had we printed the last sale, the market spun around and began plunging, ten points at a tick. To say we were whipsawed is inadequate. Fifty, eighty, one hundred, one-eighty, two hundred—there was no letup. At minus two-fifteen, the market hiccuped and paused.

Between 11:00 A.M. and noon, trading was to be halted in eighty-three stocks. Some of them accounted for more than half of the XMI. Now we *really* didn't know what to do. We were back where we started from and had left off the day before.

At quarter to twelve, the chicken-fat brigade arrived, bearing the usual overstuffed and overpriced deli sandwiches. At $8.95 for a rare roast beef on rye, extra for the half-sour pickles, it was comforting to know that at least the debacle hadn't dampened the free-enterprise spirit of the Wall Street deli owners. Get it while you can . . .

I remember the moment. There was no more shouting or screaming or fighting. An eerie silence had settled over the pit, broken only by the sound of sandwiches being unwrapped. But who could eat? I happened to glance at the Quotron. At about ten minutes to twelve, the Major Market Index futures were starting to rally, while everything else seemed frozen in the down position. At first we paid no attention because, with just twenty underlying stocks, it's a small index. Also, it was hard to determine the going price of the index because some of the stocks had not traded for almost two hours. The old prices were still being averaged in with the current prices. Then we started borrowing each other's eyeglasses because we were so convinced that we weren't seeing the screens properly anymore.

After a few minutes everyone was pointing at the market minders and trying to decipher the sudden rally. Was International Paper *really* going up five points or were the green numbers finally running together and our eyesight slipping away with our minds? Procter & Gamble, Union Carbide, Merck were all going up so fast that the Quotron began to look like a taxi meter going down Park Avenue on a Sunday morning.

Something must have been taking place at the Chicago Board of Trade because, nine minutes after the Dow hit a low of 1708, it started running up past 1800. And the XMI futures were going up ten points at a tick.

Isn't this what happened back in 1929 after the House of Morgan pumped in money to prop up the market? To us, what was happening was nothing short of a bloody miracle—a fluke, maybe—but at this point, who dared trust even miracles?

"Is it real?" we asked one another. "What's *happening?*" No news. "Is there another rumor?" "No, let me guess. They just found out that Reagan is only fifty-eight . . ."

All the stocks that had closed that morning started to open. For me, there was a new problem to contend with: Where did I price my once-beloved options, which I was now beginning to loathe with all the passion of a jilted bride?

Between 12:30 and 1:00 P.M., the market gained 115 points. The crash of 1987 was declared over.

Brokers and traders were fighting to get long in the market—options, futures, stocks, it didn't matter what you bought. If someone were to have priced all the uneaten sandwiches, undoubtedly someone would have bid on them.

"Don't be short" was the new battle cry. An army of bargain

hunters, those who had shorted in anticipation of a continued slide, as well as profit takers, flocked to the buy side. The market closed early on Tuesday and Wednesday because the back offices were so jammed up with paperwork. Going out into the bright afternoon sunshine at 2:30, I felt like a kid with a half day off because of parent-teacher conferences.

When I first came to the floor of the Exchange back in 1984, Sheila told me, "A year on the AMEX is like ten years in the real world." I never appreciated the truth in that bit of hyperbole until I reread John Kenneth Galbraith's 1954 book, *The Great Crash*. Apparently, I'd not only witnessed but survived an instant replay of the 1929–1939 boom-and-bust cycle—albeit compressed into a few days in October. It would take me another six months to make back for the firm the $1.6 million I'd blown earlier that week. By then, I'd grown a thicker skin. I called my grandfather in Huntington to tell him the latest joke going around the pit.

Seems this guy comes home to his Park Avenue duplex late in the afternoon of Terrible Tuesday. He tells his wife, "Honey, we lost everything." She gasps. "Not the household staff!" "*Everything*," he repeats. "The condo, the cars, your furs and jewelry, the summer house!" Terrified, she runs out to the terrace, twenty-eight floors up, and dives off. He walks over to the parapet, looks down, and smiles. "Thank you, PaineWebber!"

19

Checkout Time

I DIDN'T THINK I heard him right, so Dr. Kaplan, an otolaryngologist at Manhattan Eye, Ear & Throat Hospital, repeated the question: "Do you want throat cancer by the time you're twenty-five? I can help you get rid of the polyps, the penicillin will alleviate your strep throat and swollen glands, but the cancer will take more time."

I was twenty-three, and I had spent nearly six years at the Exchange, more than five of them in what now seems like one long perpetual primal scream. Every October, I would go in for a complete physical workup. Everything below the neck still seemed to be in working order. I had no ulcers, developed no junk-food-related allergies, slept soundly, and went to the bathroom regularly.

That is to say, more or less. Ever since losing ten thousand dollars on account of a sudden urge to go, I'd made it a point not to continually gulp water. But then one of my clerks, whose father must have been on dialysis, pointed out that if I persisted in not drinking, I'd risk uremic poisoning and possible loss of a kidney. That's when I started sucking on hard candies. Seven new cavities later, I took up sucking on ice cubes. I figured my kidneys wouldn't be able to tell the difference. So much for below the neck. Above it, I knew I was fast turning into a basket case. How bad, I was about to find out.

My throat was as raw as a slab of sushi and didn't taste half as good. My vocal chords were strained. I was going on my third case of strep throat that year and rued the days I hadn't invested in P & G—makers of Chloraseptic—or for that matter, Beechnut Lifesavers.

Mary Pyne, my roommate, woke up in the middle of the night at hearing drawers being opened and shut. I was like a chain smoker, her last pack gone, going through ashtrays looking for half- or three-quarters-smoked cigarette butts. Mary had awakened thinking a burglar was loose. No, I reassured her, it was only me, desperately seeking something sweet to suck on and ease my burning throat. "Go back to sleep, Mary," I said, and to myself: "Where the hell did I put those Lifesavers?"

Dr. Robert Keuchle, my dentist, took to reading the inside of my mouth like an archaeologist reading the wall art in prehistoric cave dwellings. "Mmmmmm," he'd say during prophylaxis, "what have we here?" I was in no position to say. He seemed to be doing some sort of tango, lunging forward into my mouth, then taking two steps back, putting down his tools, scratching his head as if confounded, then renewing the attack.

"What is it?" I asked when he finally pulled all his tools out of my mouth.

"Strangest damn decay pattern on the outside of your teeth," he said, "roundlike."

"Does the pattern have a hole in the middle?" I asked, helpfully.

"It *does*! How did you know?" I told him I went to sleep each night with six Lifesavers wedged firmly between my teeth and the inside of my cheek. The sugar had worked like acid. As only a dentist would, he first went into a tirade about tooth decay and only then about the risk I was taking of choking to death.

My hearing wasn't improving. I was told by a special auditory examiner at Manhattan Eye, Ear & Throat that I had lost three frequencies. I hadn't misplaced them. I knew precisely where I'd left them. When I explained what I did for a living, she smiled. "You're lucky you've only lost ten or twenty percent of your hearing. Why, I've had some rock musicians come in who . . ." The woman wouldn't shut up. I was getting an earache.

I learned there's a difference between throat and ear problems. Once it goes, hearing doesn't come back.

Already Mary would come into the apartment, screaming, "Why d'you have the TV up so loud?"

And I would respond, "Wha-a-at?"

Some of the traders wore the kind of earplugs doctors recommend to Con Edison tunnel drillers or shipyard sandblasters, but I hadn't done this, as I worried about missing a critical trade. When the object of the game is to be faster than the next guy, you don't put handicaps in your own path. That would be like a cop wearing a Sony Walkman while directing traffic.

My eye muscles were contracting and "forgetting to relax," I was told. I certainly exercised them a lot, watching eight computer screens at the same time that I followed the two Trans-Lux electronic tapes. The first opthalmologist I visited asked if perchance I was into refereeing tennis matches. I had to explain to him what I did for a living. He grasped the situation immediately. My eyes would dart from trader to trader, up to the broad tape, the ticker, down and to the side monitors, the market minders, then back to the traders—all within seconds. "You're abusing yourself," he warned me.

I began referring to my affliction as "the pogo-stick syndrome" because, after trading, people began to look as if they were jumping up and down. I mentioned it to Frankie Borenzo and he recommended an implant of a vertical-hold button. "That way you'll always win the slots at Atlantic City."

On most trading days, by 2:00 P.M. I'd place my open hands over my face, peering through my fingers to cut the glare. There were days when the big digital clock appeared to me like one of those *National Enquirer* space aliens. In fact, the only point in the day when I knew the exact time was at 2:22, because everyone in the pit would yell out "ducks on the water"—traders insisting that digital two's look like ducks.

Even my friendly podiatrist urged me to quit. He'd declared me "the most anxiety-ridden patient" ever to come for treatment and ordered me to wear special shoe inserts he'd fabricated with plaster impressions of my feet.

I   I   I

It became necessary to do a "financial health audit." At NYU we'd learned how companies place dollar values on such intangibles as trademarks and goodwill. I started in 1985, itemizing those assets of mine at greatest risk: throat (valued at $50,000), hearing ($40,000), eyes ($30,000).

The numbers were not entirely arbitrary. I figured that as long as my posttax earnings exceeded the damages, I'd stay in the pit.

In 1986, all the figures moved up a notch, but not enough for me to give them much thought. But after the 1987 crash, throat had shot up to $100,000, hearing to $75,000, and eyes to $50,000. I was still ahead. Not so by the time the second crash (October 1989) came and went. I was in a negative position. It just wasn't worth it anymore. Four years earlier, I'd been a varsity soccer player and a bicycle racer. I skied and played volleyball. Now I was beginning to feel thirty going on seventy-five—and that was just physically.

The trader who doubled as a human-skin collector walked around with a tape measure, offering to fit any of us for a body bag, which we could then fold up and keep in the coat room. Actually, I wasn't worried about dying, but most of the guys worried about dying of a coronary. Or at least they did until a floor trader actually had a heart attack, was pronounced dead, but then was brought back to life in about ten minutes by the paramedics. He returned to the floor and told all the coronary candidates that dying was a breeze: "Like taking your profits on a good trade." It was just like going to sleep, he said. He didn't know whether he had been out ten years or ten minutes.

Afterward, all the guys went back to the bars, the greasy food, and a strict no-exercise regimen. Some, whose incomes had been sharply reduced by the crash, started taking side jobs until the market recovered.

Mark Meade, a pit broker, signed up to drive a New Jersey suburban bus to and from Wall Street. He'd regale us with tales of life behind the big wheel, such as the three worst enemies of the suburban bus driver, which, he insisted, were (1) pedestrians, (2) inclement weather, and (3) the flu. He actually seemed to enjoy his second career, but it didn't last. One day he showed up for work earlier than his bus route would have allowed. We were curious. "I got fired," Mark said. "I went to pull what I thought was the emergency brake but instead emptied the latrine."

| | | |

It was in July 1987—three months before the crash—that I got my first qualms about the career path I'd picked out. I was involved in industry functions that I no longer believed in. In talking to people back home, kids I'd grown up with and who were making a small fraction of what I was taking home, I had trouble justifying what was happening on Wall Street.

The Boesky business had just begun to have an impact upstate. The old suspicions that the game was fixed in favor of the Big Guys were coming back in spades. While I was still convinced that we were performing a valuable service making markets in options—making stock trading more efficient—a sense of detachment was taking hold of me that I could not explain. Only later would I learn that this was the earliest stage of burnout. One could see the flames, but the brain had not yet begun to process the pain.

Certainly there were tip-offs. My nightmares seemed to be all about bad trades. In the shower all I could think of were the trades that got away. On dates, over dinner in some of the most expensive restaurants in town, I'd pick at the food because my mind was on something else: Would the last trade clear? Or would it be a fifty-thousand-dollar error? Then there were those awful moments when I was all thumbs. All my powers of coordination failed me one day as I got set to use the Touchtone phone: I couldn't punch in the numbers because they weren't in fractions.

In such odd behavior I was not alone.

Michael Gann's clerk, Linda, had left the year before. She was smart and pretty and very good at her job. She was two years older than me. Clerking for a spread broker is like being both an air-traffic controller and a mind reader. One day I saw her leaning over the balcony signaling Michael to buy six thousand options—a staggeringly huge order. Those who weren't trading at that exact moment looked up in disbelief. Michael began buying. "Are you sure?" he yelled up, a rare question. There was never time for checking orders; it was assumed that the numbers signaled down were correct.

"Yes!" she yelled back down. Then, a split-second later, an agonizing "NO! Only six hundred. STOP! Only six hundred!"

I saw the vein in Michael's temple start to throb and turn purple. I glanced up at the balcony. Linda seemed to be in shock.

The following week she was gone. They didn't fire her. She was too good. She quit. On her last day with Michael's firm, I ran into her in the ladies' room. "I heard one thing and started signaling something else," she said. "It just didn't make sense for a minute. My ears told my brain one thing, and it blew up and told my hands something else. I watched my hands and knew something was wrong but I couldn't stop. I lost it, I completely lost it."

And I was losing it.

Clearly, I was no longer a True Believer. Oh, sure, the system worked, and probably always would. But it had grown too big, too fast, and the people who ran it were in too far, too deep, to see it needed an overhaul. Not reform, just fine tuning is what they were saying as they hunkered down by releasing one statistical study after another to support the contention that program trading and portfolio insurance were actually lessening market volatility.

To paraphrase President Eisenhower's former defense secretary, "Engine Charlie" Wilson: "What's good for Wall Street is good for America."

I was no longer convinced that was so. After the 1987 crash, there was a lot of talk about "reform." With great fanfare, the Commodity Futures Trading Commission (CFTC) doubled the margin requirement for the S&P 500 index futures to $15,000; two weeks later, it quietly pared it back down to a precrash $7,500. The NYSE convened a special nineteen-member "Blue Ribbon Panel on Volatility and Investor Confidence." Predictably, it found little wrong with the system that couldn't be taken care of in-house. It found nothing innately wrong with the concept of program trading. On the panel were people like Salomon's John Gutfreund, CBOE's Leo Melamed, Fred Graver of Wells Fargo Nikko Investment Advisors. What did Claude Rains say in *Casablanca?*—"Round up the usual suspects."

I knew for certain that I was losing it when for the first time I sided with the Securities & Exchange Commission's call for a single regulator over all forms of trading—in effect, serving notice on the CFTC, Chicago Mercantile Exchange, and Chicago Board of Trade that they had failed to adequately control their people.

And I lost it finally on October 13, 1989, when, just as predictably, the market crashed again, this time the Dow-Jones Industrial Average dropping 190.58 points to 2569.26 in the last half hour of trading. That afternoon, after United Airlines announced that its long-awaited leveraged buy-out had collapsed, all three markets—stocks, options, and futures—went into free-fall. The big brokerage houses hadn't been sufficiently hedged against what they owed their big institutional clients who were big into options, so they began unloading stock. Not an orderly retreat but a panic dumping operation. In a postmortem report, the SEC found that, with eleven minutes remaining in the trading day, three of the largest firms dumped 2.5 million shares. The infrastructure just couldn't take that kind of pressure and gave way.

That the self-styled reformers were only playing word games came across when Salomon's house semanticist, Louis Margolis, called for a new lexicon of trading terms. For example, he wanted to do away with that bad term "margin" and replace it with "good-faith deposit."

Appearing before an AMEX conference of futures and options traders in the spring of 1990, Margolis spoke of "episodic volatility" (as if describing an epileptic seizure to a conference of neurosurgeons) and indicated that it could not be linked to program trading or to that newest wrinkle on an old discredited theme, "portfolio puts." Rather, such "episodic volatility" was more an act of God.

Margolis's views, so reflective of current congressional thinking, prompted business writer Susan Antilla of *USA Today* to observe, "It's kind of like saying you don't really live on the fault line, you just have these unexplained earthquakes once in a while."

I came in the following Monday and Tuesday to clean up the mess. I was exhausted, angry, but had given no thought to quitting. I was not about to flush six years down the drain.

Actually, "mess" wasn't the right word for what faced me. The trading mistakes were horrendous. Having lost my voice as a result of the frantic action on Friday, I was relegated to ironing out the costliest of the errors—those *starting* at one hundred thousand. There were reams of them, over a million dollars' worth of errors. In between straightening out the errors, I had to deal with a number of pit traders who wanted to square their accounts with Spear Leeds. Some of them were out of business, history. They'd been wiped out in less than an hour. Swallowed up and spat out.

I spent most of Monday on the phone with the Exchange, pleading for time extensions so that we could at least find out where the money went. Useless. By the close of business that day, the firm was in the hole for five hundred thousand dollars, just in the previous day's mistakes. It was more of the same Tuesday. On Wednesday, I called in sick. I wrote it off to PMS, but over the weekend the truth hit home. The job had become humanly impossible.

My friend Suzy Benzinger, the Broadway costume designer, came over to the loft to which I moved after the 1987 crash. My ambivalence was driving her crazy. I told her, "It's October and I should really hang in there till December to get my bonus."

Suzy said, "Lou"—she still called me by whatever name popped into her head—"when I was two weeks short of graduation at SUNY Stonybrook, I got so fed up that one night I packed up my car and left. It was two in the morning, I was slightly drunk and I packed four years of stuff myself. Down six flights and into the hatchback. Sometimes you can't take it for another minute. Then I put the refrigerator into the back of that car and drove eight hours to Buffalo and went to bed. When I got up the next day I couldn't figure out how I ever got that fridge in, because it wouldn't come out."

Suzy never went back to get her diploma, and the fridge never came out of the car, which she sold six months later with the fridge still in it filled with food.

On Monday morning I sat down with Ron Shear and told him I was packing it in. I said it was either my money or my life, and I valued my life more. I didn't tell him of my disenchantment. I don't know if he would understand.

"You sure, kid?"

"Look at me," I whispered. "I can barely speak, I can barely hear, I feel like shit, and I just turned twenty-four. Yeah, I'm sure."

"Let me know if you change your mind."

I went downstairs to the lockers. I pulled out a shopping bag and emptied my hoard of patent medicines, OTC drugs, and assorted Lifesavers and candy bars; I pulled out all the Cross pens that had been foisted on me over the years by member companies; and a whoopie cushion, three water guns, a shoebox filled with such novelties as rubber vomit and plastic dog shit, two clean shirts, three ruined ones, one jar of Play-Doh, the Perrier bottles I had practiced on when I first got to Dritz, some coloring books, and a dog-eared paperback entitled *Voodoo for Beginners*. I went next to the cloakroom to retrieve a couple of pairs of high-heeled shoes and headed for the door.

As I left the cloakroom I heard the opening bell go off. This was not the time to head up to the pit and say my good-byes. Eddie the security guard held open the door for me. "Have a nice vacation, Laura, you look like you need it."

I thanked him and headed out into the sunlight of Trinity Place. Turning left, I headed for the World Trade Center to catch the subway. When I got there, there was a long line of people waiting to buy tokens. I reached into my pocket and pulled out a couple of tokens. I approached the people at the end of the line and sold them two one-dollar tokens for two dollars apiece.

I swore I had put trading behind me forever. Obviously it was something I would have to work out of my system.

Slowly.